332.6
N67
Noddings, T.
The Dow Jones-Irwin guide to convertible
   securities.

JUL-8

CARNEGIE PUBLIC LIBRARY
OF PARKERSBURG & WOOD COUNTY
725 GREEN ST.
PARKERSBURG, W. VA. 26101

Parkersburg & Wood County Public Library
A CONTEMPORARY LIBRARY... A VITAL INSTITUTION

In Memory of
Donald E. Martin

The Dow Jones-Irwin
Guide to
Convertible Securities

The Dow Jones-Irwin Guide to Convertible Securities

THOMAS C. NODDINGS

1973

DOW JONES-IRWIN, INC.   Homewood, Illinois   60430

© DOW JONES-IRWIN, INC., 1973

All rights reserved. No part of this publication may be reproduced, stored in a retrieval system, or transmitted, in any form or by any means, electronic, mechanical, photocopying, recording, or otherwise, without the prior written permission of the publisher.

This publication is designed to provide accurate and authoritative information in regard to the subject matter covered. It is sold with the understanding that the publisher is not engaged in rendering legal, accounting, or other professional service. If legal advice or other expert assistance is required, the services of a competent professional person should be sought.

From a Declaration of Principles jointly adopted by a Committee of the American Bar Association and a Committee of Publishers.

First Printing, July 1973

ISBN 0-87094-059-7
Library of Congress Catalog Card No. 73-80102
Printed in the United States of America

Preface

THIS BOOK was written for the serious and patient investor who is willing to devote time and energy toward achieving above-average long-term investment success—the investor who desires to compound his equity at a rate in excess of 15 percent annually by the use of conservative and proven techniques. I believe it will also be of significant use to stockbrokers in helping them guide their clients in the constantly expanding field of convertible securities.

Through planned and systematic investment in convertible securities, which are the safest form of equity investment I know of, the investor may reasonably expect to achieve superior performance over the long term.

I am well aware that the concepts and techniques that I propose in this guide will not provide a panacea for the entire investment community—this specialized investment system simply cannot accept all the billions of dollars that flow into Wall Street. But I am confident that professional money managers and individual investors alike will be able to profit from them.

I do not claim that the reader can breeze through this book and then attack the investment world, armed with its sophisticated weaponry. The book must be studied. However, once the techniques are mastered—and they are not really too difficult—the average investor-reader can expect to have a very substantial advantage over the rest of the investment community.

The book begins with a study of warrants—the backbone of the investment system developed in subsequent chapters.

This book was years in the making and represents the advice and assistance of several investment professionals—some through direct consultation and others by their writings. I am especially indebted to Richard Horton and George Peugeot, two business executives who are also exceptionally sophisticated investors.

Dick Horton made invaluable contributions during the countless hours of analysis and development of the basic concepts. Without his help, encouragement, and sincere enthusiasm, I might not have persisted through the years of study and effort that led to the writing of this guide.

George Peugeot, a professional investment advisor, was most helpful in the area of portfolio design for maximum success regardless of stock market trends. Through his direct guidance, the scope of my initial manuscript was substantially broadened to reflect his highly developed concepts of money management.

The author also gratefully acknowledges editorial help from Daniel Turov, an expert in the field of convertible securities with Halle & Stieglitz, Filor Bullard, Inc., and to The Value Line Convertible Survey for their truly outstanding investment service. My thanks also to authors of books and other investment services referred to or cited as references in this guide.

June 1973   THOMAS C. NODDINGS

Contents

1. Warrants   1

Where Do Warrants Originate? Where Are They Traded? Exercise Terms. Scheduled Changes of Exercise Terms. Protection against Stock Splits and Stock Dividends. Expiration Date. Senior Securities Usable at Par Value. Are There Enough Bonds for Full Warrant Conversion? Callable Warrants.

2. Warrant/Common Stock Price Relationships   11

Conversion Value. Speculative Value. The Warrant/Common Stock Price Curve.

3. Normal Value Curves for Long-Term Warrants   17

The Normal Value Curve. Adjusted Warrant and Exercise Prices. Factors Affecting Normal Value. Warrant Leverage.

4. Undervalued Warrants   30

A Normally Priced Warrant Is More Conservative Than Its Common Stock. Undervalued Warrants. The Basic System. General Guides for Buying Warrants.

5. Hedging Undervalued Warrants   38

The Warrant Hedge. An Actual Warrant Hedge Position in Ling-Temco-Vought. A Graphical Analysis of Alternate Hedge Positions in Ling-Temco-Vought Warrants. Conclusion of the

Ling-Temco-Vought Story. Hedging Warrants with Borrowed Funds. General Guides for Hedging Warrants.

6. **The Basic System** 53

   Procedures for Evaluating, Establishing, and Maintaining Hedge Positions. Specific Buy, Hold, and Sell Actions. Anticipated Performance in Different Types of Markets.

7. **The Basic System in Action** 60

   The Six-Year Study: *January 1967—January 1969: A Major Bull Market. January 1969—July 1970: A Major Bear Market. July 1970—July 1971: A Market Rebound. July 1971—January 1973: A Sideways Market.* Summary of All Positions Taken during the Six-Year Study. A Close Look at Warrants in January 1973.

8. **Performance Results form the Basic System** 70

   Common Stock Performance. Warrant Performance. Warrant/Cash Performance. Buying on Margin. Warrant Hedge Performance—The Basic System. Warrant Hedge Performance on Margin.

9. **Alternatives to the Basic System** 86

   Continuous Review of All Warrant Opportunities. Over-the-Counter Warrants. Fine Tuning the Hedge Portfolio. Trading against Warrants for Profits during Sideways Markets. Predicting Major Market Swings.

10. **Convertible Bonds and Convertible Preferred Stocks** 93

    Investment Value. Conversion Value. Latent Warrants. Opportunities in Undervalued Convertibles. Convertible Bonds versus Convertible Preferred Stock. Convertibles versus Warrants/Cash. Convertible Funds: *Mutual Funds. Closed-End Funds.* General Guides for Buying Convertibles.

11. **Hedging Undervalued Convertibles** 105

    Hedging XYZ Company Convertible Bonds. Closing Out a Convertible Bond Hedge on the Upside. An Actual Convertible Bond Hedge Position in Gulf Resources & Chemical. General Guides for Hedging Convertibles. Possible Risks.

12. **Reverse Warrant Hedging** 115

    General Guidelines. An Actual Reverse Warrant Hedge Position—American Telephone & Telegraph. Actual Reverse Warrant Hedge Positions Taken by the Author.

13. Special Situations and Call Options 127

Delayed Convertibles Having Fixed Conversion Terms. Delayed Convertibles Having Conversion Terms Based on a Specified Formula: *Continental Investment Corp. United National Corp. Pan American World Airways*. Real Estate Investment Trusts—Delayed "Warrants." Fabricated Convertibles. Buying Call Options. Buying Call Options on Undervalued Warrants. Writing Call Options. General Guides for the Use of Call Options in a Convertible Hedging Program. Dual-Purpose Funds.

14. Margin Regulations 149

Application of Margin Regulations in a Hedging Program.

15. Portfolio Management 153

Your Brokerage Account. Selecting a Brokerage Firm. Selecting a Broker. Operating at Maximum Leverage. Portfolio Selection and Diversification. Investment Services. Income Tax Considerations. Portfolio Turnover Strategy. Record Keeping. Acion. Recommended Readings for Investors Interested in Warrants, Convertibles, and Options.

16. Can Anything Go Wrong? 168

Tender Offers. Merger Proposals. Far West Financial Warrants—What Went Wrong? National General Warrants—What Went Wrong?

Appendix A Straight Bonds Usable at Par Value in Exercising Warrants 181

Appendix B Calculations for Plotting the Normal Value Curve for Long-Term Warrants (common stocks have high-price volatility and pay no dividends) 182

Appendix C Stock Volatility Calculations 183

Appendix D Selling Securities Short 184

Appendix E Optimum Short to Long Ratio for Hedge Positions in Undervalued Warrants 187

Appendix F Warrants Evaluated during the Six-Year Study—1967 through 1972 190

Appendix G Exercise Terms for Warrants Having Common Stocks Listed on The New York or American Stock Exchanges 200

Appendix H Terms Applying to Convertibles, Warrants, and Hedging 206

Index 217

1

Warrants

WARRANTS are the least understood, but potentially the most profitable, of all securities. They are the backbone of this investment system.

A warrant may generally be defined as: "a negotiable security issued by a company which represents a long-term option to purchase common stock from the company on specified terms." The terms are sometimes extensive and complex, thus contributing to unusual opportunities for the informed investor and disappointment for others.

Warrants are often referred to as "high-risk" or "speculative" investments. "Funny money" was a popular description prior to the prestigious American Telephone & Telegraph issue in 1970. Like most clichés, these terms are frequently inapplicable and have often discouraged conservative investors from considering warrants for their portfolios. Under certain circumstances, a warrant may actually be a more conservative investment than its common stock and should be purchased by the prudent investor as a superior *alternative* to the common. It is the conservative, *undervalued* warrant that offers potential for spectacular stock market success when combined with sophisticated investment techniques. Techniques that most investors are capable of executing but are frequently overlooked or misused; even by the professionals. These techniques will be presented in subsequent chapters, but first, one should attain a basic knowledge of the most important factors which influence a warrant's value.

WHERE DO WARRANTS ORIGINATE?

Warrants have come into being in numerous ways, limited only by the imagination of the issuing company. In recent years of tight money, they were frequently issued with bonds to broaden the bonds' investment appeal and to permit the company to market them at lower interest rates than would be possible without the warrant "sweetner." They have also been issued as units with common stock as a means of increasing the marketability of the common. Other methods have included direct sale, dividend payments, reorganization, mergers, acquisitions, recapitalization, and compensation to underwriters.

WHERE ARE THEY TRADED?

Warrants are bought and sold in the same manner as common stock. They used to be primarily traded over-the-counter with but a few listed on the American Stock Exchange or on regional exchanges. However, in the fall of 1970, A.T.&T. warrants became the first to be accepted by the New York Stock Exchange and they have since been followed by several warrants of other major companies. Today, there are in excess of 300 actively traded warrants. Over 100 of these warrants are listed on a stock exchange.

EXERCISE TERMS

The *exercise price* is the amount of money to be submitted with each warrant upon surrendering them to the company for a stated number of common stock shares. If the exercise terms for XYZ Company warrants are one share of common for $10, then $10 would be submitted with each warrant and an equal number of common shares would be received in return. If the exercise terms are two shares for $10, then $10 would still be submitted with each warrant but twice as many common shares would be received. In both cases, the exercise price is $10. As will be demonstrated later, when other than one share of common stock is received in the exchange, the exercise price must be *adjusted* before determining warrant values.

SCHEDULED CHANGES OF EXERCISE TERMS

Warrant terms occasionally contain provisions for periodic changes in the exercise price. These changes are usually upward and can therefore retard the warrant's appreciation potential. They must be taken into consideration when computing values. For example, the exercise price for Loews Corp. warrants, which expire in 1980, was $35 until November 1972, at which time it was automatically increased to $37.50. A further increase to $40 will take place after November 1976. Warrant provisions may also include periodic reductions in the number of common stock shares to be received which, in effect, is comparable to increasing the exercise price.

PROTECTION AGAINST STOCK SPLITS AND STOCK DIVIDENDS

The amount of common stock to be received for each warrant may also be changed as a result of stock splits, but this type revision should have little effect on the warrant's value. Braniff Airways warrants were originally exercisable into one share of common for $73. A 3 for 1 stock split in 1968 required that the exercise terms be revised to three shares for $73. The stock split had no effect on the warrant's inherent value or market price.

Through antidilution clauses in warrant agreements, most warrants are also protected against stock dividends (small stock splits) and for issuance of additional common stock or convertible securities by the company at prices below the warrant's exercise price. These factors may result in occasional small adjustments to the exercise terms and will also have little or no effect on the warrant's value or trading price. Braniff Airways also issued a stock dividend in 1972 causing an additional revision to the warrant's exercise terms to 3.183 shares for $73.

EXPIRATION DATE

In addition to the number of shares of common stock to be received and the price to be paid to exercise the privilege, the time period during which the option is valid is of major importance. This may be a few months, several years, or even perpetual. The majority of new warrants currently being issued have a life of 5 to 10 years.

A warrant with a remaining life of over three years is generally considered to be long-term and may be evaluated with other long-term warrants by the use of standardized techniques to be developed in the following chapters. As the expiration date draws to within two years or less, the degree of risk may be substantially increased and special evaluation methods must then be used. This guide will concentrate on those warrants having a life of three years or more, as it has been the author's experience that an undervalued short-term warrant is a rare exception.

Where the exercise price is to be periodically increased, it may be necessary to evaluate the warrant as both short term and long term. Prior to November 1972, the Loews warrant would have been considered short term at an exercise price of $35 and long term at $37.50. Except where otherwise indicated, all exercise terms used in our warrant computations will be those prevailing three years hence. A study of the Loews warrant would, therefore, have been based on the higher exercise price of $37.50. As time draws to within three years of the next scheduled increase in November 1976, the new exercise price of $40 will be considered.

Note that when warrants expire, those holding them during the final days must exercise them to salvage any value that they may have at the time. Prior to the expiration date, warrants should seldom be purchased with the intention of exercising them. An exception to this rule would be if one were interested in purchasing the common stock and the warrants were available at or below their conversion value. Purchase and exercise of the warrants would then result in a savings to the investor.

SENIOR SECURITIES USABLE AT PAR VALUE

When warrants are issued with bonds, the bonds may often be used at full par value in lieu of cash in exercising the warrant, at the option of the warrant holder. If the bond is selling above par value, it would not be considered as it would be more economical to use cash instead of the bond. If the bond is selling below par, usually the case since the bond normally drops in price when the warrant is detached after issuance, the *effective* exercise price may be reduced quite drastically.

Appendix A lists those senior securities which are currently usable at par value in exercising warrants on listed stocks. For example, Loews Corp. 6.875's–93[1] bonds, trading at 85,[2] would re-

---

[1] The bond coupon is 6.875 percent at par value, or $68.75 annually. The bond maturity date is 1993.

[2] Bonds are quoted as a percent of par value. For a $1,000 bond, "85" means 85 percent of $1,000 or $850. The par value for the vast majority of bonds is $1,000.

duce the $37.50 exercise price to an effective exercise price of $31.88 ($37.50 × 85/100 = $31.88). In other words, if one were planning to convert his Loews warrants into common, he would submit bonds purchased for $850, but valued at $1,000 for exercise purposes, instead of cash.

One must be extra cautious of deeply discounted bonds in applying the effective exercise price to warrant price projections. An improvement in the prospects of the particular company under study will normally result in a higher bond price. The appreciation potential of the warrant would then be reduced accordingly as the bond's price increased.

An example of an excessively discounted bond was Ling-Temco-Vought's 5's-88 which sold near 20 in the fall of 1970. This 80 percent discount from par value reduced the warrant's exercise price from $115 all the way down to an effective exercise price of $23 ($115.00 × 20/100 = $23.00). Any advance by LTV common stock would certainly have been accompanied by higher price levels for the bond. For warrant evaluation purposes at that time, one should have assigned a higher value to the LTV bond, a price that was comparable to other bonds of similar quality (assuming favorable prospects for the company's future).

Be careful to also note the length of time that the bonds may be usable at par value as it may be less than the warrant's life. The Ling-Temco-Vought warrants do not expire until 1978 but the bonds were only usable until January 15, 1973. At that time, the effective exercise price was increased back up to $115. As when a warrant's exercise price is increased, if the usable bond life expires prior to the warrant, the warrant may have to be evaluated from both short-term and long-term standpoints. Appendix A also indicates the usable bond life where it is less than the warrant life.

If a bond is not usable at par until some time in the distant future, do not consider it for current warrant evaluation purposes.

Budget Industries 6's-88 bonds are usable only after November 1, 1978, and would, therefore, not be available for conversion purposes if one were to exercise his warrants prior to that time.

ARE THERE ENOUGH BONDS FOR FULL WARRANT CONVERSION?

Another important factor which must be considered is the size of the bond issue in relation to the number of bonds required for exercise of the entire warrant issue. Although most bond issues exceed the exercise quantity, some fall far short. Only 30 percent of the General Host warrant issue could presently be exercised by the use of their 7's-94 bonds. And this percentage could be reduced still further if the company were to make additional purchases of their own bonds on the open market; a practice frequently employed by many companies to reduce interest payments and to improve net worth. This could cause a "squeeze" on the bonds if the common stock were to rise to the point where exercise was desired or, in certain cases, mandatory. A significant and abrupt decline in warrant value could result under these conditions. A conservative analysis of the General Host warrant would therefore exclude the bonds from consideration. An alternate approach would be to purchase bonds along with the warrants to assure availability for future conversion. This, of course, would require additional cash and hence reduce the leverage afforded by purchase of warrants only. Appendix A also indicates the size of the bond issue in relation to the number required for converting all outstanding warrants.

CALLABLE WARRANTS

Warrants that are callable by the company may present annoying problems to the investor that are often encountered with convertible bonds selling above their call prices. Fortunately, only a few warrant terms include such provisions, but, when they do, special precautions must be taken since any premium above conversion value would be immediately lost if the warrants were called.

An extreme example, one that was most detrimental to the warrant holders, was Keyes Fibre. This warrant was issued in 1960 with a stated life of 10 years. Its exercise terms varied during the life of the warrant and were one share of common for $25 between November 1965 and the November 1970 expiration date. However, the warrant provisions permitted the company to call them at any time for redemption at only $1 each. This disastrous event occurred in September 1967 while the warrants were trading over-the-counter near the $4 level. Because the common stock was selling below the warrant's $25 exercise price at the time, the warrants had no tangible value. They immediately dropped to $1; their cash value upon redemption. Any prior purchase of Keyes Fibre warrants above the $1 level, while the common was selling below $25, would have simply been a gamble that the company would not call the warrants. It is this kind of gamble that one should avoid. He should seek opportunities elsewhere.

A current example of a callable warrant, but one that is much less risky than the Keyes Fibre warrant, is Daylin, Inc. The Daylin warrant terms contain a provision that they may be called at a price of $5.35 each. But this provision cannot be implemented by the company unless and until Daylin common stock sells at $28 per share or above for 30 continuous trading days. Assuming that the Daylin 5's-88 bonds, which are usable at par value, would advance to the 80 level when the stock reached $28, the effective exercise price would be $18 ($22.50 exercise price $\times$ $80/100$ = $18.00). This would result in a minimum warrant value of $10 when the stock traded at $28 ($28.00 − $18.00 = $10.00), well above the $5.35 call price.

In effect, a call by the company would force the warrant holders to purchase the bonds, since they would be selling below par value, for use in exercising their warrants. Providing that the warrant does not trade at a sizable premium above the $10 level as the common stock nears $28, the financial risk of a call for warrant holders is not too great. A factor that complicates the analysis of the situation, however, is the possibility of a "squeeze" on the bonds as the warrant holders rush to purchase them for exercise purposes. This sudden demand could force the bond's price toward par while reducing the warrant's exercise value and related market price. Of course, the common stock could also be selling well above $28 when the warrants are called. If the common was at $35, for example, the warrants would be worth at least $12.50 ($35.00 − $22.50 = $12.50) even if the bonds were "squeezed" all the way up to par.

Anyone interested in the Daylin warrant should also consider purchase of the bonds to avoid these complications if the warrants were called. As will be demonstrated in Chapter 13, warrants plus usable bonds are similar to the familiar convertible bond.

A more frequent warrant provision can be a call in effect but one that can actually be of extra value to the warrant holder. This is where the company has the option to reduce the exercise price for a limited period of time, usually 30–60 days. This event would tend to increase the price of the warrant during this short-time period and would force exercise to avoid the loss of this windfall since the warrant's price would likely drop back upon expiration of the period. Since such action by the company could cause severe price gyrations, the major stock exchanges have reportedly banned this privilege for warrants listed there in an effort to assure orderly trading markets.

EXHIBIT 1-1

WORK SHEET

CHECK LIST FOR THE INITIAL EVALUATION OF A WARRANT

1. Exercise terms are_____share(s) of common stock for $_____until_____, at which time the warrants:

   _____expire or,
   _____the terms change to_____share(s) for $_____until_____.

2. The remaining warrant life is_____years and_____months. This is:

   _____long-term (three years or more) or,
   _____short-term (less than three years).

3. Is there a bond which is usable at par value for exercising the warrant?

   _____no
   _____yes The bond is usable until_____, it is currently selling at _____, and it is traded on the_____Exchange. _____percent of the entire warrant issue may be exercised with the quantity of bonds presently outstanding.

4. Are the warrants callable by the company?

   _____no
   _____yes They are callable under the following provisions:_____ _____.

5. Can the company modify the exercise terms?

   _____no
   _____yes Terms may be changed under the following provisions:_____ _____.

6. Is the warrant protected against stock dividends?

   _____yes
   _____no The company may pay a stock dividend up to $_____or _____percent of the stock price without adjusting the exercise terms.

7. Other factors: _____
   _____
   _____

2

Warrant/Common Stock Price Relationships

SINCE a warrant is an option to purchase common stock, its market price is directly related to its exercise terms, its remaining life before expiration, the current market price of the common, and the future appreciation potential of the common. This market price is composed of two separate elements: conversion value and speculative value.

CONVERSION VALUE

Conversion value is the present worth of the warrant assuming that it would be immediately exercised to obtain the common stock. It equals the current market price of the common less the warrant's exercise price. For example, if XYZ Company stock was trading at $15, and the XYZ warrant was exercisable into one share for $10, then the conversion value is the difference between these two prices, or $5. Conversion value may also be referred to as minimum value, tangible value, exercise value, or intrinsic value.

Except for occasional short-term price fluctuations, a warrant will always sell at or above its conversion value. The reason is simple. If XYZ warrants were selling at only $5 each with the common at $15, the commission expense for purchasing the common would be less by buying the lower priced warrant and forwarding the warrant plus the $10 exercise price to the company in return for the common. At current commission rates, the alert investor would save $15.10 for 100 shares of stock obtained by effecting this conversion. Obviously, if the warrants could be purchased below their $5 conversion value, an even greater savings would be achieved. Note, that if you ask your brokerage firm to provide this conversion service for you, there may be a small service fee charged, depending on the firm's policies. The time required for effecting the conversion may also make this approach impractical for the "in and out" stock trader.

Although a warrant should theoretically never sell below its conversion value, the real or imaginary complications in exercising them, and in certain cases possible tax considerations, will cause some investors to sell their warrants at a small discount rather than convert them. If there are no investors available to take advantage of this fortunate situation at the time, professional arbitragers stand ready to buy these discounted warrants. The arbitrager will simultaneously sell the stock and pocket a small but sure profit in the exchange. Because the arbitrage transaction is accomplished with a very modest investment and at the low commission expenses applicable to exchange members, a small but quick gain can result in significant annualized profits.

SPECULATIVE VALUE

Since conversion value is the immediate worth of the warrant if one were to exercise it, a warrant has no conversion value if its common stock is trading below the exercise price. Nevertheless, since the warrant is an option to purchase the common stock and since the common might rise to well above the exercise price during the warrant's lifetime, it will have speculative value in the marketplace. This speculative value, the excess over conversion value, is the premium paid for the warrant. Or stated in another way, the speculative value that investors or speculators are willing to pay for the option privilege is the difference between the market price of the warrant and its conversion value.

Let's examine possible price levels for XYZ warrants having exercise terms of one share of common for $10 and a remaining life of several years.

Common Stock Price	Warrant Price	Conversion Value	Speculative Value
$ 5.00	$ 1.50	$ 0	$1.50
10.00	4.00	0	4.00
20.00	12.00	10.00	2.00
30.00	20.00	20.00	0

While XYZ common is selling at $10 per share or below, the entire amount paid for the warrant is speculative value. As the common rises above $10, the warrant's market price includes both conversion value and speculative value. At some high price for the common, the warrant loses all of its speculative attraction as an option and it will trade at or near its conversion value: the $30 price level for the common in the above table illustrates this characteristic.

An examination of these warrant/common stock price relationships for XYZ Company reveals why investors are willing to pay substantial premiums for long-term options to purchase common stock. At first glance, it would seem that $4 would be an excessive amount to pay for the warrant when the common is only selling at the $10 exercise price. At this point it has no conversion value. But examine what happens if the common stock were to double to $20, as the buyers of the common are certainly hoping will take place. The warrant would be expected to advance from $4 to $12 for a 200 percent profit. If the common were to triple to $30, the warrant must increase to at least its $20 conversion value: a 400 percent price appreciation versus but 200 percent for the common.

To achieve these above-average gains in rising markets, the buyer of the warrant must normally assume extra risks if his expectations do not materialize. As shown in the above table, a decline of 50 percent by the common from $10 to $5 would be expected to cause a larger percentage loss by the warrant of 62.5 percent as the warrant declines from $4 down to $1.50. And, of course, if the warrant expires with the common still at $10 or less, the warrant holder would lose his entire investment. In addition, the warrant buyer does not receive dividends as might the investor in the common stock, nor does he usually have voting rights.

THE WARRANT/COMMON STOCK PRICE CURVE

The anticipated price relationships between XYZ warrants and common stock may be plotted as illustrated in Exhibit 2–1. This chart permits one to quickly ascertain the expected warrant price at any common stock price level, assuming of course that the warrant's life to expiration is still long term. The stock price is normally plotted on the horizontal axis and the warrant price on the vertical axis, as shown. Note that the warrant's conversion value price line represents the minimum expected warrant price. It intersects the stock price axis at the $10 exercise price and slopes upward to the right on the chart on a point for point basis with the common stock.

A maximum warrant price line is frequently referenced in the literature and is also presented in Exhibit 2–1 for illustrative pur-

EXHIBIT 2-1

Typical Warrant/Common Stock Price Relationships—XYZ Company

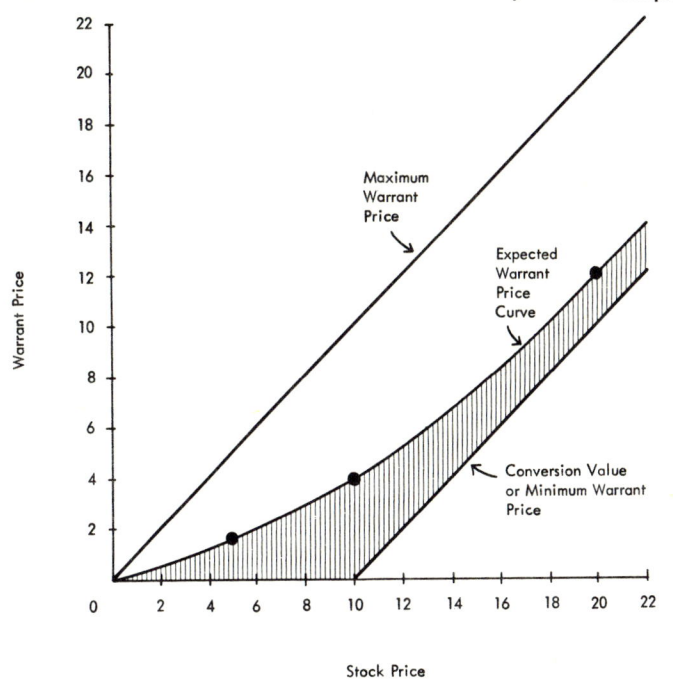

Exercise terms are 1.0 share of stock for $10. Warrant life is three years or more.

poses. A warrant's maximum price is supposedly the market price of the common stock since no investor should pay more for an option on the stock than he would pay for the stock itself. This is of only academic interest as there are no circumstances where a prudent investor or even an incorrigible gambler should purchase a warrant at a price anywhere near this theoretical maximum. Nevertheless, there have been times when warrants have actually sold at, or even above, this maximum price line. These absurd conditions were almost always caused by complicated exercise terms that the warrant buyers did not understand. The maximum price line will be deleted from subsequent charts as it serves no useful purpose and can only lead to possible confusion and abuse.

The warrant's speculative value is indicated by the shaded area on the chart and can readily be seen to equal the price of the warrant less its conversion value. Note that the expected speculative value is always greatest when the common stock is trading at the warrant's exercise price. In the following chapter, we will explore warrant/stock price curves in greater detail as they will provide the basis for all of our warrant studies.

3

Normal Value Curves for Long-Term Warrants

THE PREVIOUS chapter demonstrated a convenient method for illustrating warrant and common stock price relationships. The anticipated warrant price, at any price level for the common, could be easily determined from the expected warrant price curve. But, how is it possible to construct such a curve for XYZ Company or for any other warrant under study? Is there a standardized method for evaluating all warrants against a theoretical norm value?

THE NORMAL VALUE CURVE

Several different "normal value" curves for warrants are referenced in the literature. Each are similar in construction but contain significant differences depending on the formulas used or personal observations of historical warrant price patterns. The author has found the following simple formula to be conservative, and the most practical, for use as a basis in his studies of long-term warrants on *speculative* common stocks.[1]

---

[1] S. T. Kassouf, *Evaluation of Convertible Securities,* Analytical Publishers Co., New York, 1966.

$$W = \sqrt{E^2 + S^2} - E$$

Where:

W = warrant price
E = exercise price
S = stock price

This formula may be used to plot a curve for each warrant under consideration; similar to the XYZ warrant in Chapter 2. Fortunately, it is not necessary to prepare individual curves for every warrant. Since the formula is the same for all long-term warrants (on speculative stocks) except for different exercise prices, a standardized normal value curve may be constructed which can be used for all applicable warrants. This is accomplished by dividing both the warrant and stock prices by the exercise price in the above formula. A standardized curve may then be plotted for W/E (warrant price divided by exercise price) versus S/E (stock price divided by exercise price). This will allow one to conveniently plot prices on a single chart, for all warrants under study, for comparison with the theoretical norm.

The standardized normal value curve is illustrated in Exhibit 3–1 and is noted to be similar to the warrant price curve presented for XYZ Company in the previous chapter. The only difference is the use of W/E and S/E factors instead of actual warrant and stock prices. Appendix B provides the factors for construction of this standard curve for stock prices ranging from 0 to 4 times the exercise price.

To illustrate the application of Exhibit 3–1, National General (NGC) warrants were exercisable into one share of common stock for $15. At stock and warrant prices of $24 and $13, calculations were:

S/E = $24.00 ÷ $15.00 = 1.60
W/E = $13.00 ÷ $15.00 = .87

These values are plotted on Exhibit 3–1 and it is noted that the National General warrant was trading close to the theoretical normal value curve.

ADJUSTED WARRANT AND EXERCISE PRICES

When the exercise terms provide for other than one share of common stock for each warrant, or if there is a usable senior security selling below par value, the warrant price and exercise price must first be adjusted before computing W/E and S/E factors.

a) The warrant price is adjusted by dividing it by the number of shares of common stock to be received for each warrant.
b) The exercise price is first reduced, if there is a usable bond selling below par, to determine the *effective* exercise price. The effective exercise price is then adjusted by also dividing it by the number of shares of common stock to be received for each warrant.

Two examples will serve to illustrate these procedures:

Pacific Southwest Airlines (PSA) warrants were exercisable into one share of common stock for $23.40. Their 6's-87 bonds were usable at par value and were selling at 75. At stock and warrant prices of $25 and $16, calculations were:

$$\text{Effective exercise price} = \$23.40 \times 75/100 = \$17.55$$
$$S/E = \$25.00 \div \$17.55 = 1.42$$
$$W/E = \$16.00 \div \$17.55 = .91$$

Braniff Airways (BNF) warrants were exercisable into 3.0 shares of common stock for $73. Their 5.75's-86 bonds were usable at par value and were selling at 76. At stock and warrant prices of $15 and $18, calculations were:

Adjusted warrant price = $18.00 ÷ 3.0 = $6.00
Effective exercise price = $73.00 × 76/100 = $55.48
Adjusted exercise price = $55.48 ÷ 3.0 = $18.49
S/E = $15.00 ÷ $18.49 = .81
W/E = $6.00 ÷ $18.49 = .32

EXHIBIT 3–1

Normal Value Curve for Long-Term Warrants on Speculative Stocks

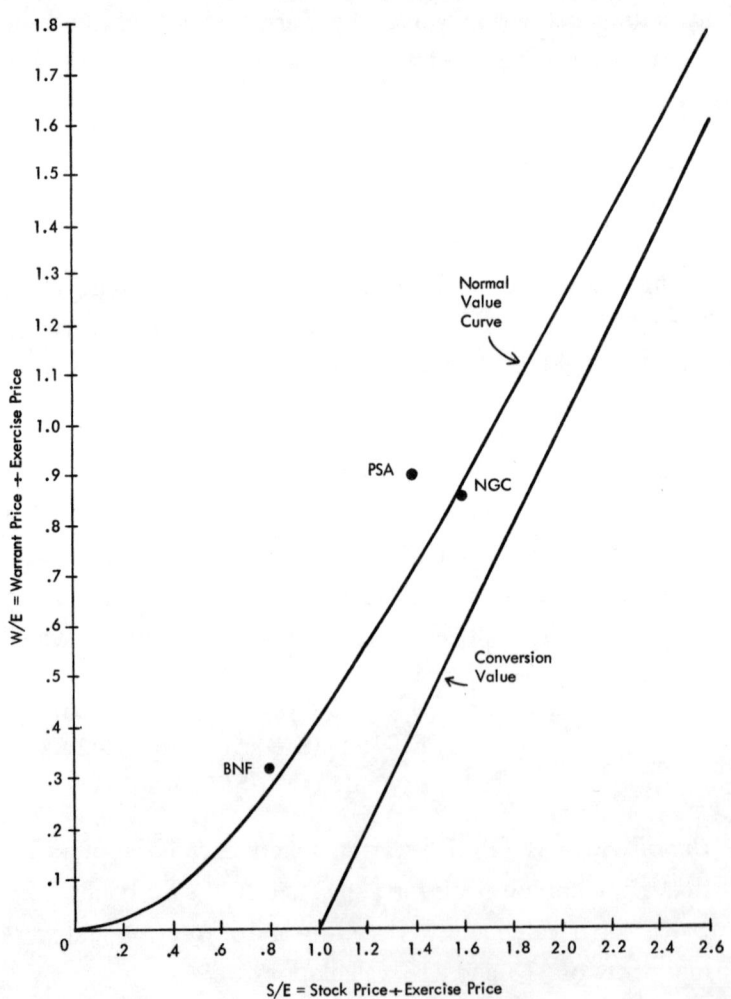

These warrants are also plotted on Exhibit 3–1 and it is noted that they both fell somewhat above the normal value curve.

FACTORS AFFECTING NORMAL VALUE

An option to purchase common stock is naturally worth most when there is the possibility of a substantial increase in the price of the common. Conversely, warrants to purchase stable, high-quality stocks would be expected to command lower premiums.

A major factor relating to a stock's quality and stability, and, therefore having a pronounced influence on a warrant's normal value, is the dividend payout on the common stock. All other factors being equal, stocks with high yields will appreciate in value at a slower rate than the stocks of companies which do not distribute part of their earnings to their shareholders. The return on investment to the common shareholders may be the same in both cases when both dividends and price appreciation are considered. However, since a warrant does not receive any benefits from dividends, it will be worth considerably more in the case where no dividend is paid on the common. A simple example will serve to illustrate this characteristic.

Assume that both A and B common stocks are selling at $50 and both have five-year warrants that are exercisable into one share of common for $50. A's common stock yields 5 percent while B's pays no dividend. If after five years, A's common stock appreciates in value by 25 percent to $62.50, the stockholders would have received a total return on their investment of $25 or 50 percent ($12.50 price appreciation plus $12.50 in dividends). To equal this total return, the price of B's common must appreciate in price by the full 50 percent to $75. At the expiration date, B's warrants would have a conversion value of twice that of A's—$25 versus but $12.50. One would, therefore, expect that

B's warrants would have sold at a greater premium than A's when both stocks were trading at the initial $50 price level.

An extreme example of high dividend-paying stocks with warrants, but a common occurrence in recent times, are the Real Estate Investment Trusts (REIT). To qualify as a trust, and to thereby receive favorable tax considerations, these companies must distribute at least 90 percent of their earnings to shareholders. One must, therefore, evaluate the warrants of REITs with extra caution as the possibility for significant price increases by their common stocks is seriously retarded by their exceptionally high dividend payouts.

Exhibit 3–2 illustrates empirically derived modifications to the normal value curves based on common stock yield. Experience indicates that these curves are representative of the majority of warrants that one will encounter and will, therefore, contribute to the accuracy of one's warrant evaluations. Five different value bands are shown based on a warrant's common stock yield as follows:

Band 5 = 0–2 percent stock yield
     4 = 2–4 percent
     3 = 4–6 percent
     2 = 6–8 percent
     1 = above 8 percent

Note: Area 6 represents all warrants selling above band 5.

For example, if a warrant's common stock yields 5 percent, the warrant would be considered properly priced if it were selling in band 3. Above band 3, it would be overpriced and below band 3 it would be believed to be undervalued. Note that a stock dividend will have the same negative effect on a warrant's normal value as a cash dividend if the warrant's terms are not adjusted to reflect these small stock splits. The assignment of a normal value band must therefore take into consideration both cash dividends and unprotected stock dividends.

EXHIBIT 3-2

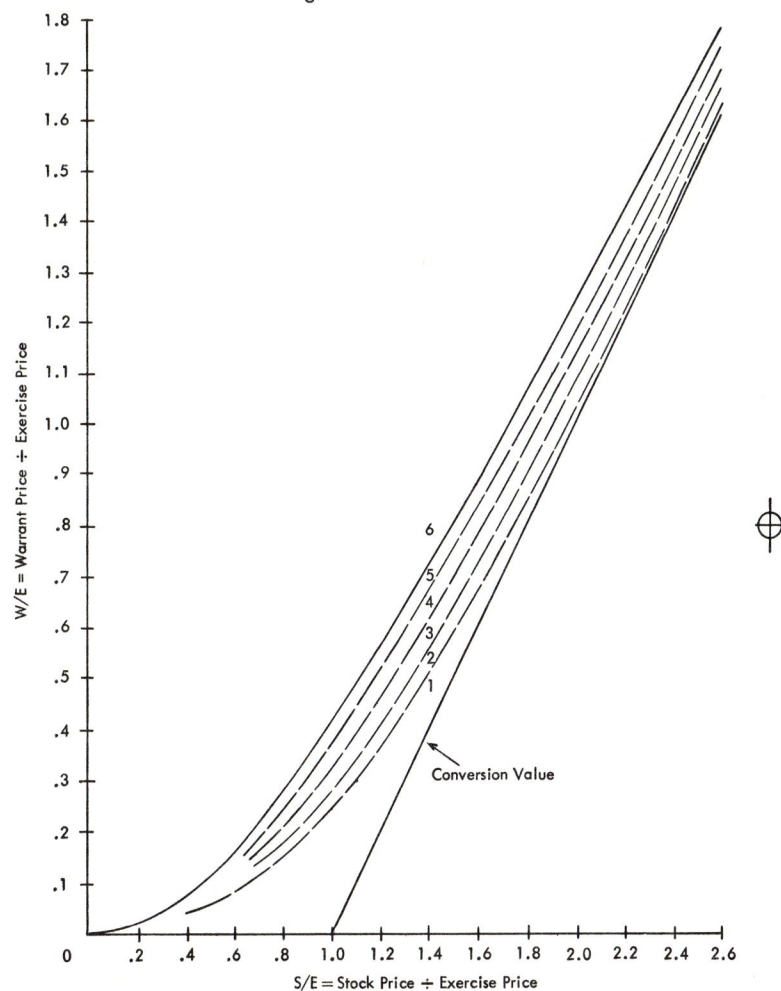

Normal Value Curves for Long-Term Warrants Based on Stock Yield

Band 5 = 0–2 percent yield
    4 = 2–4 percent
    3 = 4–6 percent
    2 = 6–8 percent
    1 = above 8%
Note: Area 6 represents all warrants above band 5.

If a common stock exhibits a higher than normal degree of price stability, its warrant should be assigned to a value band below that based on yield alone. Although historical price fluctuations may not be fully representative of future price action, they are certainly useful facts for evaluation purposes. Appendix C presents volatility calculations, over a three-year period, for a representative list of common stocks with potentially attractive warrants available at the present time. The conclusions drawn from a study of these volatility calculations by the author, indicates that the value bands for relatively stable stocks like **Carrier, Goodrich,** and **Louisiana Land** should be reduced one level below their normal band based only on yield. Those with extremely low price volatility, like **A.T.&T., Commonwealth Edison,** and **Tenneco** should be reduced by two value bands. Of course, if there are valid reasons to expect that a stock will exhibit greater or less relative price volatility in the future than it did in the past, then the above rules should be modified accordingly. Remember, also, that the normal value curves shown in this book are for long-term warrants, those having a remaining life in excess of three years. Additional downward adjustments would have to be made to these curves for shorter term warrants.

WARRANT LEVERAGE

A warrant possesses leverage when it is expected to appreciate in value at a greater percentage rate than the common stock upon a price increase by the common. This leverage may be determined from the normal value curves by assuming that the common will advance to a given price and then estimating the corresponding price advance for the warrant. For example, if the warrant was expected to increase 200 percent upon a 100 percent rise by the common, it would have an upside leverage factor of 2.0.

Since warrants should only be considered for purchase when

they offer significant leverage advantages over their common stocks, a most useful addition to the normal value curves are the leverage lines as illustrated in Exhibit 3–3. These leverage lines are based on the common stock advancing 100 percent in price while the warrant is still long term and assuming that it remains on its normal value curve during the stock's advance. For example, the 2.0 leverage line intersects the top curve at $S/E = 1.0$ and the conversion value line at $S/E = 2.0$. A warrant trading on the top curve would be expected to advance 200 percent (from $W/E = 0.414$ up to $W/E = 1.236$—per Appendix B) if the common stock doubles ($S/E = 1.0$ up to $S/E = 2.0$). A warrant trading on the conversion value line would also advance 200 percent (from $W/E = 1.0$ up to $W/E = 3.0$) as the common stock doubles from $W/E = 2.0$ up to $W/E = 4.0$.

As will be noted from a study of these curves, greater leverage is attained when the stock is selling below the exercise price. As the common stock rises above the exercise price, the warrant leverage diminishes. At some high price level for the common, the warrant will lose most of its leverage and will advance or decline at about the same percentage rate as the common.

These varying leverage characteristics are perfectly logical. When the common is selling below the warrant's exercise price, the entire price paid for the warrant is premium and, therefore, one would expect greater potential gain to compensate for the possibility that the warrant may have little or no value upon expiration. As the common stock moves above the exercise price, part of the warrant's price is conversion value and the risk is, therefore, reduced because the warrant may still have substantial value upon expiration.

A good rule of thumb is that warrants should be considered for purchase when they possess upside leverage of 2.0 or higher. They would then be selling in the area to the left of, or below, the 2.0 leverage line shown in Exhibit 3–3. They should, of course, also

EXHIBIT 3-3

Normal Value Curves for Long-Term Warrants Based on Stock Yield

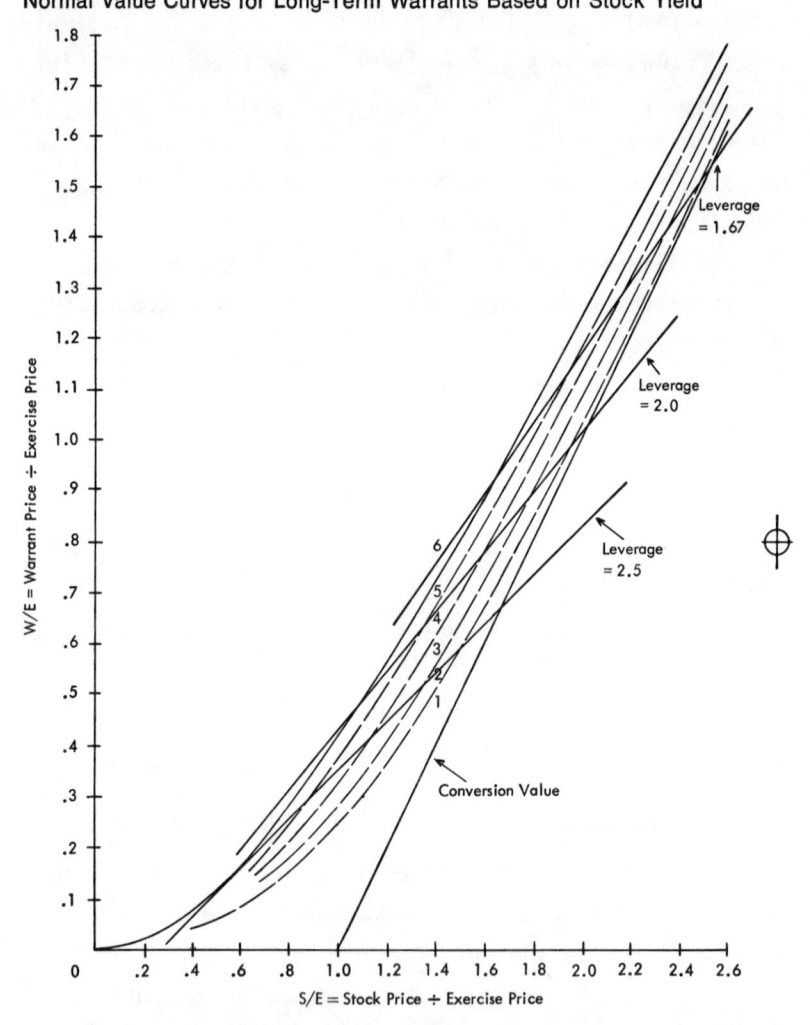

Band 5 = 0–2 percent yield
    4 = 2–4 percent
    3 = 4–6 percent
    2 = 6–8 percent
    1 = above 8 percent
Note: Area 6 represents all warrants above band 5.

be selling in, or below, their normal value band. The area between the leverage lines of 2.0 and 1.67 would be considered by the author as a "hold" area and to the right or above the 1.67 line, a "sell" area. In any event, a warrant should never be purchased unless its common stock has been evaluated and a favorable decision made on the common. The warrant should only be considered as an alternate investment to the common stock.

To facilitate more precise application of the normal value curves, they are repeated on Exhibit 3–4 for an S/E range from 0 up to 1.4. The larger scales will contribute to ease of plotting W/E and S/E factors.

28   *Dow Jones–Irwin Guide to Convertible Securities*

EXHIBIT 3–4

Normal Value Curves for Long-Term Warrants Based on Stock Yield

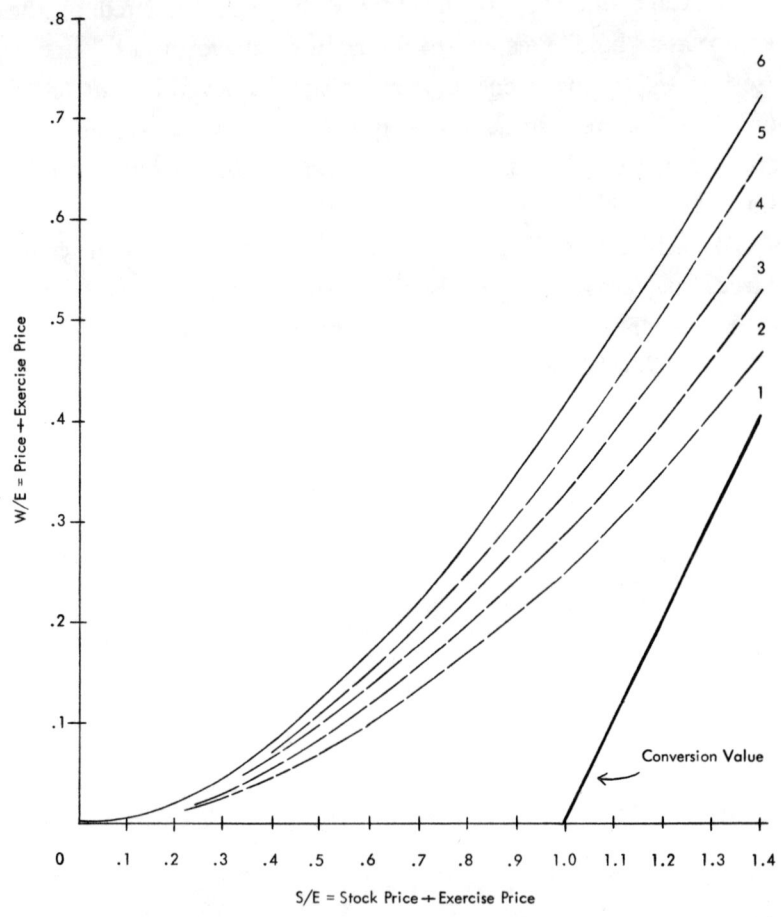

S/E = Stock Price ÷ Exercise Price

W/E = Price ÷ Exercise Price

Band 5 = 0–2 percent yield
    4 = 2–4 percent
    3 = 4–6 percent
    2 = 6–8 percent
    1 = above 8 percent
Note: Area 6 represents all warrants above band 5.

3 / Normal Value Curves for Long-Term Warrants

EXHIBIT 3-5

WORK SHEET FOR EVALUATING LONG-TERM WARRANTS

1. Company_____ Date_____

2. Stock price _____ (a)
   Warrant price _____ (b)
   Usable bond price _____ (c)

3. Exercise terms (three years hence) are _____ (d) shares of stock for $_____ (e).

4. Stock yield = _____ percent cash + _____ percent unprotected dividends = _____ percent total.

5. Stock price volatility is:

   _____ high (use normal value bands)
   _____ moderate (one lower value band)
   _____ low (two lower value bands)

6. S/E and W/E Calculations

   Adjusted warrant price = $_____ (b) / _____ (d) = $_____ (f)
   Effective exercise price = $_____ (e) x _____ (c) / 100 = $_____ (g)
   Adjusted exercise price = $_____ (g) / _____ (d) = $_____ (h)
   S/E = $_____ (a) / $_____ (h) = _____
   W/E = $_____ (f) / $_____ (h) = _____

7. By plotting the S/E and W/E factors from item 6 on Exhibit 3-3 (or 3-4) the warrant falls in:

   band _____

8. From an evaluation of items 4 and 5, the warrant's normal value should be band _____.
   The warrant is therefore considered to be:

   _____ overpriced
   _____ normally valued
   _____ undervalued

9. Other factors: _____
   _____
   _____

4

Undervalued Warrants

CHAPTER 3 developed a standardized approach for determining a warrant's normal value by the application of a mathematical formula and rating bands based on the dividends paid on the common stock. It was shown that a normally priced warrant would often advance at a percentage rate in excess of twice that of its common stock. To obtain this favorable leverage during an upside move, one must expect the warrant to also decline faster than the common in a down market. It might, therefore, be expected that the positive upside leverage would be offset by negative downside leverage. Although this is frequently the case for overpriced warrants, normally priced warrants, as evaluated by the previously discussed procedures, provide an overall mathematical advantage over purchase of their common stock.

Referring again to Exhibit 3–3 in Chapter 3 (or Appendix B for exact figures), consider a long-term warrant whose common stock pays no dividend and has exhibited high price volatility—the warrant would be expected to sell on its normal value curve at the top of band 5. If the common stock were trading at the warrant's exercise price ($S/E = 1.0$), the W/E factor for the warrant would be 0.414. Assuming a 100 percent price advance by the common (to $S/E = 2.0$), the warrant would be expected to increase in value by approximately 200 percent (to $W/E = 1.236$). On the downside, if the common were to decline 50 percent (to $S/E = 0.5$), we would expect the warrant to decline 71.5 percent to a W/E factor of 0.118. The warrant would have positive upside leverage and negative downside leverage, characteristics common to all normally priced warrants. These price relationships may be expressed by a simple formula which permits computation of an overall mathematical advantage (MA) for the warrant versus its common stock.

$$MA = \frac{\text{upside leverage}}{1.0} \times \frac{.50}{\text{downside leverage}} = \frac{2.0}{1.0} \times \frac{.50}{.715} = 1.4$$

A NORMALLY PRICED WARRANT IS MORE CONSERVATIVE THAN ITS COMMON STOCK

An investment in the above warrant would be a superior alternative to common stock. A prudent investor, who is interested in purchasing the common stock, might consider the following position in lieu of a $1,000 investment in the common.

Warrants purchased..............................	$ 700
Cash retained.....................................	$ 300
Total investment.................................	$1,000

If the common stock were to double, a net profit of $1,400 would be expected from the warrant/cash position as the warrant advances 200 percent in value ($700 × 2.0 = $1,400)—$400 more than if one had purchased the common stock. If the stock declined 50 percent, a $500 loss for the investor in the common stock, the warrant/cash position would also be expected to experience a $500 loss as the warrant price declined by the anticipated 71.5 percent ($700 × .715 = $500). In addition to these more favorable investment results, the warrant/cash position provides interest on the $300 cash portion of the investment whereas the common stock pays no dividend. Brokerage commissions paid would also be somewhat less.

A more conservative investor, one who recognizes the importance of preserving capital in declining markets for long-term investment success, would consider this position in lieu of the common stock.

Warrants purchased	$ 500
Cash retained	$ 500
Total investment	$1,000

This alternate position would be expected to appreciate in value, on an upside move by the common stock, just as much as if one had purchased the common while providing substantially greater downside safety. Assuming a one-year investment, and considering interest income associated with the investment position, the following table summarizes the anticipated results for a $1,000 investment in the common stock versus warrants and cash in equal amounts.

As illustrated below, the normally priced warrant, combined with retained cash, may offer as much to gain as its common stock at substantially less risk. The interest received on the cash retained

	Stock Price Move	
	−50%	+100%
Stock Position		
Upside capital gain		$1,000
Downside capital loss	($500)	
Dividends received	0	0
Net profit or (loss)	($500)	$1,000
Return on investment	−50%	+100%
Warrant/Cash Position		
Upside capital gain = $500 × 2.0		$1,000
Downside capital loss = $500 × .715	($360)	
Interest received = $500 × .06	30	30
Net profit or (loss)	($330)	$1,030
Return on investment	−33%	+103%

will frequently exceed dividends paid by the stock and the commission expenses for securing and closing out the warrant/cash position are usually less. Numerous examples of actual warrants that have exhibited the above characteristics in the past may be sighted —warrants on common stocks that are typically held by mutual funds and in other institutional portfolios. An examination of these portfolios has consistently shown a surprising lack of warrant understanding on the part of the professional investment community.

UNDERVALUED WARRANTS

An even greater advantage is gained when a warrant is selling below its normal price level. These undervalued warrants offer unique opportunities for spectacular investment success. An undervalued warrant may advance several times faster than its common stock during a bull market move while declining only slightly faster than the common stock on the downside.

Consider a warrant which should be selling on the normal value curve at the top of band 5, as in the previous example, but is actually trading at a price 18 percent lower ($W/E = .414 \times .82 = .34$). As shown in Exhibit 4–1, the warrant would be priced near the lower limit of band 4. Assuming that this undervalued condition is temporary, let's determine what performance can be expected if the warrant returns to its normal value after either an advance of 100 percent or a decline of 50 percent by the common, as in the previous example.

Upside gain............ 260% (from .34 up to W/E of 1.236)
Downside loss.......... 65% (from .34 down to W/E of .118)
Mathematical advantage.. $\dfrac{2.6}{1.0} \times \dfrac{.50}{.65} = 2.0$ (compared to 1.4 for the normally priced warrant)

With the above undervalued warrant opportunity, the conservative investor could again apportion his investment funds equally

EXHIBIT 4–1

Undervalued Warrant

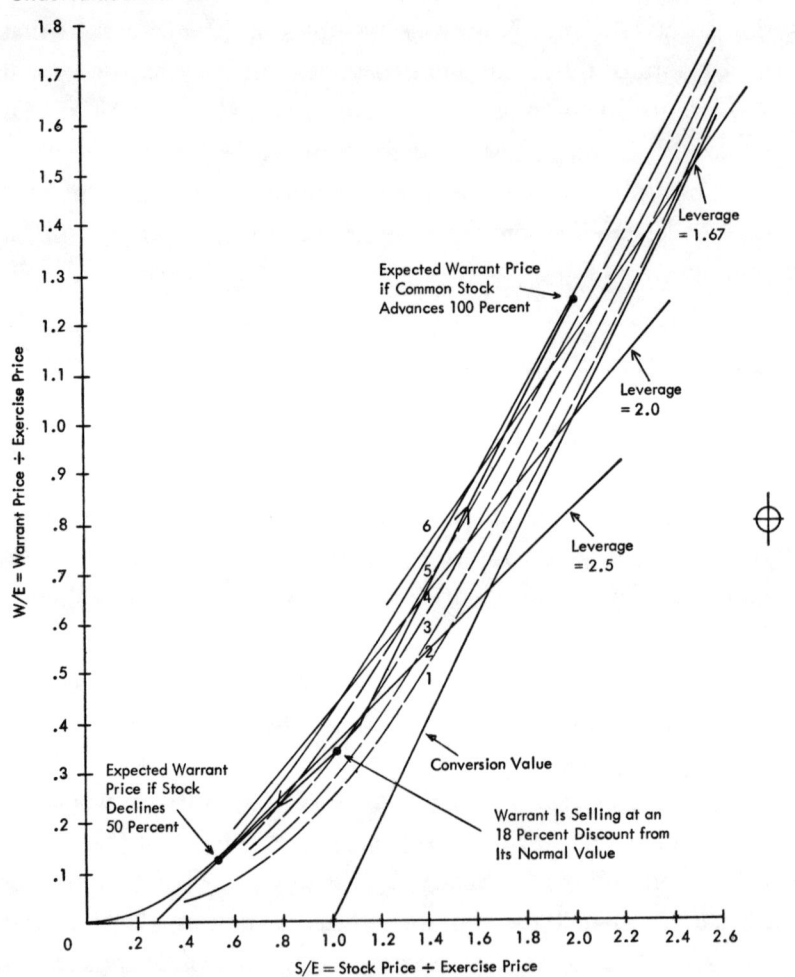

Band 5 = 0–2 percent yield
4 = 2–4 percent
3 = 4–6 percent
2 = 6–8 percent
1 = above 8 percent
Note: Area 6 represents all warrants above band 5.

between warrants and cash as a superior alternative to investing in the common stock. Potential results from his $1,000 warrant/cash position, again assuming that the stock either advanced 100 percent or declined 50 percent would be:

	Stock Price Move	
	−50%	+100%
Warrant/Cash Position		
Upside capital gain = $500 × 2.6		$1,300
Downside capital loss = $500 × .65	($325)	
Interest received = $500 × .06	30	30
Net profit or (loss)	($295)	$1,330
Return on investment	−30%	+133%

A comparison of the above alternate investments in common stock with normally valued warrants, or undervalued warrants, combined with 50 percent of one's investment funds retained in cash is summarized below.

	Stock Price Move	
	−50%	+100%
Common stock	−50%	+100%
Normally priced warrant/50 percent cash	−33%	+103%
Undervalued warrant/50 percent cash	−30%	+133%

THE BASIC SYSTEM

It would appear from the previous analysis that an investment in undervalued warrants combined with cash offers the optimum alternative to the conventional purchase of common stock—more to gain on the upside with less risk in declining markets. As exceptional as this approach may be, there is an even superior way for the conservative investor to capitalize on the fortunate existence of an undervalued warrant—techniques that offer more to gain at substantially lower risk—a simple mathematical system that can preserve one's capital in the worst bear markets while achieving above-average capital appreciation in bull markets!

As will be demonstrated in the following chapters, the "basic system" involves hedging techniques of selling short common stock against undervalued warrants. Before proceeding, it is recommended that Appendix D be carefully studied by one not experienced with the techniques of selling stock short.

GENERAL GUIDES FOR BUYING WARRANTS

1. Warrants should be evaluated only as an alternative investment to their common stock. Be sure you have studied and like the stock before buying the warrant.
2. Warrants should be long-term (three years or more) to minimize the downward price pressure caused by an approaching expiration date.
3. The warrant should provide an advantage over purchase of the common—greater potential upside reward that more than compensates for the expected higher downside risk. Application of the normal value curves and leverage lines previously illustrated will help to assure that the warrant is fairly priced. A mathematical advantage, or risk/reward ratio, may be calculated as follows:

$$MA = \frac{\%\text{ warrant advance}}{100\%\text{ stock advance}} \times \frac{50\%\text{ stock decline}}{\%\text{ warrant decline}}$$

A ratio in excess of 1.0 would indicate a positive advantage but 1.4 would be considered a more desirable ratio to compensate for other disadvantages of warrant ownership (look for an even higher ratio if the stock pays a large dividend or is relatively stable).

4. Never purchase an overpriced warrant simply for its upside leverage—there are superior means of obtaining leverage if desired, i.e., buying the common stock on margin.

5. Unless you are a skilled trader, do not buy warrants on margin. Your equity could be totally eliminated in a bear market. In fact, it is recommended that a cash reserve be retained to permit bargain hunting after major market declines.
6. Be prepared to close out the position, even at a loss, when the warrant's life is only about two years—an approaching expiration date may seriously affect the warrant's price.
7. Sell the warrant if it becomes mathematically overpriced, even if the common stock has not changed appreciably—the funds should be switched into the common or employed in another warrant having more favorable risk/reward characteristics.
8. All other factors being equal, select warrants which are listed on a major stock exchange that are also actively traded.
9. Since warrants are generally volatile securities, they should not be bought and then forgotten. The price action of both the warrant and its common stock should be watched weekly or even more frequently for maximum success.
10. The warrant certificates should be kept in street name at your brokerage firm to permit prompt action when the circumstances require it.

5

Hedging Undervalued Warrants

IT WAS demonstrated in Chapter 4 that a most acceptable technique for capitalizing on the availability of an undervalued warrant was the apportionment of one's investment funds between warrants and cash. This approach permitted the achievement of better performance than owning the common stock during rising markets while significantly reducing risk in a declining market. It was also indicated that there was an even superior alternative available to the conservative investor.

The combination investment of undervalued warrants and cash, while superior to the purchase of the common stock, does not make the most efficient use of one's capital. Only a portion of the investment funds are placed in the favorably leveraged security—the warrants. The balance was held in a passive cash position. The safest, and the most profitable long-term approach, is the *warrant hedge*.

THE WARRANT HEDGE

A hedge position involves the short sale of common stock against a convertible security—in this case, against a warrant. The hedged investor plans to take advantage of the mathematical advantage afforded by the undervalued warrant without exposing his investment capital to unnecessary risks. He is not particularly concerned about the fundamentals of the common stock as he would be if he were considering purchase of the stock or warrants only. He is, however, even more concerned about the price volatility of the common and its dividend payout.

In a rising market, the profits secured from the favorably leveraged warrant are expected to exceed losses on the common stock sold short by a significant amount. In declining markets, it would be expected that profits received from the short sale of common would partially or even completely offset losses on the warrants held long. This approach permits the conservative investor to be fully invested in the warrant without having a portion of his capital tied up in an inactive cash position. Also, as noted in Appendix D, no funds or other collateral are required to be held in deposit on the short sale since it is made against a convertible security.

Let's examine a possible warrant hedge position for the same undervalued warrant discussed in the previous chapter having the following characteristics.

```
Upside leverage............................... 2.6
Downside leverage............................. 0.65
Mathematical advantage........................ 2.0
```

Our entire $1,000 investment will be utilized to purchase warrants —no cash will be retained. Against this $1,000 investment on the long side, we will sell short $1,300 worth of common stock—our net investment is only $1,000. Excluding brokerage commissions, as in previous examples, the following results are anticipated.

	Stock Price Move	
	−50%	+100%
Warrant Hedge Position		
Downside		
Profit on stock sold short = $1,300 × 50%...... $650		
Loss on warrants purchased = $1,000 × 65%...... (650)		
Upside		
Profit on warrants purchased = $1,000 × 260%.....		$2,600
Loss on stock sold short = $1,300 × 100%.....		(1,300)
Net profit or (loss).................................	$ 0	$1,300
Return on investment...............................	0%	+130%

Presto—as if by magic—the warrant hedge position completely eliminated downside risk while actually outperforming ownership of the common stock on the upside. Compare this hedge position with the alternate unhedged investments presented in Chapter 4.

	Stock Price Move	
	−50%	+100%
Common stock...	−50%	+100%
Normally priced warrant/50 percent cash................	−33%	+103%
Undervalued warrant/50 percent cash...................	−30%	+133%
Undervalued warrant hedge position....................	0%	+130%

Chapters could be written about the theoretical ramifications of hedging undervalued warrants. However, it is believed that an actual case history will best serve to illustrate the numerous techniques and factors involved. Fortunately, for review purposes, this example also includes the majority of skills required for evaluating warrants as discussed in previous chapters.

AN ACTUAL WARRANT HEDGE POSITION IN LING-TEMCO-VOUGHT

In early January 1969, Ling-Temco-Vought's common stock was trading at $100 per share on the New York Stock Exchange, having declined from its high of $169. Numerous investment services and brokerage firms were recommending purchase at that time. However, few of these professionals were aware of vastly superior alternatives to the purchase of LTV common.

LTV warrants were concurrently trading on the American Stock Exchange at $42 per share. These warrants were the option to purchase 1.113 shares of LTV common for $115 until their January 1978 expiration date. The LTV 5's-88 straight bonds were usable at par value in lieu of cash for conversion purposes through January 15, 1973 and were selling at 60 on the New York Stock Exchange.

At prices of $100 and $42 for the common and warrant, the warrant was a far superior purchase. As do all undervalued warrants, it offered unique investment opportunities compared to purchase of the common stock. A step-by-step evaluation of possible hedge positions in Ling-Temco-Vought warrants would have proceeded in the following manner.

1. *Warrant Life.* Long-term, even though the usable bonds were effective for a shorter time than the warrant expiration date, since they could be used at par value for conversion purposes for a period of four years.

2. *S/E and W/E Calculations.* Following the procedures presented in Chapter 3, calculations were:

Adjusted warrant price = $42.00 ÷ 1.113 = $37.74
Effective exercise price = $115.00 × $60/100$ = $69.00
Adjusted exercise price = $69.00 ÷ 1.113 = $62.00
S/E = $100.00 ÷ $62.00 = 1.61
W/E = $37.74 ÷ $62.00 = .61

The S/E and W/E factors are plotted on Exhibit 5–1 and we were elated to discover that the warrants were selling right on their conversion value line! Since the yield on LTV common was only 1.3 percent, these warrants were trading at a discount of approximately 30 percent from their normal value (band 5). In ad-

EXHIBIT 5–1

The Ling-Temco-Vought Warrant in January 1969

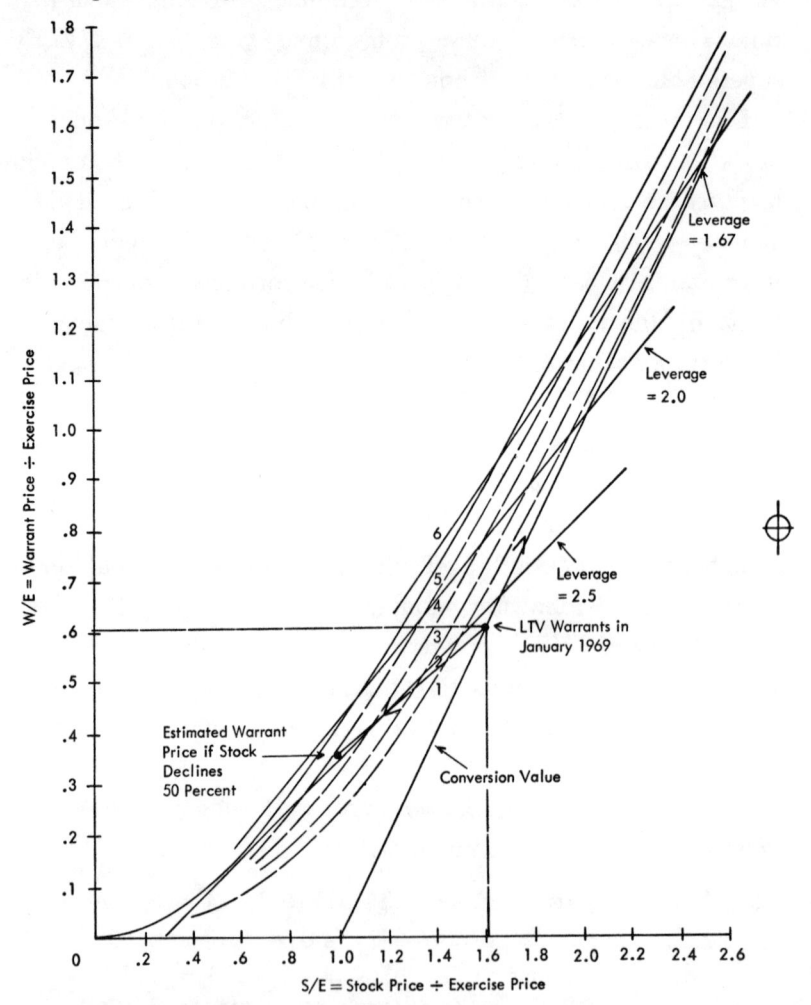

Band 5 = 0–2 percent yield
 4 = 2–4 percent
 3 = 4–6 percent
 2 = 6–8 percent
 1 = above 8 percent
Note: Area 6 represents all warrants above band 5.

dition, the speculative appeal of Ling-Temco-Vought enhanced the attraction of a long-term LTV warrant. A very fortunate opportunity was presented to alert and sophisticated investors.

3. *Considerations Given to the 5's-88 Bonds.* The LTV 5's-88 bonds were obviously speculative—not of investment grade caliber. Disregarding possible changes in money rates, we could expect these bonds to fluctuate in price somewhat in harmony with the common stock. Stock price changes would certainly reflect the future prospects for Ling-Temco-Vought and accordingly its ability to meet bond interest payments. We would, therefore, have considered bond price changes in our future price projections and would have assigned bond prices of say 50 and 70 in the event the stock declined 50 percent or advanced 100 percent, respectively.

4. *Warrant Price Estimate if Stock Declined 50 Percent.* Due to the speculative nature of LTV common and the long warrant life, it would have been reasonable to expect that the warrant would have sold at its normal value rating if the stock dropped 50 percent to $50 per share. If LTV maintained the $1.33 dividend on the common stock, the normal value rating would have been band 4. If the dividend were passed, a reasonable possibility if the stock price were to drop in half, band 5 would have been the normal value rating for the LTV warrant at that time. A conservative assumption would have been that the warrant would have sold at the top of band 4, in which case calculations to determine the warrant's probable price would have been:

Effective exercise price = $115.00 × $50/100$ = $57.50
Adjusted exercise price = $57.50 ÷ 1.113 = $51.66
S/E = $50.00 ÷ $51.66 = .97
W/E from Exhibit 5–1 = .35
Adjusted warrant price = .35 × $51.66 = $18.08
Estimated warrant price = $18.08 × 1.113 = $20.00

Note that the above steps are the reverse of the normal procedures for determining whether a warrant is fairly valued based on current price levels. In this case we are estimating the warrant's price after a major move by the common stock.

5. Warrant Price Estimate if Stock Advanced 100 Percent. Assuming that the warrant would remain at its conversion value upon a price rise by the common stock to $200 per share, calculations would have been:

$$\text{Effective exercise price} = \$115.00 \times {}^{70}\!/_{100} = \$80.50$$
$$\text{Adjusted exercise price} = \$80.50 \div 1.113 = \$72.33$$
$$S/E = \$200.00 \div \$72.33 = 2.77$$
$$W/E \text{ at its conversion value} = 1.77$$
$$\text{Adjusted warrant price} = 1.77 \times \$72.33 = \$128.00$$
$$\text{Estimated warrant price} = \$128.00 \times 1.113 = \$142.00$$

6. Leverage Projections. Leverage calculations and a determination of the mathematical advantage of the LTV warrant confirmed the initial conclusion that the warrant was substantially undervalued.

$$\text{Upside leverage} = (\$142.00 - \$42.00) \div \$42.00 = 2.38$$
$$\text{Downside leverage} = (\$42.00 - \$20.00) \div \$42.00 = .52$$
$$\text{Mathematical advantage} = \frac{2.38}{1.00} \times \frac{.50}{.52} = 2.3$$

Upon completion of the above analysis of the LTV warrant, the investor would have had several choices as to how to best take advantage of the situation. Depending on the investor's objectives and his opinion of future prospects for Ling-Temco-Vought, a variety of different hedge positions could have been evaluated. For example, consider the following alternatives:

Bullish Hedge—profits on the upside at no downside risk.
Bearish Hedge—profits on the downside at no upside risk.
Neutral Hedge—profits on both the upside or the downside.

Assuming the purchase of $1,000 worth of warrants, and excluding brokerage commissions as in the previous examples, anticipated performance results for these alternate hedge positions are presented in Exhibit 5–2. The "bullish hedge" position offered a

EXHIBIT 5–2

Alternate Hedge Positions in LTV Warrants

		Stock Price Move	
		−50%	+100%
Bullish Hedge: Stock sold short = $1,040			
Downside			
Profit on stock sold short	= $1,040 × 50%.....	$ 520	
Loss on warrants purchased	= $1,000 × 52%.....	(520)	
Upside			
Profit on warrants purchased	= $1,000 × 238%....		$2,380
Loss on stock sold short	= $1,040 × 100%....		(1,040)
Net profit or (loss)............................		$ 0	$1,340
Return on investment..........................		0%	+134%
Bearish Hedge: Stock sold short = $2,380			
Downside			
Profit on stock sold short	= $2,380 × 50%.....	$1,190	
Loss on warrants purchased	= $1,000 × 52%.....	(520)	
Upside			
Profit on warrants purchased	= $1,000 × 238%....		$2,380
Loss on stock sold short	= $2,380 × 100%		(2,380)
Net profit or (loss)............................		$ 670	$ 0
Return on investment..........................		+67%	0%
Neutral Hedge: Stock sold short = $1,700			
Downside			
Profit on stock sold short	= $1,700 × 50%.....	$ 850	
Loss on warrants purchased	= $1,000 × 52%.....	(520)	
Upside			
Profit on warrants purchased	= $1,000 × 238%....		$2,380
Loss on stock sold short	= $1,700 × 100%....		(1,700)
Net profit or (loss)............................		$ 330	$ 680
Return on investment..........................		+33%	+68%

134 percent potential gain at no downside risk—heads you win but tails you don't lose! The "bearish hedge" indicates a 67 percent downside potential at no upside risk—tails you win but heads you don't lose! The "neutral hedge" offered profits either way—heads you win and tails you win!

A GRAPHICAL ANALYSIS OF ALTERNATE HEDGE POSITIONS IN LING-TEMCO-VOUGHT WARRANTS

The anticipated return on investment for each of the alternate hedge positions may be graphically displayed as in Exhibit 5–3. It was assumed that no action was taken to modify the position while the common stock either advanced to $200 or declined to $0. Note that maximum profits are anticipated upon a major price

EXHIBIT 5–3

A Graphical Analysis of Alternate Hedge Positions in LTV Warrants

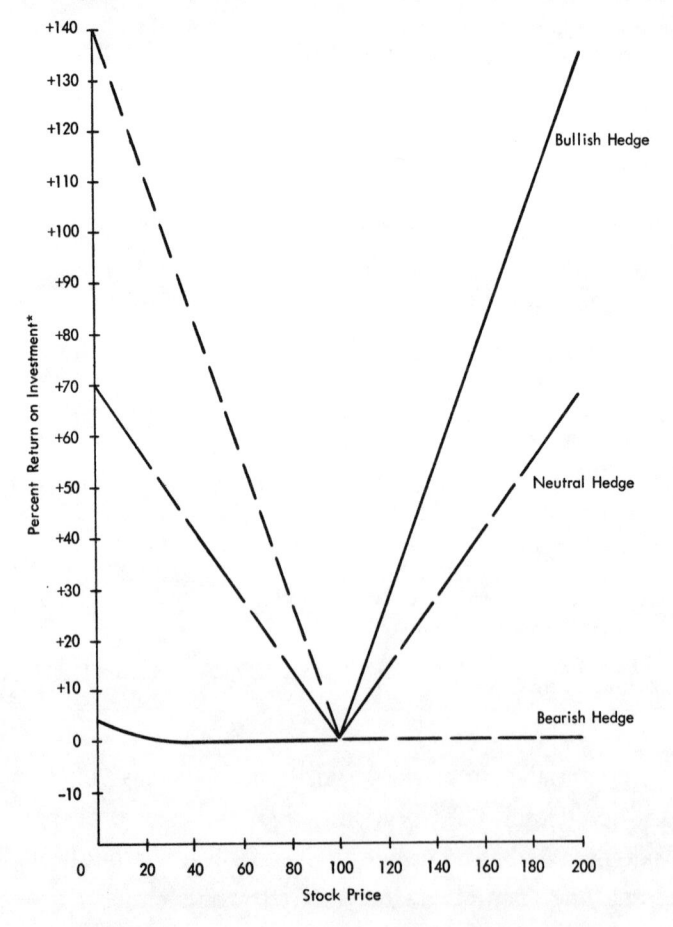

* Excluding commissions and other investment expenses.

move by the common—a situation which is typical of all warrant hedge positions. If the common were to trade only in a narrow price range, of say $80 to $120, none of the hedge positions could be closed out at significant profits—particularly when commissions and related investment expenses are considered. An exception would be the possibility that the warrants might become overpriced upon a minor price move by the common. The investor should always be ready to take advantage of such an event, but it is not normally to be expected. It cannot be overemphasized that the best warrant hedge positions are in stocks having high price volatility. Ling-Temco-Vought certainly met this requirement.

CONCLUSION OF THE LING-TEMCO-VOUGHT STORY

As was painfully evident to buyers of LTV common stock in January 1969, or to those who had purchased the stock at even higher price levels, the price subsequently dropped like a "one-way elevator" to under $10 per share in December 1970, and was still trading at this level two years later. Those who held LTV stock during this debacle suffered a 90 percent loss. Those speculators who had purchased LTV common on margin saw their equity completely evaporate long before the stock hit bottom. Those who maintained hedge positions in the LTV warrants would have lost nothing or enjoyed profits, depending on the specific hedge. In fact, the bearish hedge position, if established on margin as would normally be the case, could have been closed out near the bottom at a net profit far in excess of 100 percent!

HEDGING WARRANTS WITH BORROWED FUNDS

Since a warrant hedge position can substantially reduce or even eliminate investment risks, the conservative investor can safely consider the use of borrowed funds to provide leverage on his investment positions. This is accomplished by the purchase of warrants at the prevailing margin rate obtainable from the brokerage firm. During recent years, margin requirements for listed securities have fluctuated between 55 and 80 percent, as specified by the Federal Reserve Board's Regulation T. For simplification purposes, 70 percent will be used for most of our studies throughout this book. In some cases, actual examples may be based on the specific margin rate prevailing at the time the positions were evaluated.

For those unfamiliar with margin buying, 70 percent margin means that the buyer of securities must only deposit funds equaling 70 percent of their purchase costs with the brokerage firm. The 30 percent balance is borrowed from the brokerage firm and interest must be paid on the resulting loan (see Chapter 14 for a detailed discussion of margin regulations). Margin buying is a technique which should normally be employed only by the stock market speculator as it requires keen judgment and fast response to changing conditions. Since it amplifies both potential profits and losses, one's capital could be quickly erroded in a severe market decline.

In a carefully designed hedge position, the use of borrowed funds can actually amplify potential profits without significantly contributing to additional risk. Exhibit 5–4 presents calculations for a margined "bullish" hedge position in the LTV warrant on a standard work sheet for evaluating warrants. Since we expected large profits if the prices advanced, the use of margin amplified these potential profits by an additional 50 percent. On the downside, we were expecting to about break even so the additional leverage from margining our position did not contribute to additional downside risk. Also, the interest expense for carrying the position on margin was very small compared to the potential capital gains.

It is hoped that by now that the reader is beginning to appreciate the enormous profit potential available to the alert and knowl-

EXHIBIT 5-4

```
                            WORK SHEET
                     WARRANT HEDGE EVALUATION
```

COMPANY _Ling-Temco-Vought_   DATE _January 1969_

A. DESCRIPTION OF SECURITIES

Security	Description	Traded	Price	Yield %
Common stock		NYS	100	1.3
Warrant		ASE	42	
Usable bond	5's-88	NYS	60	

Warrant exercise terms: _1.113_ shares for $ _115.00_ to _1-15-78_

B. POSSIBLE HEDGE POSITION: Bullish __✓__, Neutral _____, or Bearish _____

Warrants purchased: _200_ shs. at $ _42.00_ each = $ _8,400_
Stock sold short: _100_ shs. at $ _100.00_ each = $ _10,000_
Investment = ($ _8,400_ + $ _110_ comm.) x _70_ % margin = $ _5,950_
Initial debit balance = $ _8,510_ - $ _5,950_ = $ _2,560_

C. PROFIT AND LOSS ESTIMATES—ASSUMING A 12-MONTH POSITION

Assumed stock price change	-50%	+50%	+100%	Other
Stock price	50		200	
Estimated warrant price	20		142	
Profit or (loss) - warrants	(4,400)		20,000	
- stock	5,000	( )	(10,000)	( )
Commissions	(320)	( )	.380	( )
Estimated capital gain or (loss)	280		9,620	
Estimated return on investment	+ 4.7%	%	+160 %	%

D. ESTIMATED ANNUAL MAINTENANCE EXPENSE

Dividends paid on stock sold short   = $(_130_)
Estimated margin interest* = $ _2,560_ x _6.0_ % = $(_155_)
Estimated negative cash flow   = $(_285_) = _4.8_ %

*Based on the initial debit balance, however, this will fluctuate as the short account is marked to the market. The indicated interest rate is also subject to change.

E. OTHER FACTORS _____

edgeable investor. A potential that the author sincerely believes will permit one to compound investment profits at a rate in excess of 15 percent annually. For those who lack the "wisdom" or "foresight" for projecting stock or market trends, the following chapters will develop and document historical performance results by the use of a simple "mechanical system" for hedging undervalued warrants. A system that anyone with a basic knowledge of arithmetic can master and execute by following the fundamentals presented in this guide.

GENERAL GUIDES FOR HEDGING WARRANTS

1. Warrants should be substantially undervalued—a mathematical advantage (risk/reward ratio) of 1.5 or higher.
2. Warrants should be long term (three years or more) to minimize the downward price pressure caused by an approaching expiration date.
3. Select warrants on common stocks which pay little or no dividends—the short seller must pay these dividends.
4. Since a properly designed hedge would be expected to protect one against major loss, even in the event of bankruptcy, best hedge positions are in stocks having high price volatility.
5. Make sure that the stock is available for short selling and that there is a reasonable probability that it can be held short as long as desired.
6. Both warrants and common stock should be actively traded to permit establishing and closing out positions at favorable price relationships.
7. The dollar amount of common stock sold short versus warrants purchased should be designed to meet one's specific objectives for that situation. This ratio will generally fall within a range of 1.0 to 2.0
8. Warrants are held in the brokerage account, even if purchased for cash, to permit the short sale of common stock without having to deposit margin on the short side. Most hedge investors purchase listed warrants on margin to obtain leverage.
9. A major price move is usually required before closing out a

position for profit—do not consider warrant hedging for short-term trading.
10. Close out the position if warrants become overvalued—the funds should be employed in another situation having more favorable risk/reward characteristics.
11. Be prepared to close out the position, even at a loss, when the warrant's life is only about two years.
12. Avoid situations where the common stock will likely be tendered or merged with another company.
13. It is recommended that one have at least five different positions for diversification and preferably 10 or more.

Possible Risks in Warrant Hedging

Risk	Recommended Action to Minimize Risk
1. A major market decline will substantially reduce warrant prices.	Amount of stock sold short should be carefully selected to minimize downside risk (bullish hedge) or to achieve profits on the downside if desired (neutral or bearish hedge).
2. Warrant price will go to its conversion value upon expiration.	Hedge positions should normally be closed out within about two years of the expiration date—even if a loss must be taken.
3. A sideways market will cause warrant prices to drift downward in relation to their stocks as time passes.	Only long-term warrants should be selected to minimize downward price pressure. Common stocks should have high price volatility to improve the chances for major price moves within a sideways market.
4. Short sales cannot be protected as a result of a tender offer or other circumstances which could cause a forced closeout of the position at unfavorable price relationships (i.e., the common rises in response to a tender offer while the warrants lag behind).	Avoid obvious problem stocks where possible. Diversification will limit overall portfolio risk.
5. Warrant values are reduced as a result of a merger whereby the common stock is exchanged for less volatile securities.	Avoid obvious problem stocks where possible. Diversification will limit overall portfolio risk.
6. Dividends paid on stocks sold short will cause an equity deterioration unless offset by profit opportunities.	Select common stocks which pay little or no dividends.
7. Margin interest paid will also cause an equity deterioration unless offset by profit opportunities.	If leverage is employed for hedging warrants, it is recommended that income type situations also be included in the overall portfolio to offset the margin interest.
8. Warrants, in general, become out of favor during a sideways market movement as they did during the later half of 1972.	There is no direct action that can be taken to avoid this risk. Trading the short side against the warrants will reduce it somewhat at the expense of lower profits if the market were to sustain a major price advance.

6

The Basic System

WAS THE highly leveraged Ling-Temco-Vought warrant an unusual occurrence? Or was it representative of frequently available situations upon which one could establish a broad and continuous investment program? The author believes that there have been an adequate number of undervalued warrants available on a continuous basis during recent years to permit a sizable portion of one's investment portfolio to be placed in warrant hedge positions. And there are positive indications that future opportunities will be even greater as more nonconglomerate type companies employ warrants in their new financing packages.

The other question, which was continuously pondered, was how should one best utilize his skills in selecting undervalued warrants and in executing hedge positions for optimum long-term performance. Should the amount of common stock sold short be determined based on one's judgment of the future price action of the stock—or the market? Are most investors capable of projecting price trends with a high degree of accuracy—is anyone truly capable of doing so including professional money managers? The conclusion reached by the author was that, over a long period of time, even the most astute professionals have difficulty in outperforming the market by a significant degree.

To accommodate those who possess few skills in forecasting future price movements, could a mechanical type system be devised to permit one to select, maintain, and to close out warrant hedge positions on a routine and predetermined basis? In the belief that a mechanical system was feasible, a specific set of warrant hedging procedures were developed as outlined below. As confirmation that the system would have worked over a reasonable period of time, and to obtain an indication of possible future profitability and potential risks, the procedures were applied to the six-year investment period from 1967 through 1972.

PROCEDURES FOR EVALUATING, ESTABLISHING, AND MAINTAINING HEDGE POSITIONS

1. Only warrants having their common stocks listed on the New York or American Stock Exchanges would be considered since it is most difficult to sell short over-the-counter securities or even those traded on regional exchanges. The warrants could be either listed or traded over-the-counter.
2. All warrants must be long-term to receive consideration, a life to expiration of three years or more. Exercise terms prevailing three years hence would be used for calculation purposes where the warrant terms were scheduled to be changed in the interim.
3. Warrants would be purchased when they were computed to be undervalued, in relation to their common stock, and regardless of anyone's good or bad opinion on the prospects for the common. It was felt that everyone with an opinion had probably already cast his vote in the marketplace and

those opinions were therefore reflected in the current price of the stock.
4. Undervalued warrants were defined as those trading in a rating band one or more levels below their normal value band. If there was a usable bond selling at an excessive discount, alternate calculations would be based on a more representative higher bond price assuming improved prospects for the company. Note that no consideration was given to possible future changes in money rates as this area also requires unusual forecasting skills.
5. If the common stock had historically low price volatility, the warrant had to be two or more rating bands below the normal value band to be considered undervalued.
6. Real estate investment trust warrants, as a group, were excluded completely from consideration due to their extremely high dividend payout and low price volatility.
7. Upside leverage for the warrant had to equal or exceed 2.0 as determined from leverage lines previously shown on the normal value curves.
8. The evaluation would include both warrants purchased for cash (nonleveraged) as well as purchases at the prevailing margin rates obtainable from the brokerage firm. Note that over-the-counter warrants must be margined at a full 100 percent and, depending on specific rules of the brokerage firm and portfolio makeup, low priced warrants might also have to be margined at up to 100 percent (refer to Chapter 14 for current margin regulations).
9. The amount of common stock sold short was to be 130 percent of the market value of the warrants purchased. This 1.3 ratio was established to compensate for the negative downside leverage inherent in even most undervalued warrants so as to achieve an approximate break-even position in declining markets. Note that, although a neutral position

involving additional short selling could produce profits in both rising and declining markets, mathematics indicate that a break-even, downside position would produce optimum performance results over the long-term, even assuming no long-term upward bias for stock prices (refer to Appendix E for the determination of the optimum amount of short selling).
10. Periodic adjustments would be made to the amount of common stock sold short to maintain the 1.3 ratio. These adjustments were for the purpose of keeping the portfolio in a continuous low-risk downside posture. Additional short sales would be made in rising markets to "lock in" profits and partial covering of short sales would be effected in declining markets to take profits.
11. Positions would be closed out if the warrants became overpriced or if their upside leverage was reduced below 1.67. Positions would also be closed if the remaining warrant life was reduced to less than two years.

SPECIFIC BUY, HOLD, AND SELL ACTIONS

1. *Establish* hedge positions when:
    a) Warrants are undervalued *and,*
    b) Upside leverage is greater than 2.0 *and,*
    c) Warrant life exceeds three years.
2. *Hold* hedge positions when:
    a) Warrants are normally valued *and,*
    b) Upside leverage is greater than 1.67 *and,*
    c) Warrant life exceeds two years.
3. *Closeout* hedge positions when:
    a) Warrants become overpriced *or,*
    b) Upside leverage is less than 1.67 *or,*
    c) Warrant life is less than two years.

ANTICIPATED PERFORMANCE IN DIFFERENT TYPES OF MARKETS

Prior to application of the above procedures to the six-year test period, it will be of interest to review the anticipated performance results for different types of market conditions which we can expect to encounter.

Declining Markets. During broad declining markets, similar to the 1969–70 collapse, we would expect the equity in the account to remain relatively constant as profits on the short sales would offset warrant losses. However, since the account's equity margins the long side of the portfolio only, buying power is developed as the security prices fall. Additional investments would be established with this surplus buying power. Also, since the warrants are expected to decline at a faster rate than the common stock, short positions will be periodically reduced, or additional warrants purchased, to maintain the 1.3 short to long ratio. As erratic prices can be expected during a market panic, there will probably be opportunities to close out positions for profit as some warrants become temporarily overpriced in relation to their common stock. The funds obtained would be shifted into more favorable situations to constantly upgrade our portfolio.

To illustrate the above points, consider the following hedge position for a warrant having the previously discussed leverage characteristics of 2.6 on the upside and .65 on the downside.

Warrants purchased........................... $1,000
Common stock sold short...................... $1,300
Investment at 70 percent margin.............. $ 700

If the common stock and warrants were to decline 50 percent and 65 percent, respectively, profits on the short side would exactly equal losses on the warrants. Equity would have remained constant at our initial investment of $700. The status of our margin account after this decline, assuming that this was the only position in the account, would be:

Value of warrants held long.................... $350 ($650 loss)
Value of common stock sold short.............. $650 ($650 profit)
Equity.. $700
Required margin = $350 × 70%................. $245
Excess margin = $700 − $245.................. $455
Short to long ratio = $650 ÷ $350............. 1.86

If, after this price decline, the warrants were still undervalued in relation to the common, additional warrants would be purchased to reestablish the 1.3 ratio of stock sold short to warrants purchased. If the warrants were normally valued at this point, a portion of the short position would be covered instead of buying additional warrants. If the warrants were overpriced, the entire position would be closed out and the funds redeployed in another situation having better risk/reward characteristics.

Advancing Markets. In broad advancing markets, similar to the 1967–68 period, we would anticipate an increase in our equity as warrant profits would be expected to exceed losses on the common stock sold short. Since the popularity of various stock groups will rotate during bull markets, our portfolio of hedged investments will naturally do best when the secondary and speculative stocks, which we prefer for warrant hedging, are in favor.

Consider again the previous hedge position based on the common stock and warrants advancing 100 percent and 260 percent, respectively. Our equity would have increased by $1,300 ($2,600 − $1,300) and the status of our margin account would be:

Value of warrants held long.................... $3,600 ($2,600 profit)
Value of common stock sold short.............. $2,600 ($1,300 loss)
Equity = $700 + $1,300 profit................. $2,000
Required margin = $3,600 × 70%............... $2,520
Margin deficit = $2,520 − $2,000.............. $ 520
Short to long ratio = $2,600 ÷ $3,600.......... .72

Upon a major upside move, additional buying power is not expected even though our equity should increase by a substantial amount. In the above example, the account has become restricted, or undermargined by $520. However, no action is required to correct this situation unless the equity were to drop to below 30 percent of the market value of the long side of our portfolio—it is 55 percent in the above example ($2,000 ÷ $3,600 = 55%). If the equity did drop to below 30 percent, the brokerage firm would issue a maintenance margin call requiring the deposit of additional funds or the sale of a portion of our long positions to bring the account back up to the 30 percent level.

If the warrants were still undervalued after the above price advance, additional common stock would be sold short to reestablish the 1.3 ratio. If the warrants were normally valued, a portion of the warrants would be sold instead of shorting more stock. If they became overpriced, the total position would be closed out.

Sideways Market. This is the most unpredictable and difficult type market for the warrant hedger to encounter. By periodically adding to or reducing short sales as required to maintain the 1.3 ratio, some profits may be obtained if the price swings of individual positions are broad enough to permit these trades. From the negative aspect, it is possible to experience a slow decline in one's equity resulting from margin interest plus dividends paid on stock sold short. The warrants will probably also decline in value relative to the stock as time passes depending on the time remaining to their expiration date. Probably the most important variable is whether speculative securities are in favor or not during the period that the overall market is in the sideways movement. If they are in favor, there will most likely be sufficient market action to produce some profits. If they are not, it will probably be a very dull and disappointing market for the warrant hedger.

The following chapters will demonstrate how the mechanical hedging system would have performed during the six-year period between 1967 and 1972—a period in the stock market's history that includes each of the typical types of markets discussed above —a period when most everyone had difficulties achieving satisfactory profits from their equity investments.

7

The Basic System in Action

To DETERMINE how the mechanical system would have performed during the six-year test period, from 1967 through 1972, the procedures developed in Chapter 6 were applied with these modifications.

1. Only listed warrants were considered as it was felt that historical price data available on over-the-counter warrants, many of which were not actively traded, was of questionable accuracy. Also, most OTC securities have small floating supplies thus they cannot accept large amounts of capital without significantly affecting their price levels. It was believed, therefore, that the study, being limited to listed warrants only, would provide a more accurate documentation of historical performance as well as a better indication of future profit potential for warrant hedging.
2. Warrants were evaluated and specific buy, hold and sell decisions were made but once every six months—January and July of each year. By limiting the study to six-month intervals,

it was felt by the author that it would contribute to more conservative results and also be of meaningful value to those investors unable to monitor their portfolios on a continuous basis.

3. Only warrants having normal value bands of 4 or 5 were considered so as to minimize the cost of dividends paid on stock sold short. This limitation also improved the probability of the common stock having high price volatility—an important characteristic of a successful hedge program. It was assumed, that at the end of each six-month period, that portfolio adjustments would have been made so that: all positions represented an equal portion of the portfolio; the short to long ratio would be 1.3 for each position; and the account's equity was 70 percent of the market value of the securities held long. These adjustments were necessary to assure that performance for the subsequent six-month period would not be distorted by prior results.

To assure a realistic study, deductions were made in the profit and loss calculations for applicable investment expenses: commissions, margin interest, and dividends paid on stock sold short.

THE SIX-YEAR STUDY

Appendix F lists all warrants which were possible candidates for selection beginning January 1967. S/E and W/E calculations were made for each in accordance with previously established procedures. Each warrant was assigned to a normal value band based on its common stock yield. Its actual value band was then determined by plotting its S/E and W/E factors on the normal value curves and noting in which band those factors fell. Buy, hold, and sell actions, as indicated, were made by application of the mechanical rules previously developed.

As will be noted from an analysis of Appendix F, there were only seven warrants available for consideration in January 1967. During the ensuing years, increased warrant popularity swelled the selection list to 40 by mid-1970. At this point, numerous nonconglomerate type companies began employing imaginative financing arrangements in an effort to reduce the excessive cost of borrowing brought about by the historically high interest rates prevailing at that time. Other companies also found warrants to be a helpful aid in their new equity financing.

Following are the semiannual warrant selections and a review of the portfolio during the six-year study.

January 1967–January 1969: A Major Bull Market

January 1967. Hedge positions were initially established in two of the seven warrants available for consideration as the market began a substantial upward move—an advance that featured speculative type securities. It was the era of the "go-go" money managers. The two initial positions were Hilton Hotels and Uris Buildings.

July 1967. Of the initial two positions, Hilton Hotels was still rated a "buy" while Uris Buildings was rated "hold." Realty Equities was added to the portfolio which now included: Hilton Hotels, Reality Equities, and Uris Buildings.

January 1968. The common stock of Uris Buildings, having more than doubled in price from the original buy level, decreased the warrant leverage to below 1.67, thus forcing a "sell" decision. No new positions were available at that time and the portfolio included these two positions: Hilton Hotels and Realty Equities.

July 1968. During this period, Realty Equities substantially increased in price and the hedge position was closed out since the warrant leverage fell to below 1.67. Braniff Airways was purchased to give us a portfolio of the following two positions: Braniff Airways and Hilton Hotels.

January 1969–July 1970: A Major Bear Market

January 1969. As we entered our third investment year, the other one of our initial purchases, Hilton Hotels, was closed out as the stock climbed to $134 from the original level of $32 and the warrant leveraged dropped to below 1.67. Gulf & Western Industries, Ling-Temco-Vought (remember it?), McCrory, and Wilson & Company were added. Our portfolio included five positions as we headed into the worst bear market since the thirties: Braniff Airways, Gulf & Western Industries, Ling-Temco-Vought, McCrory, and Wilson & Company.

July 1969. Braniff Airways and Gulf & Western were closed out as their warrants became overpriced during the market decline. General Host and National General were added so our portfolio still contained five different situations: General Host, Ling-Temco-Vought, McCrory, National General, and Wilson & Company.

January 1970. As the market continued downward, General Host, Ling-Temco-Vought, and National General warrants all became overpriced and were closed out. Four new positions were added to our portfolio bringing the total number of hedge positions to six: Gould, Kaufman & Broad, Kinney National Services, Loew's Theatres, McCrory, and Wilson & Company.

July 1970–July 1971: A Market Rebound

July 1970. The stock market debacle during the first half of 1970 dropped three of the positions to price levels which placed the warrants in an overpriced condition and they were closed out. Despite the increase in the number of warrants trading, no new issues were favorably priced to permit addition to our portfolio. It contained three positions as the market turned upward: Kaufman & Broad, Kinney National Services, and McCrory.

January 1971. The hedge position in McCrory was closed out and two new warrants were selected: Continental Telephone and Loews (formerly Loew's Theatres). The portfolio contained four positions as we entered our fifth year: Continental Telephone, Kaufman & Broad, Kinney National Services, and Loews.

July 1971–January 1973: A Sideways Market

July 1971. The Kaufman & Broad position was closed out as the warrant leverage fell to below 1.67 upon an advance by the common stock. A position was again established in Gould and a new position in Daylin provided us with a portfolio of five situations: Continental Telephone, Daylin, Gould, Kinney Services (formerly Kinney National Services), and Loews. At this point, the stock market began a long sideways movement.

January 1972. As a result of a very stable market during the last half of 1971, all of our hedge positions remained in a narrow price range and none were closed out. A position was reestablished in National General and new positions were taken in General Development and Louisiana Land & Exploration. As we entered the sixth year of our study, our portfolio was swelled to eight different situations: Continental Telephone, Daylin, General Development (warrants issued by City Investing), Gould, Kinney Services, Loews, Louisiana Land & Exploration (warrants issued by Amerada Hess), and National General.

July 1972. The stock market continued to trade in a narrow price range during the first half of 1972 and gave us no opportunities to close out any of our hedge positions. Our portfolio contained the eight positions which we had in January plus a new position taken in Carrier Corp.

January 1973. The market continued its sideways movement which began in July 1971. The hedge position in Continental Telephone was closed out as the warrant's life to expiration dropped to less than two years. The position in General Development was also closed as the warrant became overpriced upon a substantial decline by the common stock. Positions were reestablished in Braniff Airways and General Host and new positions taken in LCA Corp., NVF Co., and United National. Our portfolio contained 12 different situations as we concluded the six-year study and entered the seventh year: Braniff Airways, Carrier, Daylin, General Host, Gould, LCA, Loews, Louisiana Land & Exploration, National General, NVF, United National, and Warner Communications (formerly Kinney Services).

Upon examining the above portfolio of warrant hedge positions, the author cannot resist commenting that the common stocks by themselves would have made an interesting portfolio of speculative and aggressive growth securities—many were included in mutual funds and other institutional type accounts at the time. How many of these professional money managers were aware of the fact that hedge positions in the warrants of these stocks actually offered as much (or more) to gain if the stocks appreciated in price, as they hoped and expected, at little risk if their expectations did not materialize. If their bylaws precluded short selling, they still could have improved their risk/reward prospects by the combination of warrants and cash.

SUMMARY OF ALL POSITIONS TAKEN DURING THE SIX-YEAR STUDY

Exhibit 7–1 presents a summary of all positions established during the six-year study. A few pertinent conclusions may be drawn.
1. The chance that a warrant will become overpriced is greatest during a major market decline as most investors apparently place excessive values on "cheap" warrants.
2. An undervalued warrant will generally remain undervalued as its common stock advances. A hedge position will not normally be closed out on the upside until its leverage is reduced to the point where little more can be gained by holding the position (the 1.67 leverage line).

EXHIBIT 7-1

Positions Taken in Undervalued Warrants—January 1967 through January 1973

Warrant	Date Purchased	Date Closed	Months Held	Stock Gain or Loss	Warrant Gain or Loss	Reason Position Was Closed
Hilton Hotels	1-67	1-69	24	+319	+1115	A
Uris Buildings	1-67	1-68	12	+105	+ 271	A
Realty Equities	7-67	7-68	12	+104	+ 228	A
Braniff Airways	7-68	7-69	12	− 37	− 42	C
Gulf & Western	1-69	7-69	6	− 49	− 54	C
Ling-Temco-Vought	1-69	1-70	12	− 72	− 82	C
McCrory	1-69	1-71	24	− 51	− 68	C
Wilson & Company	1-69	7-70	18	− 76	− 76	C
General Host	7-69	1-70	6	− 40	− 38	C
National General	7-69	1-70	6	− 35	− 26	C
Gould	1-70	7-70	6	− 36	− 44	C
Kaufman & Broad	1-70	7-71	18	+ 29	+ 84	A
Kinney National Services†	1-70		36+			
Loew's Theatres	1-70	7-70	6	− 46	− 50	C
Continental Telephone	1-71	1-73	24	+ 2	− 29	E
Loews	1-71		24+			
Daylin	7-71		18+			
Gould	7-71		18+			
General Development	1-72	1-73	12	− 47	− 56	C
Louisiana Land & Exploration	1-72		12+			
National General	1-72		12+			
Carrier	7-72		6+			

* A.—Warrant leverage was reduced to below 1.67 upon an upside move.
   B.—Warrant became overpriced upon an upside move.
   C.—Warrant became overpriced upon a downside move.
   D.—Warrant became overpriced upon a sideways move.
   E.—Warrant life remaining was less than two years.
† Present name is Warner Communications.

3. Most warrants will decline at a greater percentage rate than their common stocks thus confirming the need for excess short selling to preserve capital (the 1.3 short to long ratio).
4. The vast majority of hedge positions were held for a year or longer indicating that patience is required for warrant hedging as in other long-term investment programs.
5. Warrants closed out on the upside increased percentagewise by more than twice their common stock as we had anticipated

7 / *The Basic System in Action* 67

EXHIBIT 7-2

Warrants in January 1973

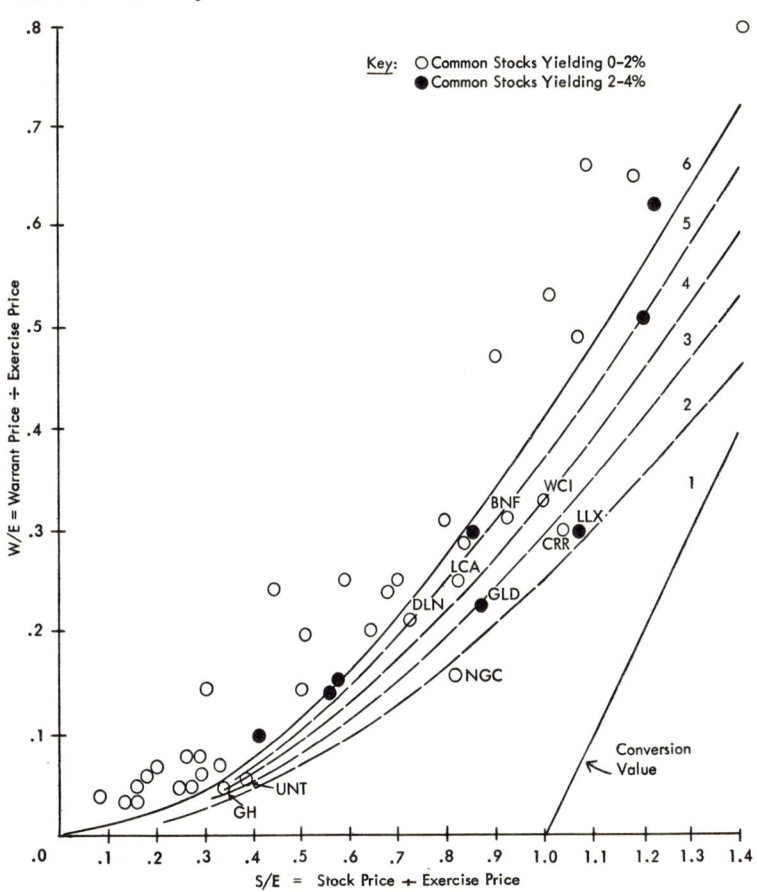

Key: ○ Common Stocks Yielding 0-2%
● Common Stocks Yielding 2-4%

Y-axis: W/E = Warrant Price ÷ Exercise Price
X-axis: S/E = Stock Price ÷ Exercise Price

Band 5 = 0-2 percent yield
     4 = 2-4 percent
     3 = 4-6 percent
     2 = 6-8 percent
     1 = above 8 percent
Note: Area 6 represents all warrants above band 5.

—even though they remained undervalued during the advance.

A CLOSE LOOK AT WARRANTS IN JANUARY 1973

Exhibit 7–2 presents the warrants from the January 1973 listing plotted on the familiar S/E versus W/E normal value curves (up to $S/E = 1.4$). This provides a graphical picture of typical warrant/common stock price relationships. Note that the majority of warrants trading at that time were considered to be overpriced—especially at the lower end of the S/E scale. Those warrants given a "buy" rating are identified by their stock's ticker symbols.

A close examination of Exhibit 7–2 reveals that when the common stocks were selling at half their warrant's exercise price, or less ($S/E = 0$ to .5), 16 of the 18 warrants were considered to be overpriced—the only exceptions being General Host and United National. This phenomenon may be partially due to the conservative nature of our warrant value curves at the lower end of the S/E scale. However, since most of these warrants were selling below $3, their overpriced condition is believed to be primarily the result of excessive enthusiasm by the investing public for low-priced securities; regardless of their inherent speculative worth. It is also possible that certain warrant services have misled investors by recommending warrant purchases when the warrants were, in fact, mathematically overvalued. Buying on a "scale down," for example, could artificially support the warrant's price while the common stock was falling more rapidly.

Most "normal value" ratings for warrants referenced in the literature also reflect these excessive prices paid for low-priced warrants. Although these ratings may accurately depict historical price relationships, they should not be used indiscriminately for investment purposes. A closer review of the 16 overpriced warrants will prove why. The average S/E and W/E factors for these

16 warrants are .26 and .08, respectively. If their common stocks were to advance, on average, by about 300 percent to bring them up to the warrant exercise price ($S/E = 1.0$), the warrants would only increase by about 400 percent if they were to sell at their normal values at that point—"normal values" that are surprisingly consistent among different warrant raters at an S/E factor of 1.0. And this warrant advance assumes that all of the 16 warrants would still have over three years of life remaining after their common stocks advanced 300 percent—an extremely improbable likelihood. This insignificant and theoretical leverage advantage is no reasonable compensation for the higher risks assumed by the warrant buyer—particularly since at their present price levels there are good possibilities that many of the warrants will become worthless upon expiration. The application of the more conservative normal value curves presented in this book will help to assure that the warrant investor receives an acceptable risk/reward opportunity for his investment dollars.[1]

---

[1] An article published in the July-August 1967 issue of *Financial Analysts Journal* presented a statistically developed formula for determining reasonable market price for warrants. This formula would assign a W/E factor of .105 to a three-year listed warrant on a nondividend paying stock which is selling at $S/E = .26$. In this author's opinion, such an excessive warrant price would be absurd.

8

Performance Results from the Basic System

EXHIBIT 8–1 presents performance data for the warrants and their common stocks for each of the 12 six-month periods during the six-year study from January 1967 to January 1973. Gains or losses for each warrant and stock were determined and average gains or losses were calculated on the basis that equal amounts of each position were held in the portfolio. The following points of interest may be drawn from an analysis of this data.

1. Of the 12 six-month periods, stock prices advanced six times, declined three and were essentially neutral three times (a neutral or sideways market is arbitrarily defined as one where the common stocks advanced or declined by less than 10 percent during the six-month period). The price movements were in general harmony with stock market averages—especially those that reflect a broad spectrum of stocks, i.e., Value Line's 1,500 stock average.
2. During the nine periods of advancing or declining prices, the warrants advanced or declined, on average, at greater percentage rates than their common stocks, as expected.

EXHIBIT 8–1

The Six-Year Study—Stock and Warrant Performance

	Stock Prices			Warrant Prices		
Position	*Beginning*	*Ending*	*% Gain or Loss*	*Beginning*	*Ending*	*% Gain or Loss*
January–June 1967						
Hilton Hotels............	32.00	59.12	+ 84.8	6.75	19.75	+192.6
Uris Buildings............	16.25	21.25	+ 30.8	6.12	11.88	+ 93.9
Average gain or loss.....			+ 57.8			+143.2
July–December 1967						
Hilton Hotels............	59.12	82.50	+ 39.5	19.75	32.12	+ 62.6
Realty Equities...........	12.38	10.00	− 19.2	6.25	6.12	− 2.0
Uris Buildings............	21.25	33.25	+ 56.5	11.88	22.75	+ 91.6
Average gain or loss.....			+ 25.6			+ 50.7
January–June 1968						
Hilton Hotels............	82.50	104.62	+ 26.8	32.12	58.88	+ 83.3
Realty Equities...........	10.00	25.25	+152.5	6.12	20.50	+234.7
Average gain or loss.....			+ 89.6			+159.0
July–December 1968						
Braniff Airways..........	22.88	21.88	− 4.4	28.50	28.50	0
Hilton Hotels............	104.62	134.00	+ 28.1	58.88	82.00	+ 39.3
Average gain or loss.....			+ 11.8			+ 19.6
January–June 1969						
Braniff Airways..........	21.88	14.50	− 33.7	28.50	16.50	− 42.1
Gulf & Western Industries..	51.25	26.25	− 48.8	18.12	8.25	− 54.5
Ling-Temco-Vought.......	98.00	40.00	− 59.2	41.25	13.12	− 68.2
McCrory.................	36.00	24.25	− 32.6	16.25	8.88	− 46.1
Wilson & Company........	37.12	24.25	− 34.7	13.75	6.88	− 50.0
Average gain or loss.....			− 41.8			− 52.2
July–December 1969						
General Host.............	24.00	14.50	− 39.6	5.62	3.50	− 37.8
Ling-Temco-Vought.......	40.00	27.00	− 32.5	13.12	7.62	− 41.9
McCrory.................	24.25	23.75	− 2.1	8.88	7.62	− 14.1
National General.........	29.62	19.38	− 34.6	8.62	6.38	− 26.1
Wilson & Company........	24.25	19.75	− 18.6	6.88	5.25	− 23.6
Average gain or loss.....			− 25.5			− 28.7
January–June 1970						
Gould...................	36.75	23.50	− 36.1	8.50	4.75	− 44.1
Kaufman & Broad.........	49.00	32.12	− 34.4	22.25	13.88	− 37.6
Kinney National Services...	30.25	21.88	− 29.3	8.75	5.50	− 37.1
Loew's Theatres...........	37.38	20.00	− 46.3	16.00	8.00	− 50.0
McCrory.................	23.75	15.38	− 35.3	7.62	3.50	− 54.1
Wilson & Company........	19.75	8.88	− 55.1	5.25	3.25	− 38.1
Average gain or loss.....			− 39.4			− 43.5

EXHIBIT 8–1 (Continued)

	Stock Prices			Warrant Prices		
Position	Beginning	Ending	% Gain or Loss	Beginning	Ending	% Gain or Loss
July–December 1970						
Kaufman & Broad.........	32.12	44.75	+ 39.3	13.88	23.75	+ 71.2
Kinney National Services...	21.38	29.00	+ 35.7	5.50	7.25	+ 31.8
McCrory..................	15.38	17.75	+ 15.4	3.50	5.12	+ 46.4
Average gain or loss.....			+ 30.1			+ 49.8
January–June 1971						
Continental Telephone.....	25.25	23.25	– 7.9	7.75	7.38	– 4.8
Kaufman & Broad.........	44.75	63.00	+ 40.8	23.75	41.00	+ 72.6
Kinney Services............	29.00	34.25	+ 18.1	7.25	12.25	+ 69.0
Loews....................	34.88	54.25	+ 55.6	14.00	27.88	+ 99.1
Average gain or loss.....			+ 26.6			+ 59.0
July–December 1971						
Continental Telephone.....	23.25	22.38	– 3.8	7.38	6.38	– 13.6
Daylin....................	21.25	23.75	+ 11.8	7.38	8.25	+ 11.9
Gould....................	36.25	44.25	+ 22.1	8.62	11.25	+ 30.4
Kinney Services............	34.25	31.25	– 8.8	12.25	9.75	– 20.4
Loews....................	54.25	46.38	– 14.5	27.88	22.00	– 21.1
Average gain or loss.....			+ 1.4			– 2.6
January–June 1972						
Continental Telephone.....	22.38	21.00	– 6.1	6.38	4.88	– 23.5
Daylin....................	23.75	17.75	– 25.3	8.25	6.00	– 27.3
General Development......	25.88	33.25	+ 28.5	9.00	11.88	+ 31.9
Gould....................	44.25	32.75	– 26.0	11.25	10.75	– 4.4
Kinney Services............	31.25	48.38	+ 54.8	9.75	19.12	+ 96.2
Loews....................	46.38	53.50	+ 15.4	22.00	23.62	+ 7.4
Louisiana Land & Exploration..............	51.12	44.75	– 12.5	18.50	14.50	– 21.6
National General..........	25.00	23.75	– 5.0	6.38	5.88	– 7.8
Average gain or loss.....			+ 3.0			+ 6.4
July–December 1972						
Carrier...................	29.50	28.38	– 3.9	9.83	8.25	– 16.1
Continental Telephone.....	21.00	25.75	+ 22.6	4.88	5.50	+ 12.8
Daylin....................	17.75	16.25	– 8.5	6.00	4.75	– 20.8
General Development......	33.25	13.75	– 58.6	11.88	4.00	– 66.3
Gould....................	32.75	32.38	– 1.1	10.75	8.38	– 22.1
Loews....................	53.50	46.75	– 12.6	23.62	18.12	– 23.3
Louisiana Land & Exploration..............	44.75	43.25	– 3.4	14.50	12.00	– 17.2
National General..........	23.75	32.75	+ 37.9	5.88	6.50	+ 10.6
Warner Communications*...	48.38	36.88	– 23.8	19.12	12.38	– 35.3
Average gain or loss.....			– 5.7			– 19.7

* Formerly Kinney Services.

3. During the six periods of rising prices, the common stocks advanced 40 percent, on average, while the warrants advanced 80 percent. These relative price increases confirmed our anticipated results for undervalued warrants having upside leverage of 2.0 or higher.
4. During the three periods of falling prices, the common stocks declined 36 percent, on average, versus 42 percent for the warrants. Here again the relative price performance was consistent with expected results since, as previously indicated, even undervalued warrants normally possess negative leverage on the downside.
5. From the above performance data, an overall mathematical advantage for the warrants over their common stocks may be computed as follows:

$$MA = \frac{\text{upside warrant gain}}{\text{upside stock gain}} \times \frac{\text{downside stock loss}}{\text{downside warrant loss}}$$

$$= \frac{80}{40} \times \frac{36}{42} = 1.7$$

6. During the three periods when prices were neutral, the relative performance between the warrants and common stocks was about as expected except for the last six-month period. During this period, warrants, in general, were extremely out of favor—they lagged behind when their common stocks advanced and declined appreciably faster when their stocks declined.

As a general conclusion, the actual results were surprisingly consistent with overall market movements and expected relative warrant/stock performance in spite of the small number of positions held in the portfolio throughout the study. Also, the six-year period, which included a major bull market, a major bear market, and a market of drifting prices, is probably quite representative of market cycles to be expected in the future. It would seem, therefore, that future predictions based on this study may be made with a high degree of confidence.

COMMON STOCK PERFORMANCE

Exhibit 8–2 shows the gains or losses on investments made in just the common stocks for each of the 12 six-month periods. The cumulative profit or loss column assumes that total equity would

EXHIBIT 8–2

The Six-Year Study—Common Stock Performance

Six-Month Period	Net Profit or Loss* (Percent)	Cumulative Profit or Loss (Percent)
January–June 1967	+57.8	+ 57.8
July–December 1967	+25.6	+ 98
January–June 1968	+89.6	+276
July–December 1968	+11.8	+320
January–June 1969	−41.8	+145
July–December 1969	−25.5	+ 82
January–June 1970	−39.4	+ 10
July–December 1970	+30.1	+ 44
January–June 1971	+26.6	+ 82
July–December 1971	+ 1.4	+ 84
January–June 1972	+ 3.0	+ 90
July–December 1972	− 5.7	+ 79

* Net profit or loss figures shown were taken from Exhibit 8–1. No deductions were made for commissions paid on stock purchases or sales as it was assumed that they would have been offset by dividends received.

have been equally proportioned among the indicated stocks in the portfolio at each six-month interval. As shown by the cumulative profit or loss figures, one would have increased his equity by 79 percent if he had maintained a portfolio of these stocks for the six-year period. This 79 percent appreciation appears to be reasonable for a portfolio of speculative and growth securities, selected at random, when considering overall market action during that period of time. It is very close to the average gain for growth type mutual funds having generally high volatility. It may, therefore, be concluded that the common stocks in our study were fairly representative of the general stock market for speculative and growth type securities.

WARRANT PERFORMANCE

If investments were made in the warrants only, Exhibit 8–3 shows that equity would have increased by an astounding 284 percent—almost four times that of the common stocks. This vastly superior performance dramatically illustrates the advantages offered by the undervalued warrant. Note, however, that in spite of this exceptional performance, the warrant investor still would have had many sleepless nights. He would have witnessed his equity decline by over 80 percent during the 1969–70 bear market.

EXHIBIT 8–3

The Six-Year Study—Warrant Performance

Six-Month Period	Net Profit or Loss* (Percent)	Cumulative Profit or Loss (Percent)
January–June 1967	+142.2	+142.2
July–December 1967	+ 49.7	+263
January–June 1968	+158.0	+835
July–December 1968	+ 18.6	+1009
January–June 1969	− 53.2	+ 419
July–December 1969	− 29.7	+ 265
January–June 1970	− 44.5	+ 103
July–December 1970	+ 48.8	+ 201
January–June 1971	+ 58.0	+ 376
July–December 1971	− 3.6	+ 359
January–June 1972	+ 5.4	+ 384
July–December 1972	− 20.7	+ 284

* A deduction of 1 percent was made from the figures of Exhibit 8–1 to compensate for commissions which would have been paid for warrant purchases and sales.

And how would he have felt if he had started his warrant investment program in January 1969—at the beginning of the decline? He would have still been behind by 65 percent four years later. He would have received little comfort from the fact that his warrant investments had provided mathematical advantages over their common stocks.

WARRANT/CASH PERFORMANCE

It was indicated in Chapter 4 that a conservative investor might consider a combined investment of 50 percent warrants and 50 percent cash as a superior alternative to the common stocks. This approach has considerable merit if one utilizes a constant ratio formula plan. Under this plan, as prices decline, a portion of one's cash position would be transferred to warrants to maintain the 50/50 ratio. As prices rise, some profits would be taken on the warrants and the proceeds retained as cash. The constant ratio

EXHIBIT 8–4

The Six-Year Study—50 Percent Warrants/50 Percent Cash Performance

Six-Month Period	Net Profit or Loss* (Percent)	Cumulative Profit or Loss (Percent)
January–June 1967	+72.6	+ 72.6
July–December 1967	+26.4	+118
January–June 1968	+80.5	+294
July–December 1968	+10.8	+336
January–June 1969	−25.1	+227
July–December 1969	−13.4	+183
January–June 1970	−20.8	+124
July–December 1970	+25.9	+182
January–June 1971	+30.5	+268
July–December 1971	− 0.3	+267
January–June 1972	+ 4.2	+282
July–December 1972	− 8.8	+249

* The net profit or loss was based on averaging the warrant profit or loss from Exhibit 8–3 with cash earning 6 percent interest.

formula plan thus assures that profits are taken when prices are high and that additional investments are made when prices are low.

The six-year performance results for this technique are presented in Exhibit 8–4 and it is noted that a warrant/cash investment program would also have substantially outperformed the common stock portfolio—249 percent versus 79 percent for the six-year period.

Exhibit 8–5 compares the common stock and warrant/cash performance results with Value Line's 1,500 stock average for the six-year period. Note how the warrant/cash portfolio closely paralleled the performance of the common stocks during rising markets. Although only half of one's equity was invested in the warrants, their inherent leverage on the upside permitted comparable performance to a 100 percent investment in the common stocks. On the other hand, the 50 percent cash portion of the portfolio limited downside losses compared to the common stocks.

BUYING ON MARGIN

As will be demonstrated later, the use of margin—funds borrowed from the stock brokerage firm—is a key tool for improving performance results for a convertible hedge program. Since investing with borrowed funds normally amplifies both profit and loss, could one have improved on the overall favorable results shown for both the common stocks and warrants alone if he had margined his purchases throughout the six-year test period?

The calculations presented in Exhibits 8–6 and 8–7 show surprising results. Contrary to popular thinking of market speculators, the use of borrowed money to leverage speculative investments is a self-defeating technique. As shown in Exhibit 8–6, the six-year stock performance would have been reduced from the favorable 79 percent appreciation to only 7 percent. Exhibit 8–7 shows that

EXHIBIT 8–5

The Six-Year Study—Relative Performance

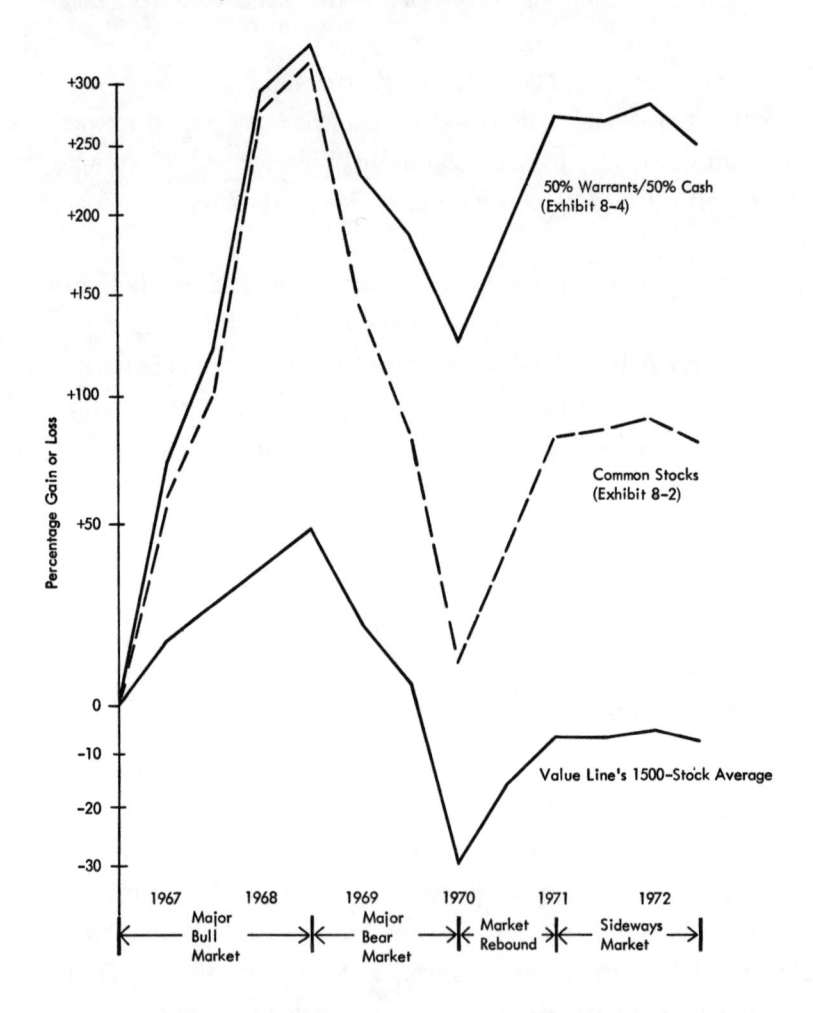

[Chart showing Percentage Gain or Loss from 1967 to 1972 for three series: 50% Warrants/50% Cash (Exhibit 8-4), Common Stocks (Exhibit 8-2), and Value Line's 1500-Stock Average. Market periods marked: 1967–1968 Major Bull Market, 1969 Major Bear Market, 1970 Market Rebound, 1971–1972 Sideways Market.]

warrant appreciation would have been lowered from 284 percent down to only 53 percent.

These figures assume that at each six-month interval, the account would have been adjusted to the 70 percent margin level. If equity had increased during the previous six months, additional purchases would have been made. If equity had declined, securities would have been sold. Margin purchases, therefore, tend to work

EXHIBIT 8-6

The Six-Year Study—Common Stock Performance on 70 Percent Margin

Six-Month Period	Net Profit or Loss* (Percent)	70% Margin† Profit or Loss (Percent)	Cumulative Profit or Loss (Percent)
January–June 1967	+57.8	+ 80.4	+ 80.4
July–December 1967	+25.6	+ 34.4	+142
January–June 1968	+89.6	+125.9	+448
July–December 1968	+11.8	+ 14.7	+528
January–June 1969	−41.8	− 61.9	+139
July–December 1969	−25.5	− 38.6	+ 47
January–June 1970	−39.4	− 58.4	− 39
July–December 1970	+30.1	+ 40.9	− 14
January–June 1971	+26.6	+ 35.9	+ 17
July–December 1971	+ 1.4	− 0.1	+ 17
January–June 1972	+ 3.0	+ 2.1	+ 19
July–December 1972	− 5.7	− 10.3	+ 7

* The net profit or loss figures were taken from Exhibit 8–2.

† A deduction of 1.5 percent was made from the net figures, to compensate for margin interest, before determining the profit or loss based on 70 percent margin.

EXHIBIT 8-7

The Six-Year Study—Warrant Performance on 70 Percent Margin

Six-Month Period	Net Profit or Loss* (Percent)	70% Margin† Profit or Loss (Percent)	Cumulative Profit or Loss (Percent)
January–June 1967	+142.2	+200.3	+ 200.3
July–December 1967	+ 49.7	+ 68.1	+ 405
January–June 1968	+158.0	+222.9	+1530
July–December 1968	+ 18.6	+ 23.7	+1916
January–June 1969	− 53.2	− 78.9	+ 325
July–December 1969	− 29.7	− 45.3	+ 133
January–June 1970	− 44.5	− 66.4	− 22
July–December 1970	+ 48.8	+ 66.9	+ 30
January–June 1971	+ 58.0	+ 80.0	+ 135
July–December 1971	− 3.6	− 8.0	+ 116
January–June 1972	+ 5.4	+ 4.9	+ 127
July–December 1972	− 20.7	− 32.4	+ 53

* The net profit or loss figures were taken from Exhibit 8–3.

† A deduction of 2 percent was made from the net figures before determining the profit or loss based on 70 percent margin. This compensates for extra commission expenses plus margin interest.

opposite to dollar cost averaging. Securities are bought at high price levels and must be sold at depressed prices.

One might argue that on a market decline he would not have sold any securities; thus they would all be working for him on the next upswing in the market. However, to comply with New York Stock Exchange regulations, brokerage firms require a minimum of 30 percent maintenance margin (or higher depending on the prices of the securities held). If the equity in the account were to drop to below 30 percent of the market value of the securities held, additional cash must be deposited or securities must be sold. During the 1969–70 bear market, the 30 percent equity level would have been quickly penetrated. And if the ensuing margin call was handled by a deposit of additional cash instead of selling some securities, the original equity would have been completely wiped out.

When one uses borrowed money for investment purposes, he had better be right in predicting price trends! Or, he should be investing in convertible hedge positions.

WARRANT HEDGE PERFORMANCE—THE BASIC SYSTEM

Calculations for determining the performance results for the warrant hedge investment program are presented in Exhibit 8–8, based on the stock and warrant gains and losses from Exhibit 8–1. The profits or losses for the common stocks during each six-month period were multiplied by a factor of 1.3 to reflect the short to long ratio as specified by the mechanical system. During periods of rising prices, the losses experienced on the common stock sold short were deducted from warrant profits. As prices fell, profits were secured from the short sales whereas the warrants produced losses. A 3 percent charge was deducted from the gross profit for each six-month period to compensate for the approximate commissions which would have been paid and for dividends paid on

EXHIBIT 8-8

The Six-Year Study—Warrant Hedge Performance

Six-Month Period		Gross Profit or Loss (Percent)	Net Profit or Loss* (Percent)	Cumulative Profit or Loss (Percent)
January–June 1967				
Profit on warrants	= +143.2			
Loss on stock = 1.3 × 57.8	= − 75.1			
Net profit	=	+68.1	+65.1	+ 65.1
July–December 1967				
Profit on warrants	= + 50.7			
Loss on stock = 1.3 × 25.6	= − 33.3			
Net profit	=	+17.4	+14.4	+ 89
January–June 1968				
Profit on warrants	= +159.0			
Loss on stock = 1.3 × 89.6	= −116.5			
Net profit	=	+42.5	+39.5	+163
July–December 1968				
Profit on warrants	= + 19.6			
Loss on stock = 1.3 × 11.8	= − 15.3			
Net profit	=	+ 4.3	+ 1.3	+167
January–June 1969				
Profit on stock = 1.3 × 41.8	= + 54.3			
Loss on warrants	= − 52.2			
Net profit	=	+ 2.1	− 0.9	+164
July–December 1969				
Profit on stock = 1.3 × 25.5	= + 33.2			
Loss on warrants	= − 28.7			
Net profit	=	+ 4.5	+ 1.5	+168
January–June 1970				
Profit on stock = 1.3 × 39.4	= + 51.2			
Loss on warrants	= − 43.5			
Net profit	=	+ 7.7	+ 4.7	+181
July–December 1970				
Profit on warrants	= + 49.8			
Loss on stock = 1.3 × 30.1	= − 39.1			
Net profit	=	+10.7	+ 7.7	+203
January–June 1971				
Profit on warrants	= + 59.0			
Loss on stock = 1.3 × 26.6	= − 34.6			
Net profit	=	+24.4	+21.4	+267
July–December 1971				
Loss on warrants	= − 2.6			
Loss on stock = 1.3 × 1.4	= − 1.8			
Net loss	=	− 4.4	− 7.4	+240
January–June 1972				
Profit on warrants	= + 6.4			
Loss on stock = 1.3 × 3.0	= − 3.9			
Net profit	=	+ 2.5	− 0.5	+239
July–December 1972				
Profit on stock = 1.3 × 5.7	= + 7.4			
Loss on warrants	= − 19.7			
Net loss	=	−12.3	−15.3	+187

* 3 percent was deducted from the gross profit or loss for each period to compensate for commissions paid on warrants and stocks and for dividends paid on stocks sold short.

stock sold short. All calculations shown in Exhibit 8–8 assume the use of no leverage—this will be evaluated later. Following is a review of the warrant hedge program for each of the four distinctive market periods experienced during the six-year study.

January 1967–January 1969. The overall stock market produced a major bull market move during this two-year period as demonstrated by Value Line's 1,500 stock average which advanced nearly 50 percent. As previously illustrated in Exhibit 8–2, a portfolio of the common stocks represented in our warrant hedge positions would have gained 320 percent during this same period —they were obviously much more speculative than the average stock. Along with this strong advance by the common stocks, our warrant hedge positions turned in a very respectable performance gain of 167 percent.

January 1969–July 1970. This was the worst period in the stock market's history since the depression. The blue chip Dow Jones Industrial Average dropped 37 percent from the 1,000 area down to 630—Value Line's 1,500 stock average declined more than 50 percent. The more speculative stocks represented in our warrant hedging program "bombed" by almost 75 percent, giving back nearly all of their gain of the previous two years. The warrant hedge program, however, turned in a stellar performance and actually provided a net gain of 5 percent during this 18-month bear market. Our overall performance from the hedge program increased to 181 percent from the 167 percent level at the end of 1968.

July 1970–July 1971. The market rebounded sharply from its depressed condition and was led by blue chip and glamour stocks. Value Line's average turned in a modest 28 percent gain and our more volatile stocks advanced 65 percent. The warrant hedge program also provided a modest gain of about 30 percent. The hedge program performance stood at plus 267 percent whereas the overall stock market had still not reached its pinnacle of earlier years.

July 1971–January 1973. Except for a handful of blue chip and glamour stocks, the overall stock market drifted sideways during this 18-month period—Value Line's 1,500 stock average remained essentially unchanged as did the stocks represented in our hedge program. The warrants acted more poorly than their stocks as was expected due to the passage of time plus the fact that speculative securities were definitely out of favor during this market cycle. Although it was a disappointing 18 months, our six-year performance was still up by 187 percent—an annualized return on our investment of nearly 20 percent from a system that involved no market judgment and which was "managed" only twice a year!

WARRANT HEDGE PERFORMANCE ON MARGIN

Exhibit 8–9 presents the performance figures for the six-year warrant hedge program adjusted to reflect the leverage and extra expenses associated with investments made on 70 percent margin.

EXHIBIT 8–9

The Six-Year Study—Warrant Hedge Performance on 70 Percent Margin

Six-Month Period	Net Profit or Loss* (Percent)	70% Margin† Profit or Loss (Percent)	Cumulative Profit or Loss (Percent)
January–June 1967	+65.1	+89.4	+ 89.4
July–December 1967	+14.4	+17.0	+122
January–June 1968	+39.5	+52.9	+239
July–December 1968	+ 1.3	− 1.7	+233
January–June 1969	− 0.9	− 4.9	+217
July–December 1969	+ 1.5	− 1.4	+212
January–June 1970	+ 4.7	+ 3.1	+222
July–December 1970	+ 7.7	+ 7.4	+246
January–June 1971	+21.4	+27.0	+339
July–December 1971	− 7.4	−14.1	+277
January–June 1972	− 0.5	− 4.3	+261
July–December 1972	−15.3	−25.4	+169

* The net profit or loss figures were taken from Exhibit 8–8.
† A deduction of 2.5 percent was made from the net figures before determining the profit or loss based on 70 percent margin. This compensates for extra commission and dividend expenses plus margin interest.

Unlike the pronounced negative effect that borrowing imposed on straight purchases of either the common stock or warrants, the leveraged warrant hedge program provided improved overall performance right up until the final six months of the study. As expected, it magnified profits during advancing markets while having little adverse effect during periods of decline. During the last 18 months, when the market drifted sideways, the leveraged hedge program performed more poorly than the unleveraged investments as would be expected. Exhibit 8–10 compares both the leveraged and unleveraged hedge program with Value Line's 1,500 stock average over the six-year period.

An important reason for employing leverage in a warrant hedging program is to secure tax advantages. Assuming no other investments, the hedge program would be expected to provide net long-term capital gains during the advancing markets where profits were achieved. If, on average, an annual net profit of 15 percent were achieved from warrant hedging, it would normally consist of about 20 percent in long-term capital gains less about 5 percent paid for margin interest and dividends paid on stock sold short—both are tax deductible expense items. For an investor in the 50 percent tax bracket, the net tax would be computed approximately as follows:

Tax on long-term capital gains = 20 × 25%	=	5.0%
Less savings on deductible expenses = 5 × 50%	=	2.5%
Net tax	=	2.5%
After-tax profit	=	12.5%

Additional advantages of leveraging warrant hedge positions will become apparent as other types of convertible hedges and special situations are combined with the warrants to provide a balanced and diversified portfolio—a portfolio that would be expected to produce profits even during a sideways type market. Techniques will also be presented to improve the performance of warrant hedging, over the mechanical system, in any type of market.

8 / Performance Results from the Basic System   85

EXHIBIT 8–10

The Six-Year Study—Warrant Hedge Performance

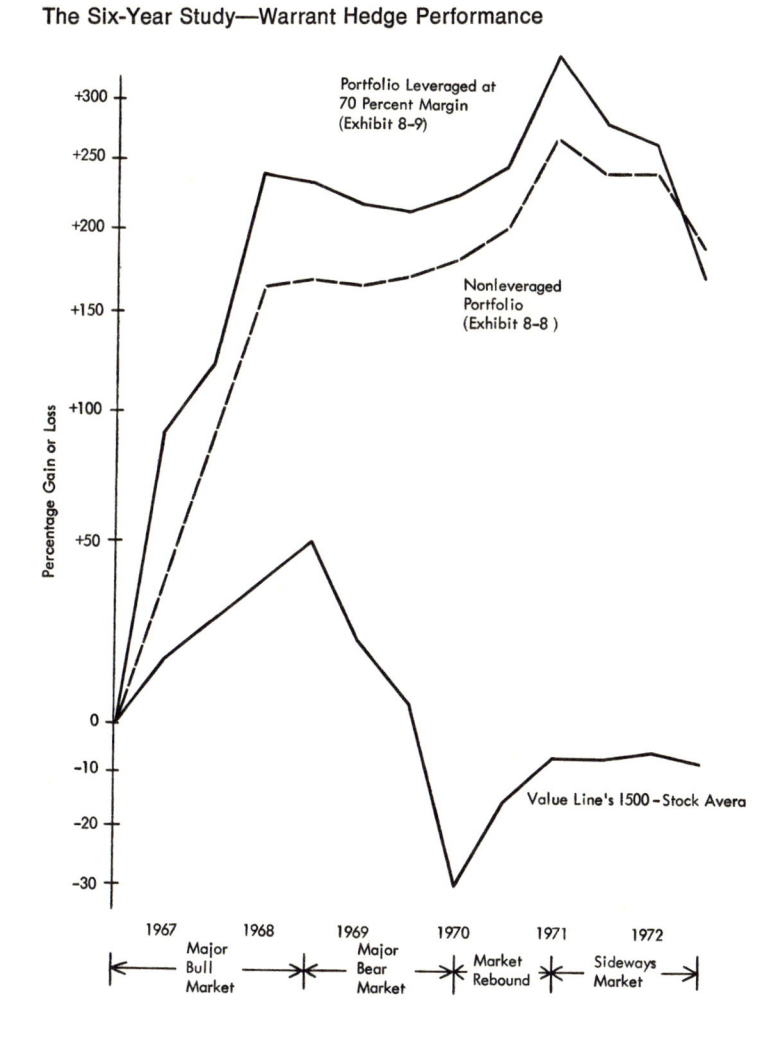

9

Alternatives to the Basic System

To CONSERVATIVELY document the anticipated performance which would have been achieved from hedging undervalued warrants during the six-year study, rigid rules were established and followed without modification. This approach eliminated all judgment factors—either on overall market direction or on individual securities. It also obviated the need to closely monitor one's portfolio as action was considered but twice each year. However, if one has the interest and the time to aggressively manage a warrant hedge portfolio, he should be able to achieve even superior results than those obtained under the basic system—and he will probably have a great deal more fun at the same time.

CONTINUOUS REVIEW OF ALL WARRANT OPPORTUNITIES

The easiest, and probably the most profitable modification to the basic system, is the continuous review of current positions and new hedging opportunities. As soon as a warrant becomes overvalued (or even normally valued depending on other available situations), the position should be closed out and the funds employed in other hedge positions offering superior risk/reward prospects. Note that many new warrants, particularly those of large issues, begin trading at depressed price levels. This is probably the result of numerous investors receiving warrants as part of an issue of bonds or other securities. As many investors probably purchase the package to obtain the senior security, they may quickly sell the unwanted warrants. This creates an unbalanced supply/demand condition that is frequently of a temporary nature. The excess supply may last for a few days or even months, but it would be expected to eventually come into balance. Some specific examples from the author's actual investment experiences will illustrate these points.

Like in the mechanical system, the author established a hedge position in Kinney National Services in early 1970. Under the basic system, the position would still have been held as of January 1973 with but nominal paper profits. However, in actual practice, the warrants became temporarily overpriced in May 1971 and the hedge position was closed out at a sizable profit. The position was reestablished later at more favorable price relationships.

National General warrants were considered to be overpriced in both January 1971 and July 1971 and were, therefore, excluded from consideration under the basic system at those times. However, during this six-month period, price fluctuations permitted a position to be established and closed out at a significant short-term profit.

In November 1970, Tenneco issued new five-year warrants having exercise terms of one share of common stock for $24.25. Despite the high yield on the common stock, the warrants were attractive for purchase. On November 24, the warrants were bought at a price of $3.625 when the stock was trading at $19.50. At the end of the year, about one month later, Tenneco stock and warrants had risen to $24 and $5.75 at which point one reviewing the warrant field would probably not have established a hedge position in Tenneco at that time. Most of the potential profit of the Tenneco hedge would have already been achieved —the short-term price advance of 23 percent by the common stock resulted in a 60 percent advance by the warrant. An investor, who evaluates his portfolio but once every six months per the mechanical system, will miss some of the more lucrative trading opportunities as illustrated by the above examples.

OVER-THE-COUNTER WARRANTS

Another area that can help to improve performance, as well as to broaden the selection list for greater portfolio diversification, is the over-the-counter market. Even those warrants which become listed, are usually first traded over-the-counter while their application for listing is being processed. The possibility that a warrant will trade at an underpriced level during this initial time period is quite high as it normally takes some time for warrant services to react and for the general public to become sold on a new warrant's merits after it is issued. Remember, that when hedging, you should not be as concerned about a company's fundamentals as you would if you were considering purchase of its common stock. When you discover an undervalued warrant, move quickly. The Tenneco warrant was actually bought in the over-the-counter market the day before it was listed on the New York Stock Exchange. Upon being listed, it quickly advanced to higher price levels as it attracted the attention of the investment public.

FINE TUNING THE HEDGE PORTFOLIO

If we can reasonably assume that professional investment analysts and advisors are earning their salaries and that stock market

9 / Alternatives to the Basic System

services are worth the expense, then it should be possible to outperform the basic system by following professional advice or even one's own personal judgment. The hedge portfolio would be fine tuned by adjusting the amount of common stock sold short for each individual position depending on the expected future price trend for that security. To illustrate this point, the author's actual investment approach to the previously mentioned Tenneco warrant may be of interest.

The author had an optimistic opinion of the future prospects for Tenneco, while watching with dismay its decline during the 1969–70 bear market from over $30 to the $19–$20 range in November 1970. A price under $20 for this blue chip security seemed absurd. It was earning $2 per share with improved prospects for the future. Its dividend was secure and provided a yield of almost 7 percent. The overall market was already recovering from its panic low in May of that year and was being led by blue chip high-yield stocks. Everything seemed to favor an improved price level for Tenneco's common stock—probably shortly after the offering of stock and warrants was consummated.

As mentioned earlier, the Tenneco warrants were purchased at the bargain price of $3.625. A hedge position could have been established at that time, and would have been, if the basic system was being followed without modifications based on judgment. Since it was felt that the price of Tenneco common was unduly and temporarily depressed, it was decided that higher price levels would be sought before selling the common stock short. This judgment proved to be correct as Tenneco common advanced to above $25 per share within the following two months. At that point, short positions were established in the common stock on a scale-up basis. It was also interesting to note that, as the stock advanced, the warrant actually moved higher on the normal rating curves. At prices of $29 and $9.50 in March 1971, the warrants were fully valued and the hedge position was closed out at a net profit in excess of 100 percent. A 50 percent price advance by the common stock since the November 24, 1970 purchase date had resulted in a 160 percent warrant price increase—an upside leverage factor of 3.2.

TRADING AGAINST WARRANTS FOR PROFITS DURING SIDEWAYS MARKETS

As was illustrated in Chapter 8, a major risk for warrant hedging is the probable deterioration of equity during a sideways market. The continuous review of one's portfolio will help to reduce this risk but it will probably not eliminate it completely.

Another technique for fine tuning a hedge portfolio to reduce the risk of a sideways market is to trade the short side of a hedge position against the warrants. This simply involves adding to the short side of the portfolio during market rallies and then covering these additional short sales on market dips. This approach would be expected to produce some profits during an extended sideways movement at the expense of reduced gains if the market sustained a major upside advance.

PREDICTING MAJOR MARKET SWINGS

An approach that can substantially improve performance, but one that is probably less predictable than individual situations like Tenneco, is the correct forecasting of future market price trends. Let's suppose that one had been able to forecast the overall market movements during the six-year test period with reasonable accuracy—there are certain investment services that claim to have accomplished this feat. What would the typical investor have done under these circumstances? He probably would have been fully invested in common stocks during the 1967–68 bull market and then have switched a portion of his equity into a cash position in early 1969, prior to the market crash. In mid-1970, he would have returned to a fully invested stock position. With luck, he might have doubled his equity during the six-year period—an admirable performance but significantly poorer than that achieved by the mechanical system for hedging warrants.

The warrant hedge investor has better alternatives at his disposal than having any of his funds tied up in a passive cash position. While remaining fully invested at all times, he can simply adjust the amount of common stock sold short against the warrants. Let's suppose that the warrant hedger was equally skilled at forecasting overall market price movements. Let's also assume that he had made adjustments to his short to long ratio in anticipation of the market trends. Instead of the mechanical 1.3 ratio we will assume that he had employed the following:

Short to Long Ratio

January 1967–December 1968	1.0
January 1969–June 1970	2.0
July 1970–January 1973	1.0

By cutting back on the short side to a 1.0 ratio during advancing markets, the hedger would have increased his upside capital appreciation over the mechanical system at a somewhat higher downside risk if his judgment proved to be incorrect—a risk that was substantially less than a conventional portfolio of common stocks. The 2.0 short to long ratio employed during the market crash promised downside profits at little or no risk if the market continued its upward movement.

By exercising accurate market judgment, but again only evaluating his portfolio but twice each year, the warrant hedge investor would have increased his equity by 1,200 percent during the six-year period! For the skeptical reader, Exhibit 9–1 provides the detailed calculations in support of this conclusion.

EXHIBIT 9–1

Warrant Hedge Performance Based on Accurate Market Judgment

Six-Month Period		Gross Profit or Loss (Percent)	70% Margin* Profit or Loss (Percent)	Cumulative Profit or Loss (Percent)
January–June 1967				
Profit on warrants	= +143.2			
Loss on stock = 1.0 × 57.8	= − 57.8			
Net profit	=	+85.4	+114.9	+ 114.9
July–December 1967				
Profit on warrants	= + 50.7			
Loss on stock = 1.0 × 25.6	= − 25.6			
Net profit	=	+25.1	+ 28.7	+ 177
January–June 1968				
Profit on warrants	= +159.0			
Loss on stock = 1.0 × 89.6	= − 89.6			
Net profit	=	+69.4	+ 92.0	+ 431
July–December 1968				
Profit on warrants	= + 19.6			
Loss on stock = 1.0 × 11.8	= − 11.8			
Net profit	=	+ 7.8	+ 4.0	+ 452
January–June 1969				
Profit on stock = 2.0 × 41.8	= + 83.6			
Loss on warrants	= − 52.2			
Net profit	=	+31.4	+ 34.9	+ 645
July–December 1969				
Profit on stock = 2.0 × 25.5	= + 51.0			
Loss on warrants	= − 28.7			
Net profit	=	+22.3	+ 21.9	+ 808
January–June 1970				
Profit on stock = 2.0 × 39.4	= + 78.8			
Loss on warrants	= − 43.5			
Net profit	=	+35.3	+ 40.4	+1,175
July–December 1970				
Profit on warrants	= + 49.8			
Loss on stock = 1.0 × 30.1	= − 30.1			
Net profit	=	+19.7	+ 21.0	+1,443
January–June 1971				
Profit on warrants	= + 59.0			
Loss on stock = 1.0 × 26.6	= − 26.6			
Net profit	=	+32.4	+ 39.1	+2,046
July–December 1971				
Loss on warrants	= − 2.6			
Loss on stock = 1.0 × 1.4	= − 1.4			
Net loss	=	− 4.0	− 12.9	+1,769
January–June 1972				
Profit on warrants	= + 6.4			
Loss on stock = 1.0 × 3.0	= − 3.0			
Net profit	=	+ 3.4	− 2.3	+1,726
July–December 1972				
Profit on stock = 1.0 × 5.7	= + 5.7			
Loss on warrants	= − 19.7			
Net loss	=	−14.0	− 27.1	+1,231

*To compensate for commissions, dividends, and margin interest, 5 percent and 7 percent were deducted from gross profit figures for periods of short sale ratios of 1.0 and 2.0, respectively, before determining the profit or loss based on 70 percent margin.

10

Convertible Bonds and Convertible Preferred Stocks

NUMEROUS publications are available which cover the investment characteristics of convertible bonds and convertible preferred stocks. Few, however, actually provide the basic tools for systematic evaluation of the merits and risks in purchasing convertibles. The essential element that is often underemphasized is that a convertible bond may be evaluated as a double security, consisting of a straight bond plus an option to purchase common stock. The option portion of the convertible is, in reality, a latent warrant and may be evaluated by procedures similar to those previously developed for long-term warrants. Convertible preferred stocks may be studied in the same manner as convertible bonds.

The two most important characteristics of convertibles are their investment value and conversion value.

INVESTMENT VALUE

The investment value of a convertible is its worth without its conversion privilege based on current interest rates, investment quality, and so on. For illustration purposes, consider the National General 4's-90 convertible bond. The owner of this bond may surrender it to the company at any time and receive 20.6 shares of common stock in the exchange. If we suppose that the bond did not include the conversion privilege, at what price would it have sold? This may be estimated by comparing it with other bonds of comparable quality or by reference to bond-rating services. In mid-1972, the National General bond sold at 65 ($650). An estimate of its investment worth at that time would have been about $500. Investors were therefore willing to pay a $150 premium over the bond's investment value to obtain the long-term option of converting the bond into common stock. Was this a reasonable price?

For analytical purposes, the premium paid for the conversion privilege may be expressed as a percentage of the investment value.

$$\text{Premium over investment value} = \frac{\$650 - 500}{\$500} = \frac{\$150}{\$500} = 30\%$$

The smaller the premium over investment value, the less susceptible is the convertible to a decline in price by the related stock since the investment value provides a price "floor" under the convertible. This "floor" may move, of course, upon changing money rates or the changing fortunes of the company.

CONVERSION VALUE

Conversion value is the other important factor to consider when evaluating convertible bonds or preferred stocks. The conversion value is its worth if the holder were to immediately exchange the convertible for common stock. It equals the current market price of the common multiplied by the number of shares received in the exchange.

10 / Convertible Bonds and Convertible Preferred Stocks

At a stock price of $27, the conversion value of the National General bond was:

$$\text{Conversion value} = 20.6 \times \$27.00 = \$560$$

At a market price of $650 for the bond, it was trading at a premium over its conversion value, computed as follows:

$$\text{Premium over conversion value} = \frac{\$650 - 560}{\$560} = \frac{\$90}{\$560} = 16\%$$

As was discussed in Chapter 2 for warrants, a convertible bond must also sell near or above its conversion value otherwise professional arbitragers will profit by purchase of the discounted bond and the simultaneous sale of the stock. The conversion value also provides a "floor" under the bond's price, a "floor" that will move as the common stock's price advances or declines.

LATENT WARRANTS

Since the National General 4's-90 is convertible into 20.6 shares of common stock, the bond actually consists of a straight bond valued at $500 plus 20.6 latent warrants to purchase common stock. Each latent warrant was in effect selling at $7.28, the $150 premium paid for the bond over its investment value divided by the number of latent warrants ($150 ÷ 20.6 = $7.28).

The exercise price for the latent warrant is the amount needed for converting it into common stock. Since the conversion process would consume a straight bond having a $500 investment value, the exercise price for each warrant is $500 ÷ 20.6, or $24.27. We can now determine whether the latent warrant was undervalued by the application of the normal value curves for warrants.

$$S/E = \$27.00 \div \$24.27 = 1.11$$
$$W/E = \$ 7.28 \div \$24.27 = .30$$

By plotting these points on Exhibit 3–4 of Chapter 3, we note that the warrant fell at the bottom of band 2 or at nearly a 40 percent discount below the normal value for a long-term warrant on a low dividend-paying, speculative stock like National General. The convertible bond was definitely undervalued at a price of 65.

Before proceeding further, let's review the procedures for evaluating the latent warrants of convertible bonds.

1. Determine the bond's investment value by reference to bond rating services or by careful comparison with straight bonds of similar quality. Be careful to recognize that convertible bonds are frequently subordinate to other debts which a company may have outstanding, thus their actual investment value will often be less than one would expect upon a cursory examination.
2. The number of latent warrants is equal to the number of shares of common stock to be received upon conversion of the bond.
3. The market price for each latent warrant is equal to the market price of the bond less its investment value divided by the number of latent warrants.
4. The exercise price is the bond's investment value divided by the number of latent warrants.
5. S/E and W/E factors are then calculated in the normal manner and compared with the normal value curves for conventional warrants. (Exhibits 3–3 and 3–4.)

Although the latent warrant approach will be helpful at first, one skilled in convertibles will normally work with the simpler investment values and conversion values along with carefully developed rules of thumb.

OPPORTUNITIES IN UNDERVALUED CONVERTIBLES

Was the 40 percent discount below normal value for the National General latent warrant an unusual occurrence or was it typical of frequent opportunities available in convertible bonds or convertible preferred stocks?

It has been the author's experience that convertibles issued by major companies seldom sell at bargain price levels. The reason for this is that they are continuously watched by the mutual funds and other large money managers who own or are considering purchase of the related common stock. They are quick to purchase the convertible if it offers advantages over the common. This is contrary to the professional money manager's approach to warrants.

The opportunities for the average investor are generally in those convertibles on the more speculative stocks like National General, stocks that are not represented in the portfolios of the large money managers. In many cases, these convertibles would also be issued in relatively small quantities thus precluding large purchases. In this respect, the small investor has a very substantial advantage over the large money manager. He can frequently find undervalued bonds that can be bought and sold in the usual 5 or 10 bond lots (or a few hundred shares of a convertible preferred).

But a word of caution is in order. The investment value of convertibles on speculative companies can be an illusive "floor." During the tight money conditions, and associated stock market crash of 1969–70, many convertibles seemed to have no investment floor at all. They plummeted right along with their common stocks. Many investors were lulled into a false sense of security by the supposed safety and high yields. The lesson, which this market panic repeated for us, was that any convertible, whether it be a warrant, a bond, or preferred stock, should only be considered for purchase as an alternative to the stock itself. If, after careful evaluation of the common stock, one would wish to have the stock in his portfolio, then by all means, purchase the convertible instead if it offers advantages. But, don't buy a convertible just because it is mathematically undervalued.

CONVERTIBLE BONDS VERSUS CONVERTIBLE PREFERRED STOCK

Since convertible bonds and convertible preferreds have many similar characteristics, they both may be evaluated by separating them into their two basic parts, their investment value and latent warrant value. Yet, there are some significant differences which the investor should be familiar with and which may make a difference in his investment strategy.

Safety. Since bondholder claims to a company's assets are senior to those of preferred stockholders, bonds are inherently safer, all other factors considered to be equal. This distinction may be of little consequence if the company is financially sound. For a speculative company, however, it may be of major importance.

Interest and Dividend Payments. Like common stocks, preferred dividends are paid quarterly and the market price of the preferred will reflect a pending dividend. On the "ex-date," the price of the preferred stock will normally decline by the amount of the dividend.

When a bond is purchased, the buyer pays the seller the interest which has accrued since the last payment date. This expense is recouped at the next semiannual interest payment date. The bondholder, in effect, receives daily interest on his investment regardless of the time period held.

Maturity. Since bonds have a fixed maturity date, they must ultimately be redeemed by the company at par value. An approaching maturity date provides additional protection against broad price swings caused by interest rate changes. It may also protect the convertible bond against a serious price decline by the common stock without limiting its upside potential. Preferred stocks have no fixed maturity date and are therefore more sensitive to changing market conditions.

Continuity of Payments. During adverse times, a company will suspend dividends on its preferred stock before discontinuing bond interest payments—the failure of a company to meet bond interest obligations places it in default, the first step toward bankruptcy.

Even though the dividends paid on preferred stock are usually cumulative (arrearages must be made up before dividends are paid to common shareholders) the holder of preferred stock may have a long wait before receiving his dividends, once suspended. Eventually, he may even have to accept some sort of exchange offer from the company and may, therefore, never see the dividend arrearages paid.

Brokerage Commissions. The buyer of preferred stock pays the same commission rate as for common stocks. The commission charged on bonds is currently only $5 per bond (there is usually a $25 minimum). Bond commissions are, therefore, almost always lower than for preferred stocks and often the difference may be quite substantial.

Margin Buying. Historically, buyers of securities on margin were able to purchase convertible bonds at substantially lower margin rates than common or preferred stocks. The differential, however, has narrowed in recent years and is presently 50 percent for convertible bonds and 65 percent for preferred stocks or common stocks.

Tax Consequences. Dividends paid on preferred stocks (or common stocks) possess unique tax advantages over interest received from bonds. Bond interest is fully taxable as ordinary income whereas the first $100 of annual dividends is excluded on individual tax returns ($200 on joint returns).

The tax advantage to corporations is even greater as they are permitted to exclude 85 percent of the dividends received on most preferreds and common stocks. These tax benefits have historically kept the yields of straight preferreds close to bonds despite the greater safety of the bond.

Bond interest paid is a tax deductible expense to the issuing corporation whereas dividends paid on common or preferred stocks must come from after-tax earnings. It is therefore, in the company's best interest to issue convertible bonds rather than convertible preferred stocks.

Call Provisions. The call price is the price at which a company may "buy back" a security if it desires to do so. Calls on convertibles are usually made to force conversion into the company's common stock. This occurs when the conversion value and hence the market price of the convertible is above the call price. Holders of the convertible must then convert rather than accept the lower value of the call price upon redemption.

One must, therefore, be extra cautious of paying a large premium over conversion value if the convertible is selling above its call price. The announcement of a call will cause any premium over conversion value to immediately vanish. In fact, a called convertible bond will drop to a discount below its conversion value if the call date is prior to the next scheduled interest payment date. In this event, the bondholder would lose the interest accrued since the last payment date as no interest would be received from the company upon the forced conversion.

When evaluating the latent warrant of a convertible subject to possible call, one should assign a normal value close to the latent warrant's actual conversion value. In fact, the normal value curves should be reduced somewhat even at the lower end of the S/E scale to reflect this reduction in upside leverage, as the latent warrant will more rapidly approach its conversion value line than would be expected for a regular warrant.

In any event, all characteristics of any convertible should be carefully checked, and the risks appraised, before purchase. The net result should be quite rewarding.

CONVERTIBLES VERSUS WARRANTS/CASH

A portfolio of convertible bonds or preferred stocks is similar to a combination of warrants plus cash—the convertibles' investment values represent the cash portion and the premium over investment values represents the warrant portion of the portfolio. The investment value of the convertibles will certainly yield a higher return than cash in the bank but is also subject to market risks.

Warrants and cash provide somewhat greater flexibility for shifting from one to the other if one were following a constant ratio formula plan as previously proposed; profits are taken as warrant prices rise and additional warrants are purchased as prices fall. To accomplish the same objectives with convertibles requires that one constantly fine tune his portfolio. As his convertibles rise in price, some must be sold and the funds placed in other convertibles selling closer to their investment value, otherwise the major portion of the portfolio would be represented by latent warrants. As prices fall, losses must be taken and funds switched into higher priced convertibles selling closer to their conversion values for participation in the next market advance.

As most investors are reluctant to take losses, they will likely find it more difficult to outperform the market with a portfolio of convertibles as compared to the warrant/cash approach. On the other hand, convertibles offer greater opportunities for selection and portfolio diversification than do warrants. Also, long-term convertibles will not be subject to price weakness as time passes as are warrants which are approaching their expiration dates. In fact, a convertible purchased below par will move upward toward par as its expiration dates approaches, regardless of its common stock's price trend.

CONVERTIBLE FUNDS

For those investors desiring to invest in high quality convertible bonds or preferreds but who lack the time for continuous portfolio management, it is recommended that consideration be given to one of the professionally managed funds specializing in convertibles. The choice presently includes one mutual fund and several closed-end investment companies.

Mutual Funds

The Harbor Fund—may be purchased at the normal sales charge for mutual funds and redeemed at net asset value.

Closed-End Funds

These are purchased or sold at regular stock exchange commissions and may trade at a premium or discount from their net asset value depending on supply/demand conditions prevailing at the time. The Monday's edition of *The Wall Street Journal* provides the net asset value for these funds as of the prior Friday and their percent premium or discount from net asset value. Closed-end funds specializing in high quality convertibles include the following:

American General Convertible Securities—New York Exchange
Bancroft Convertible Fund   —American Exchange
C. I. Convertible Fund   —American Exchange
Chase Convertible Fund   —New York Exchange

If an investor is interested in a more aggressive portfolio of convertibles, he may consider Source Capital, Inc., traded over-the-counter. This closed-end fund specializes in convertibles, or straight bonds plus warrants, obtained from private negotiations with smaller companies having unusual potential for appreciation (at higher risk). The common shares pay no dividend, and they usually sell at substantial discounts from their indicated net asset value.

GENERAL GUIDES FOR BUYING CONVERTIBLES

1. Convertible bonds and preferred stocks should be evaluated as alternate investments to their common stocks. Be sure you have studied and like the stock before buying the convertible.
2. A convertible should generally provide a yield advantage over its common stock.
3. A convertible purchased at or near its conversion value will offer equal upside potential as the common at less downside risk.
4. A convertible purchased near its investment value will provide significantly greater downside protection than the common stock.
5. The convertible should provide an advantage over purchase of the common stock. A mathematical advantage, or risk/reward ratio, may be calculated as follows:

$$MA = \frac{\% \text{ convertible advance}}{100\% \text{ stock advance}} \times \frac{50\% \text{ stock decline}}{\% \text{ convertible decline}}$$

A ratio in excess of 1.0 would indicate a positive advantage. Note that when the convertible offers a greater yield than its common stock, and it normally will, the yield differential may be included in the above risk/reward estimates.
6. Be cautious of convertibles selling above their call prices. If the convertible is called, the conversion premium plus interest accrued since the last payment date will be lost immediately.
7. All other factors being equal, select convertibles that are listed on a major stock exchange for price reporting and liquidity. Listed convertibles may also be purchased on margin, a prudent alternative to a cash purchase of common stock if the convertible has limited downside risk.
8. Convertible certificates should be kept in street name at your brokerage firm to permit prompt action when the circum-

stances require it. The investor may miss a notification that the convertible has been called if he holds the certificates. The brokerage firm will continuously monitor convertibles held in their customer accounts and, upon notification of a call, will contact their customers for instructions. Missed calls have cost the investing public sizable amounts of money in the past.

11

Hedging Undervalued Convertibles

LIKE UNDERVALUED WARRANTS, undervalued convertible bonds and preferred stocks are also excellent candidates for hedging purposes. The following parameters should be carefully applied in the selection process.

1. The bond should be selling close to its conversion value. It would then offer almost as much upside potential as the common stock.
2. The bond should be selling not too far above its investment value to limit its decline upon a drop in price by the stock.
3. The common stock should pay little or no dividends. The hedge position of long bonds versus short stock would then provide a net cash flow to the bond hedger.
4. The common stock should have a history of high price volatility to improve the chances for a major price move.

HEDGING XYZ COMPANY CONVERTIBLE BONDS

Let's develop a step-by-step evaluation of XYZ Company 6's-90 convertibles currently selling at par value. Assuming that the bonds are convertible into 100 shares of nondividend paying common stock, trading at $10 per share, the bonds are at their conversion value and are a prime candidate for hedging (conversion value = 100 shares × $10.00 = $1,000).

1. *Yield Advantage.* A current yield of 6 percent would be received by the bondholder, whereas the stock pays no dividend.

2. *Upside Potential.* The bonds *must* advance as fast as the common stock on an upside move since they are currently selling at their conversion value. If the stock were to double from $10 up to $20, the bond would sell at 200 (100 shares × $20.00 = $2,000).

3. *Downside Risk.* The bonds would decline no faster than the common stock and probably less due to their investment value providing a "floor." Upon careful study of the company and its probable ability to continue the bond interest payments during adverse times, we would *estimate* that the bond's investment value was 60 and that they would drop 30 percent from 100 down to 70 if the stock declined by 50 percent to $5.

4. *Mathematical Advantage.*

$$MA = \frac{\%\text{ convertible advance}}{100\%\text{ stock advance}} \times \frac{50\%\text{ stock decline}}{\%\text{ convertible decline}}$$

$$= \frac{100}{100} \times \frac{50}{30} = 1.67$$

Note: The MA will actually be greater if the 6 percent yield advantage is also considered.

Exhibit 11–1 provides a graphical illustration of the anticipated price relationships between the convertible bond and common stock.

5. *Alternate Bond Hedge Positions.* The amount of common stock sold short against the bonds should generally fall in

EXHIBIT 11-1

Normal Value Curve for XYZ Convertible Bonds

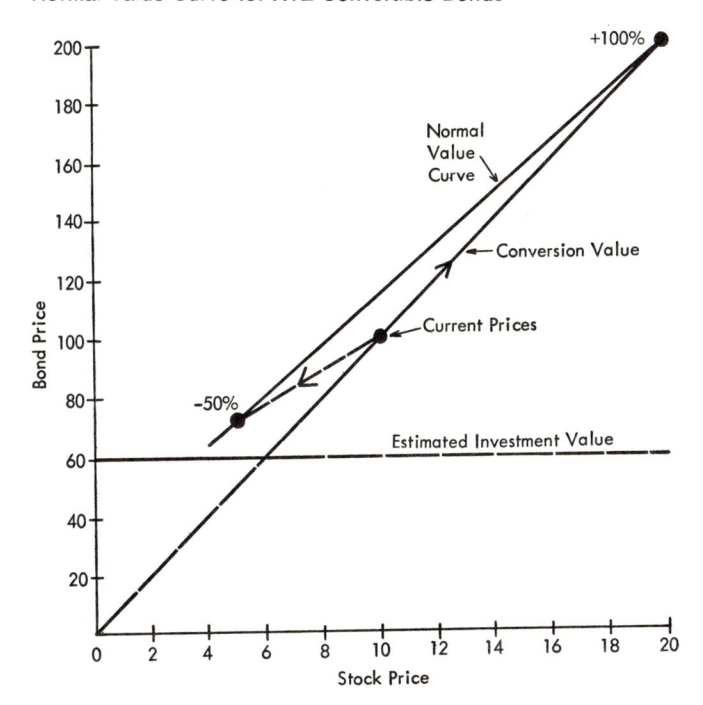

the range between half the number of shares received upon conversion (half hedge) to an equal number (full hedge)—depending on one's objectives and desired risk posture for that particular position. Assuming the purchase of 10 bonds on 50 percent margin, alternate hedge positions are illustrated in Exhibit 11-2. Note that, like warrant hedging, no margin is required for the short sales. Stock price moves of −50 percent and +100 percent are shown to be consistent with previous examples for warrant hedges. In actual practice, the bond hedge would probably be closed out on the upside before the bonds advanced as high as 200. The funds would be employed in a higher yielding bond selling near par.

EXHIBIT 11–2

Alternate Hedge Positions in XYZ Company Convertible Bonds (investment = 10 bonds × $1,000 × 50% margin = $5,000.)

	Stock Price Move	
	−50%	+100%
Half Hedge—A Bullish Posture		
Stock sold short = 500 shares × $10.00 = $ 5,000		
Downside risk		
Profit on stock sold short = $ 5,000 × 50% =	$2,500	
Loss on bonds purchased = $10,000 × 30% =	(3,000)	
Commissions =	(290)	
Upside potential		
Profit on bonds purchased = $10,000 × 100% =		$10,000
Loss on stock sold short = $ 5,000 × 100% =		(5,000)
Commissions =		(350)
Net profit or (loss)	($ 790)	$ 4,650
Return on investment	−16%	+93%
Three-quarter Hedge—A Neutral Posture		
Stock sold short = 750 shares × $10.00 = $ 7,500		
Downside risk		
Profit on stock sold short = $ 7,500 × 50% =	$3,750	
Loss on bonds purchased = $10,000 × 30% =	(3,000)	
Commissions =	(360)	
Upside potential		
Profit on bonds purchased = $10,000 × 100% =		$10,000
Loss on stock sold short = $ 7,500 × 100% =		(7,500)
Commissions =		(450)
Net profit or (loss)	$ 390	$ 2,050
Return on investment	+8%	+41%
Full Hedge—A Bearish Posture		
Stock sold short = 1,000 shares × $10.00 = $10,000		
Downside risk		
Profit on stock sold short = $10,000 × 50% =	$5,000	
Loss on bonds purchased = $10,000 × 30% =	(3,000)	
Commissions =	(430)	
Upside potential		
Profit on bonds purchased = $10,000 × 100% =		$10,000
Loss on stock sold short = $10,000 × 100% =		(10,000)
Commissions =		(560)
Net profit or (loss)	$1,570	($ 560)
Return on investment	+31%	−11%

Note: Depending on the time period, the income received from the bonds, less margin interest paid, will add to profits or reduce losses.

6. *Selection of the Best Hedge Position.* Certain sophisticated investors employ full hedge positions in convertibles to "hedge" their common stock portfolios against a market crash. The yield differential between the convertible and the shorted common is frequently as high or higher than interest paid on bank savings while substantial profits may be achieved during the market decline.

Full or neutral hedges are excellent complements to bullish warrant hedges. The net income may offset margin interest and dividend expenses associated with warrant hedges and the two types of hedge positions combined would be expected to produce some profits in a bear market. The combination of bullish warrant hedges and neutral or full convertible hedges can literally achieve the best of all worlds, profits in any kind of market.

CLOSING OUT A CONVERTIBLE BOND HEDGE ON THE UPSIDE

The convertible hedger has a choice as to how he should close out his position if prices appreciate in value. He could, of course, sell the convertibles and buy stock to cover the short sales as the warrant hedger normally will do. However, if the bonds were selling at their conversion value, as would be expected upon a major price move, he might consider converting a sufficient number of bonds and covering the short sales with the shares received. This maneuver would save much of the expense of closeout brokerage commissions. In the latter case, the bond hedger should make sure that the bond interest was just recently paid since the interest accrued from the previous payment date would be lost upon conversion. This loss could actually exceed commission expenses. Income tax considerations might also favor closeout by sale instead of conversion.

AN ACTUAL CONVERTIBLE BOND HEDGE POSITION IN GULF RESOURCES & CHEMICAL

Anticipated bond and common stock price relationships are illustrated in Exhibit 11–3. Exhibit 11–4 illustrates a "neutral" hedge position available in Gulf Resources 6¼'s–91 bonds during

EXHIBIT 11–3

Gulf Resources & Chemical 6¼'s–91 Convertible Bonds

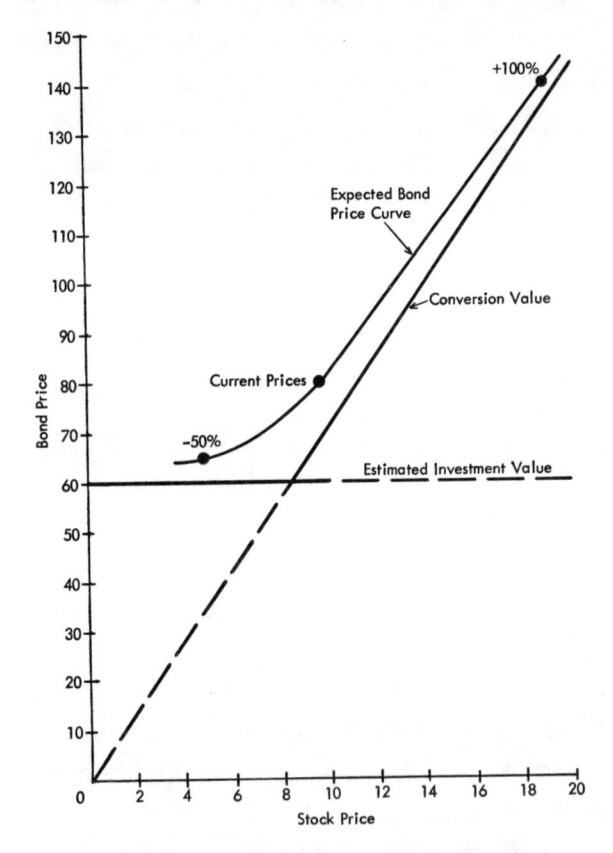

March 1973. The calculations are presented on a standard work sheet for evaluating convertible hedges and the following steps are keyed to this work sheet for ease of reference.

a) 20 bonds were purchased at $800 each.
b) 900 shares of common stock were sold short at $9.50 per share.
c) The net investment, at 50 percent margin, was $8,050.
d) The initial debit balance created by the bond purchase was $8,050.
e) Stock price changes of −50 percent and +100 percent were assumed.
f) The bond price was estimated for each of the stock prices (see Exhibit 11–3).

Note: The convertible bond provided a mathematical advantage over the common stock, computed as follows:

$$MA = \frac{\% \text{ bond advance}}{100\% \text{ stock advance}} \times \frac{50\% \text{ stock decline}}{\% \text{ bond decline}} =$$

$$\frac{75}{100} \times \frac{50}{19} = 1.97$$

g) Profit and loss calculations are based on the indicated stock and bond prices.
h) Round trip commissions and transfer taxes are included for meaningful results.
i) The estimated net capital gain or loss is determined next.
j) The estimated return on investment was the net capital gain divided by the $8,050 investment. Note that these returns are not related to a specific time frame. They could be achieved quickly or never, depending on future price actions.
k) The annual bond interest to be received is 20 bonds times $62.50 per bond, or $1,250.
l) Since the common stock currently pays no dividend, no deduction is shown for this expense item.
m) Estimated annual margin interest to be paid was based on the initial debit balance of $8,050 and 7 percent interest rate. Both of these factors are subject to change as the

market value of the shorted stock fluctuates and as interest rates change.

n) The estimated annual cash flow from the hedge position was $685, or 8.5 percent.

EXHIBIT 11-4

```
                         WORK SHEET
              CONVERTIBLE BOND HEDGE EVALUATION

COMPANY  Gulf Resources + Chemical          DATE  March 1973
A. DESCRIPTION OF SECURITIES

   Security          Description    Traded    Price    Yield %
   Common stock                      NYS      9½        0
   Convertible bond   6¼-91          NYS      80        2.8

   Bond's conversion value = 71.43 shs. x $ 9.50  = $ 678
   Conversion premium                          =   18 %
   Estimated investment value                  =   60

B. POSSIBLE HEDGE POSITION: Bullish_____, Neutral ✓, or Bearish_____

   (a) Bonds purchased:   20   M at $ 800  each       = $ 16,000
   (b) Stock sold short: 900   shs. at $ 9.50  each   = $  8,550
   (c) Investment = ($ 16,000 + $ 100 comm.) x 50 % margin = $ 8,050
   (d) Initial debit balance = $ 16,100 - $ 8,050 = $ 8,050

C. PROFIT AND LOSS ESTIMATES

   Assumed stock price change   -50%      +50%    +100%    Other
   (e) Stock price               4¾                19
   (f) Estimated bond price      65                140
   (g) Profit or (loss) - bonds (3,000  )         12,000
                       - stock   4,275  (      )   8,550  (     )
   (h) Commissions               480    (      )    600   (     )
   (i) Estimated capital gain or (loss)  795        2,850
   (j) Estimated return on investment  +10  %   %   +35 %          %

D. ESTIMATED ANNUAL CASH FLOW

   (k) Bond interest received                     = $ 1,250
   (l) Less dividends paid on stock sold short    =  (   0  )
   (m) Less estimated margin interest* = $ 8,050 x 7.0 % = ( 565 )
   (n) Estimated cash flow                        = $  685  = 8.5 %

   *Based on the initial debit balance, however, this will fluctuate as the short account is marked to the
   market. The indicated interest rate is also subject to change.

E. OTHER FACTORS  _____
```

A significant difference between Gulf Resources and the hypothetical XYZ convertible bond is that the Gulf Resources bond was selling at a 20 percent discount below par value. It was, therefore, trading closer to its investment value than XYZ but at a premium above its conversion value. By placing the hedge position on margin, it was also possible to leverage the 7.8 percent current bond yield up to a net cash flow of 8.5 percent—a major advantage in hedging high-yielding convertibles whose common stocks pay no dividends. The high cash flow available from this type of hedge position offers an excellent complement to a portfolio of warrant hedges. Or, it may be suitable by itself for the investor seeking a high income plus the potential for modest capital gains.

GENERAL GUIDES FOR HEDGING CONVERTIBLES

1. The convertible should be significantly undervalued—a mathematical advantage (risk/reward ratio) over the common stock of 1.5 or higher.
2. Select convertibles on common stocks which pay little or no dividends—the short seller must pay these dividends.
3. The convertible should be selling close to its conversion value and not too far above its investment value.
4. Make sure that the stock is available for short selling and that there is a reasonable probability that it can be held short as long as desired.
5. Both the convertible and stock should be actively traded to permit establishing and closing out positions at favorable price relationships.
6. The dollar amount of common stock sold short versus convertibles purchased should be designed to meet one's specific objectives for that situation. This ratio will generally fall within a range of 0.5 to 1.0 (half hedge to full hedge).
7. The convertibles are held in the brokerage account, even if purchased for cash, to permit the short sale of common stock without having to deposit margin on the short side.

Most hedge investors purchase listed convertibles on margin to obtain leverage.
8. A major price move is usually required before closing out a position for profit—do not consider convertible hedging for short-term trading.
9. Close out the position if the convertible becomes overvalued —the funds should be employed in another situation having more favorable risk/reward characteristics.
10. Consider closing out the position on the upside by converting the required number of convertibles to save on commission expenses.

POSSIBLE RISKS

1. The convertible could become even more undervalued—it is possible to incur losses on both the long and short sides of a position. It is recommended that one have five or more different positions for diversification.
2. Unless a full hedge is established, a bankruptcy could result in downside losses.
3. If the brokerage firm is unable to protect the short sales, the position might have to be closed out prematurely. A call by the company might also require a premature closeout.

12

Reverse Warrant Hedging

A *reverse* warrant hedge is the opposite strategy to the regular type of warrant hedging previously presented. Unlike the purchase of long-term, undervalued warrants, it involves the short sale of *overpriced* warrants nearing their expiration date. The warrants sold short are "hedged" by the purchase of common stock. Maximum success will often be achieved from different types of markets than those needed for profits from a regular warrant hedge position. Also, the cash flow characteristics are frequently similar to a convertible bond hedge as opposed to the negative cash flow of a regular warrant hedge. For these reasons, reverse warrant hedging may complement a regular warrant hedge program for portfolio balance and diversification.

"Beat the Market," by Thorp and Kassouf, developed a system for the reverse hedging of warrants and demonstrated an average yearly gain of 25 percent during those years that suitable hedge positions were available.

GENERAL GUIDELINES

1. The normal value curves in Chapter 3 may be used to roughly determine if a warrant is overpriced, bearing in mind that

these curves apply to warrants having a life to expiration in excess of three years. Specific calculations, to be presented later, will confirm whether a reverse hedge position is attractive.

2. Make certain that the company does not have the privilege of reducing the warrant's exercise price or extending its life. Either of these events could cause a sudden and sharp rise in the warrant's price. Certain real estate investment trusts have recently extended their warrant lives without specifically having that right. This adds significant risks to reverse warrant hedging.

3. Warrants should be listed on a major stock exchange to facilitate borrowing them for short selling. Since even many of the listed warrants that one will be evaluating as reverse hedge candidates will not be widely held in margin accounts, availability for short selling will be a major problem. Experience indicates that it will be difficult to maintain a diversified portfolio of reverse hedges even though there are usually as many overpriced warrants trading as undervalued warrants.

4. Warrants should generally have a life to expiration of *less* than three years to make a reverse hedge position profitable on an annualized basis. Again, the specific calculations will confirm this. Offsetting the desirability of a short-time period to expiration, for maximum *annualized* return on one's investment, is the need to establish the position early enough to assure the warrant's availability for short selling—it is important to get into a position before the "crowd."

5. Unless the common stock is trading well below the warrant's exercise price, a reverse warrant hedge will normally produce maximum profits if the common stock does not make a significant advance or decline in price. Best situations will, therefore, normally be found in high-quality stocks having low price volatility. If the common stock pays a high dividend, the reverse warrant hedge also provides an excellent vehicle for income in addition to possible capital appreciation.

6. Both sides of the reverse warrant hedge position must be margined. The funds utilized for margining the short side, however, will reduce the debit balance created from the purchase of the common stock on margin. The profit potential of a reverse hedge will generally be more affected by margin requirements prevailing at the time than the potential of regular hedges—the lower the required margin, the better.

7. Warrants must be purchased prior to their expiration date for covering the short sale. Even though they may be worthless upon expiration, the lender is still entitled to his warrant certificates. In actual practice, the reverse hedge will usually be closed out some time prior to the expiration date and the funds redeployed in better situations.

8. Best reverse warrant hedge situations will normally be found where the common stock is selling below the warrant's exercise price (S/E is less than 1.0). As was demonstrated by Exhibit 7–2, warrants are generally more overpriced toward the lower end of the S/E scale. Also, the position will offer some upside profits on the common stock in addition to the short side if the common stock's price ends up near the exercise price upon expiration.

9. The best ratio of warrants sold short versus common stock held long will be dependent on numerous factors relating to that particular position as well as the other security positions held in one's portfolio.

10. Undervalued convertible bonds or convertible preferred stocks may be substituted for the common stock to increase the expected return on investment. Convertibles may significantly improve the arithmetic if the common stock is a low dividend payer.

11. When the position is within a year of the warrant's expiration date, consider purchasing call options on the common stock in lieu of holding the stock (or convertible). This tech-

nique may substantially improve overall portfolio performance by releasing funds for other situations.

12. Keep in mind that a reverse warrant hedge will not normally be able to provide protection against a possible bankruptcy as will the regular warrant hedge. The quality of the company must therefore be more carefully considered when constructing the reverse hedge position.

AN ACTUAL REVERSE WARRANT HEDGE POSITION— AMERICAN TELEPHONE & TELEGRAPH

As was demonstrated by the Ling-Temco-Vought situation for regular warrant hedging, it is believed that an actual case history will best serve to illustrate the numerous techniques and factors involved in analyzing reverse warrant hedge situations.

In May 1972, A.T.&T. common stock and warrants were both actively trading on the New York Stock Exchange. Prices were in the area of $42 and $7, respectively. Since the warrants were to expire in three years (May 15, 1975) and were the right to purchase common stock at $52 per share, well above the stock price at the time, the warrants were excellent candidates for reverse hedging. With about 31 million warrants outstanding and a short interest of less than 1 million shares, there was no problem obtaining the warrants for short sales.

A review of the warrant terms indicated that A.T.&T. did not have the right to reduce the warrant's exercise price or extend its life. This was confirmed by a call to the company's legal department who also advised that, in their opinion, such action would require approval by the common stockholders who would most likely reject it.

Assuming the purchase of 100 shares of common stock, alternate reverse hedge positions were evaluated on standard work sheets as illustrated by the following:

12 / Reverse Warrant Hedging 119

Exhibit 12–1—100 warrants sold short—"bullish" hedge
Exhibit 12–2—200 warrants sold short—"neutral" hedge
Exhibit 12–3—300 warrants sold short—"bearish" hedge

Referring to the calculations in Exhibit 12–1, a step-by-step approach for estimating potential profit or loss proceeded as follows:

EXHIBIT 12–1

WORK SHEET
REVERSE WARRANT HEDGE EVALUATION

COMPANY __AT+T__   DATE __May 1972__

A. DESCRIPTION OF SECURITIES

Security	Description	Traded	Price	Yield %
Common stock		NYS	42	6.7
Convertible bond				
Convertible preferred				
Warrant		NYS	7	

Warrant expiration date __5-15-75__ (__3.0__ years)

B. POSSIBLE HEDGE POSITION: Bullish __✓__ , Neutral _____ , or Bearish _____

(a) Common purchased: __100__ shs at $ __42.00__ each = $ __4,200__ :+ __60__ comm. = $ __4,260__
(b) Warrants sold short: __100__ shs at $ __7.00__ each = $ __700__ :− __20__ comm. = $ __680__
(c) Total $ __4,940__

(d) Investment = $ __4,940__ × __55__ % margin = $ __2,720__
(e) Initial debit balance = $ __4,260__ − $ __2,720__ = $ __1,540__

C. PROFIT OR LOSS ESTIMATES AT EXPIRATION DATE

(f) Stock price (assumed)   30   42   52   70
    Estimated convertible price
(g) Estimated warrant price (conversion value)   0   0   0   18

(h) Profit or (loss) – warrants   700   700   700   (1,100)
                    – common   (1,200)   0   1,000   2,800
                    – convertible
(i) Commissions   (135)   (145)   (150)   (185)
(j) Estimated capital gain or (loss)   (635)   555   1,550   1,515
(k) Estimated return on investment   −23.3%   +20.4%   +57 %   +56 %
(l) Estimated annualized ROI   −7.8%   +6.8%   +19 %   +18.6%

D. ESTIMATED ANNUAL CASH FLOW

(m) Estimated stock dividends or bond interest   = $ __280__
(n) Less estimated margin interest* = $ __1,540__ × __6.0__ % = (__92__)
(o) Estimated cash flow   = $ __188__ = __6.9__ %

*Based on the initial debit balance, however, this will fluctuate as the short account is marked to the market. The indicated interest rate is also subject to change.

E. OTHER FACTORS _____

EXHIBIT 12-2

WORK SHEET

REVERSE WARRANT HEDGE EVALUATION

COMPANY __AT+T__ DATE __May 1972__

A. DESCRIPTION OF SECURITIES

Security	Description	Traded	Price	Yield %
Common stock		NYS	42	6.7
Convertible bond				
Convertible preferred				
Warrant		NYS	7	

Warrant expiration date __5-15-75__ (__3.0__ years)

B. POSSIBLE HEDGE POSITION: Bullish _____, Neutral __✓__, or Bearish _____

Common purchased: __100__ shs at $ __42.00__ each = $ __4,200__ :+ __60__ comm. = $ __4,260__
Warrants sold short: __200__ shs at $ __7.00__ each = $ __1,400__ :− __40__ comm. = $ __1,360__
Total $ __5,620__

Investment = $ __5,620__ × __55__ % margin = $ __3,090__
Initial debit balance = $ __4,260__ − $ __3,090__ = $ __1,170__

C. PROFIT OR LOSS ESTIMATES AT EXPIRATION DATE

Stock price (assumed)	30	42	52	70
Estimated convertible price				
Estimated warrant price (conversion value)	0	0	0	18
Profit or (loss) − warrants	1,400	1,400	1,400	(2,200)
− common	(1,200)	0	1,000	2,800
− convertible				
Commissions	(155)	(65)	(170)	(235)
Estimated capital gain or (loss)	45	1,235	2,230	365
Estimated return on investment	+1.5%	+40.0%	+72.2%	+11.8%
Estimated annualized ROI	+0.5%	+13.3%	+24.0%	+3.9%

D. ESTIMATED ANNUAL CASH FLOW

Estimated stock dividends or bond interest   = $ __280__
Less estimated margin interest* = $ __1,170__ × __6.0__ % = $ (__70__)
Estimated cash flow   = $ __210__ = __6.8__ %

*Based on the initial debit balance, however, this will fluctuate as the short account is marked to the market. The indicated interest rate is also subject to change.

E. OTHER FACTORS _____

a) 100 shares of common stock were purchased at $42 per share.

b) 100 warrants were sold short at $7 per share.

c) The total position, including commissions, was the sum of these two transactions, or $4,940.

d) The net investment, at the 55 percent margin rate prevailing at the time, was $2,720.

e) The initial debit balance created was the difference between the $4,260 cost for the purchase of the common stock and the $2,720 required investment, or $1,540.

f) Since the major variable (and resulting risk) is the price of

EXHIBIT 12–3

```
                         WORK SHEET
                 REVERSE WARRANT HEDGE EVALUATION

COMPANY   AT+T                                    DATE  May 1972
```

A. DESCRIPTION OF SECURITIES

Security	Description	Traded	Price	Yield %
Common stock		NYS	42	6.7
Convertible bond				
Convertible preferred				
Warrant		NYS	7	

Warrant expiration date 5-15-75 (3.0 years)

B. POSSIBLE HEDGE POSITION: Bullish _____, Neutral _____, or Bearish ✓

Common purchased: 100 shs at $ 42.00 each = $ 4,200 :+ 60 comm. = $ 4,260
Warrants sold short: 300 shs at $ 7.00 each = $ 2,100 :– 60 comm. = $ 2,040
Total $ 6,300

Investment = $ 6,300 × 55 % margin = $ 3,465
Initial debit balance = $ 4,260 – $ 3,465 = $ 795

C. PROFIT OR LOSS ESTIMATES AT EXPIRATION DATE

Stock price (assumed)	30	42	52	70
Estimated convertible price				
Estimated warrant price (conversion value)	0	0	0	18
Profit or (loss) – warrants	2,100	2,100	2,100	(3,300)
– common	(1,200)	0	1,000	2,800
– convertible				
Commissions	(175)	(185)	(190)	(280)
Estimated capital gain or (loss)	725	1,915	2,910	780
Estimated return on investment	+20.9%	+55.3%	+84.0%	–22.5%
Estimated annualized ROI	+ 7.0%	+18.4%	+28.0%	– 7.5%

D. ESTIMATED ANNUAL CASH FLOW

Estimated stock dividends or bond interest   = $ 280
Less estimated margin interest* = $ 795 × 6.0 %   = (48)
Estimated cash flow   = $ 232 = 6.7 %

*Based on the initial debit balance, however, this will fluctuate as the short account is marked to the market. The indicated interest rate is also subject to change.

E. OTHER FACTORS _____

A.T.&T.'s common stock on the warrant's expiration date, four different prices were assumed for calculation purposes. These ranged from $30 which was considered to be the maximum downside possibility, up to $70, which was believed to be the potential upside objective. The other prices selected were the stock's current price of $42 and the warrant's exercise price of $52. Note that the exercise price will always represent the maximum profit potential for any reverse hedge situation.

g) Warrant prices shown are their conversion value at the various assumed stock prices. In actual practice, one will normally buy back expiring warrants at a price slightly higher than their actual conversion value but the net effect on profit and loss calculations will be small.

h) Profit and loss calculations are based on the indicated stock and warrant prices at expiration.

i) Round trip commissions and transfer taxes are included for meaningful estimates.

j) The estimated net capital gain or loss is determined next.

k) The estimated return on investment was the net capital gain or loss divided by the $2,720 investment.

l) Annualized return on investment was determined by dividing the total return by the warrant's three-year life to expiration.

m) Annual dividends to be received were estimated at $2.80 per share during the three-year period.

n) Estimated annual margin interest was based on the initial debit balance of $1,540 and a 6 percent interest rate. Both of these factors were subject to change as the market value of the short warrants fluctuates and as interest rates change. The net results, however, would not be expected to be materially different.

o) The estimated annual cash flow was determined by deducting margin interest paid from dividends received. Note that this was actually higher than the common stock yield.

Exhibit 12–4 graphically presents the anticipated annual return on investment (including net cash flow) for each of the alternate reverse hedge positions. Also shown is the straight purchase of A.T.&T. common stock (not margined) for comparison purposes (dividends included).

EXHIBIT 12–4

Alternate Reverse Warrant Hedge Positions in American Telephone & Telegraph

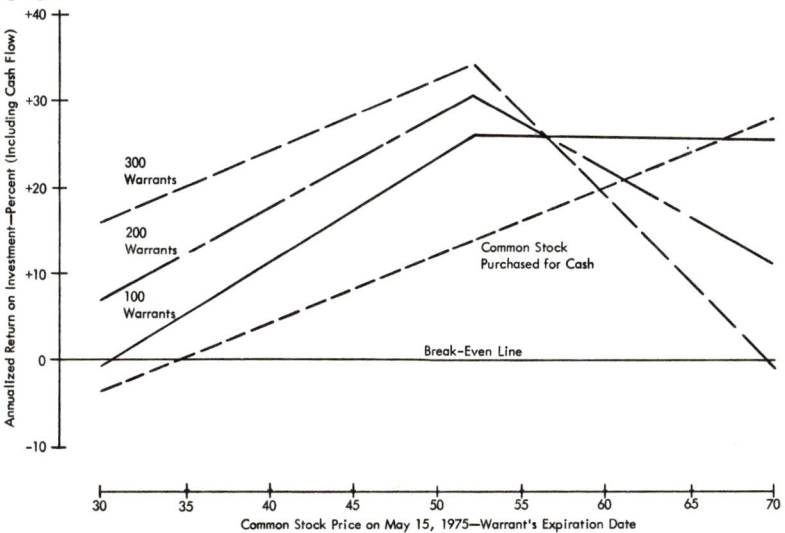

100 common stock purchased at $42.
Warrants sold short at $7 in quantities shown.

Looking first at the "bullish" 1 for 1 ratio (100 warrants sold short), it was noted that the reverse warrant hedge position was expected to outperform ownership of the common stock at all prices up to $67. If one were to have constructed a probability table for the price of A.T.&T. common stock three years hence, it would probably have shown a very low possibility that A.T.&T.

would advance to that price level. Exhibit 12–4 conclusively demonstrated that the warrants, at a price of $7, were substantially overpriced in May 1972 and that a reverse warrant hedge was a superior alternative to the common stock.

The 1 for 1 ratio was recommended for the investor who was bullish on A.T.&T. common. Others would have considered a 2 for 1 or 3 for 1 to increase their profit potential in the event that A.T.&T. would end up selling somewhere below $56 (the crossover point for the three alternate hedge positions). Also, if one had sizable holdings of other common stocks, or regular warrant hedges, a high ratio would have been considered for protection of his portfolio against a bear market or to optimize the total portfolio's performance in a sideways market.

Ratios even higher than 3 for 1 could also have been considered. However, a quick rise in the price of A.T.&T. common to the high $40s or low $50s could have resulted in a near-term loss position plus fears of substantial loss if the stock were to continue moving higher. It was believed that a 3 for 1 ratio could be closed out, if desired, at about break-even if this were to occur.

A "neutral" 2 for 1 ratio was generally believed, by the author, to be best for most investors. This offered a potential return of 20 percent annually if A.T.&T. common were to end up selling between $42 and $61.50 on May 15, 1975, with a possible return of 30 percent if the ideal price of $52 was attained. No loss would be expected on the downside unless A.T.&T. sold below $24 or on the upside above $80, both extremely unlikely events.

The actual experience with the A.T.&T. reverse hedge position was surprising. A.T.&T. common stock became the "darling" of the institutional investors during the later part of 1972. In mid-November, only six months after establishing the hedge positions, the common had risen to $52, a 10-point advance. On the other hand, the warrants lagged far behind the common and advanced only one point from $7 up to $8. This permitted a close out of the hedge position at substantial profits—the annualized return for the 2 for 1 hedge was better than 50 percent. Also, note that the capital gains on the common stock were long term and that the losses on the warrants sold short were short term for tax purposes—a desirable combination for most investors.

ACTUAL REVERSE WARRANT HEDGE POSITIONS TAKEN BY THE AUTHOR

The author's initial introduction to the field of convertible securities was the reverse warrant hedge in 1964. A total of three reverse hedge positions were taken beginning in early 1965. Since each of these positions involved different techniques, they are presented here for informational purposes and to provide an indication of the potential profit available from this type of hedging.

Sperry Rand. Reverse warrant hedge positions of long comcon stock versus short warrants were established beginning in early 1965—almost three years prior to the warrant's expiration date in September 1967. Additional positions were taken through July 1965 and then all were held until July 1966, when the common stock advanced to above the warrant's exercise price. The total position was closed out at that time as there were other situations available which had more favorable risk/reward characteristics. A net profit of 27 percent was realized on the investment which was held, on average, for 14 months.

Universal American. Reverse warrant hedge positions were established in this situation between September 1965 and July 1966—the warrants expired in March 1967. The initial hedge position included common stock purchased in the $7–$8 range—well below the warrant's $13.75 exercise price. As the common advanced to the $14 area in April 1966, the stock was sold and the funds switched into Universal American's convertible preferred stock which was trading at its conversion value and paying a generous dividend versus no yield on the common. The total position was held until the March 1967 expiration date and then closed out at a net profit in excess of 30 percent on the funds invested. The average time period that the position was held was about 10 months.

Pacific Petroleums. Like the above two reverse warrant hedges, the position in Pacific Petroleums, taken in early 1966, involved long common stock versus short warrants. As additional funds became available, the position was increased through July 1966—the warrants expired in March 1968. In September 1967, six months prior to the warrant's expiration date, all common stock shares were sold. A small portion of the proceeds received was placed in six-month call options on the common stock which were selling at only half the trading price of the warrant even though the common stock was at the warrant's exercise price—additional evidence that short-term warrants are frequently overpriced. The balance of the funds received from the sale of the common stock was placed in other convertible situations. The new hedge position of long calls versus short warrants was held right up until the warrant's expiration date. A net profit of approximately 80 percent was obtained from the total hedge position which was held, on average, for about 21 months.

Note, that in each of the above three reverse warrant hedges, the common stock was selling well below the warrant's exercise price at the time the positions were established. This price relationship is best for any reverse hedge as it offers potential profits on both the long and short sides of the position if the common advances to the area of the warrant's exercise price. In each case, the positions were closed out upon a price advance by the common stock. The exceptional results may, therefore, not be representative of the anticipated return for reverse hedging over a long period of time which includes bear markets as well as bull markets.

13

Special Situations and Call Options

INVESTORS who continuously maintain a portfolio of warrants, convertibles and/or hedge positions, and are constantly searching for new opportunities, will occasionally discover a special situation that offers unbelievable profit potential at little or no risk. Do not accept the overabused cliché, "that if it were so good the professionals would not let it happen." You have already seen how the average investor could have made 15–20 percent or more annually in regular and reverse hedges, even in such a popular and conservative situation as American Telephone & Telegraph—a stock that was normally purchased for its safety and generous dividend. Reverse warrant hedge positions offered the same high yield but at substantially less downside risk and greater profit potential. How many investors even considered the hedge position as a possible alternative to the easy and conventional purchase of the common stock? The stock market is far from a perfect system for adjudging the proper price for stocks based on their inherent values—it is also imperfect in its detection and judgment in the area of convertible securities. *Our primary interest is to take advantage of these natural and expected imperfections.*

There are no convenient investment services or other sources that one can turn to for these ideas since the profit potential will frequently diminish by the time it becomes general public knowledge. The "discovery" will probably be made during periods of routine investigation and study. Be sure to evaluate all risk/reward aspects of the special situation before investing but also be prepared to act promptly. It will probably be most helpful if you have a friend who also is an active investor in the convertible area and who you can consult with and exchange ideas.

The most exciting, and potentially rewarding, special situation is the convertible bond or preferred stock having delayed conversion features and selling at a discount below its future conversion value. These generally fall into either of two categories:

1. A convertible with fixed conversion terms which specify the number of shares of common stock to be received upon conversion. Future price action of the convertible will be related to that of the common stock.
2. A convertible which will convert into common stock, on a specific date, based upon a formula relating to the *future* price of the common. The convertible's price action will be essentially independent of the common stock's up until the date it becomes convertible.

DELAYED CONVERTIBLES HAVING FIXED CONVERSION TERMS

In late April 1967, the author "discovered" G. C. Computer bonds as he was routinely checking new convertibles being listed for trading on the American Stock Exchange. These bonds were convertible into a specified number of G. C. Computer common stock shares beginning August 1, 1967, slightly more than three months from the moment of discovery. To his amazement, the bonds were trading at about 140 while they were actually worth 150 if they were immediately convertible. There was apparently substantial profit taking by the bondholders as the common stock continued to move higher. The bond owners probably did not wish to hold them for another three months and take the risk of a possible price decline. What was the best method for taking advantage of this very fortunate opportunity? The answer was a little known provision of the Federal Reserve Board's Regulation T.

If a bond, preferred or a warrant, is convertible within 90 days, and if the purchaser indicates positive plans to his broker to actually convert them, common stock may be sold short against the convertible at only 10 percent margin on the long side of the position, thus effecting a delayed arbitrage transaction. The profit potential for this type situation may be easily calculated and the risk is of course nil (as are all true arbitrages).

The approach taken by the author to the discounted G. C. Computer convertible bond was delayed arbitrage. This effectively captured the 10 point discount at no risk. As soon as the conversion date dropped to within 90 days, the bonds were purchased at the 10 percent minimum margin rate. An equivalent number of common stock shares were immediately sold short to effect the riskless transaction. On August 1, the bonds were converted and the common stock shares received upon conversion were used to cover the prior short sales. The net return, after all expenses including margin interest and commissions, was a full 50 percent in only three months, an "unbelievable" profit that was completely predictable and without risk.

DELAYED CONVERTIBLES HAVING CONVERSION TERMS BASED ON A SPECIFIED FORMULA

Continental Investment Corp.

In late 1970, Continental Investment Corp. issued 9's–90 debentures having delayed conversion features. The bonds do not become convertible until November 5, 1973 and only at that time will the conversion terms be established. They will convert into common stock at a discount of 18 percent below the average price of the common during the five trading days immediately preceding the November 5th date. In other words, the bonds will have a conversion value of 122 (100 ÷ .82 = 122), regardless of what price the common stock happens to be selling at in November 1973.

Since the bonds also provide a generous current yield as compared to the nondividend paying common, we can expect them to actually sell at a premium over their conversion value. This will probably place them in the area of 130. It is also important to note that the bonds will be callable at the unusually high price of 130 thus alleviating any fear of losing the premium as a result of a possible call.

In November 1972, the Continental Investment convertibles could have been purchased on the New York Stock Exchange in the area of 115. Since their future price action, up to November 5, 1973, was expected to be unrelated to the action of the common stock, except for possible short-term fluctuations in sympathy with the common, the downside risk was considered to be nil. One could therefore have purchased the bonds at the 50 percent prevailing margin rate with complete "peace of mind." The anticipated return on investment, for the 12-month position, was calculated as follows:

Buy 10 bonds at 115 on 50 percent margin
Investment = ($11,500 + $50 commissions) × 50% = $5,775

	Bond Price on 11–5–73	
	122	130
Interest to be received = 10 × $90.00	$ 900	$ 900
Margin interest to be paid = $5,775 × 6.5%	(375)	(375)
Expected long-term capital gain	700	1,500
Round trip commissions	(100)	(100)
Estimated net profit	$1,125	$1,925
Estimated return on investment—one year	+19.5%	+33.3%

The Continental Investment delayed convertible bonds belonged in every conservative portfolio. They also presented the opportunity for quick profit taking as they advanced to 124 in March 1973. Sale at this point would have provided a 17 percent net profit in only four months, or greater than 50 percent on an annualized basis.

United National Corp.

Like Continental Investment Corp., United National also issued a delayed convertible—their $0.70 preferred stock with conversion terms to be established February 1, 1974, based on the average price of their common stock during the preceding month. Assuming that the common stock's price on February 1 is the same as its average trading price in January, the preferred will have a conversion value of $12.50. At a market price of $10 in February 1973, one year prior to the conversion date, the anticipated return on investment was computed as follows:

Buy 1,000 shares at $10 on 65 percent margin
Investment = ($10,000 + $172 commissions) × 65% = $6,612

Expected long-term capital gain at a price of $12.50	$2,500
Dividends to be received = 1,000 shares × $0.70	700
Margin interest to be paid = $3,560 × 7.0%	(250)
Round trip commissions	(385)
Estimated net profit	$2,565
Estimated return on investment—one year	+38.8%

Pan American World Airways

In January 1973, Pan American issued their delayed 7½'s–98 convertible bonds with unusual features. The bonds will become convertible on January 16, 1975, and similar to the above two situations, the conversion will be at a 20 percent discount below the average price of the common during the preceding 10 trading days. The indicated conversion value will therefore be 125

132 Dow Jones–Irwin Guide to Convertible Securities

(100 ÷ .80). However, the conversion price per share may not be less than $7 nor more than $13.50. Or stated another way, the minimum and maximum number of shares that may be received will be 74 ($1,000 ÷ $13.50) and 143 ($1,000 ÷ $7.00).

As a result of these limits, the bond's conversion value will be less than 125 if the common stock ends up below $8.75 and greater than 125 at a stock price above $16.875 (refer to Exhibit 13–1 for a graphical illustration of the bond's future conversion values). At any price between these limits the bond will have a

EXHIBIT 13–1

Pan American 7½'s–98 Delayed Convertible Bonds

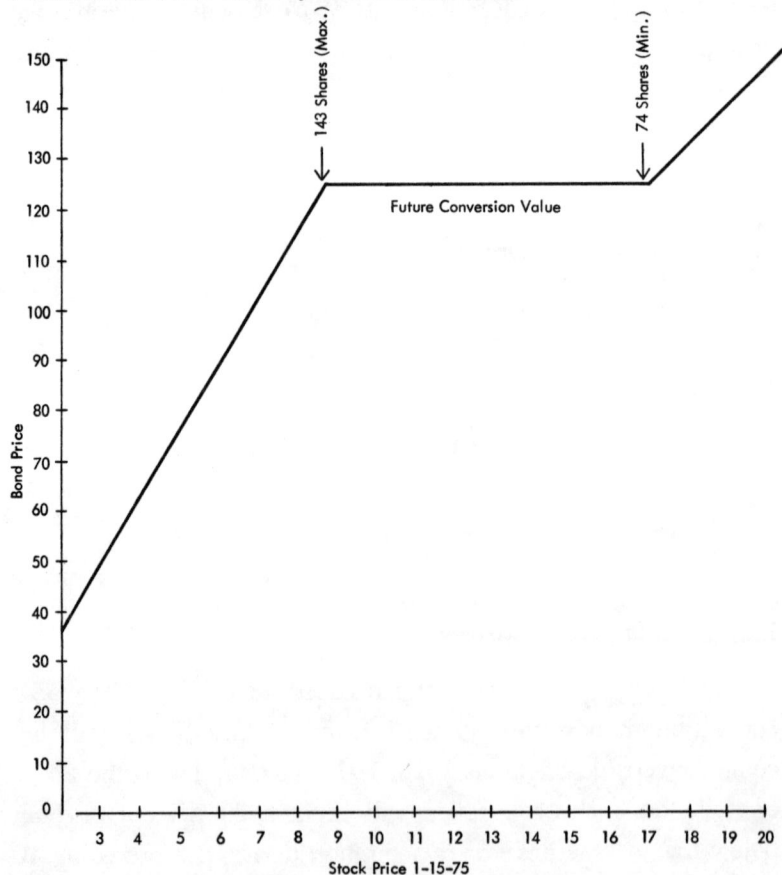

conversion value of 125 and will probably sell at a small premium reflecting its yield advantage over the common stock. The bonds therefore entail a greater risk than the Continental Investment or United National convertibles but also offer greater potential appreciation on the upside.

Any investor considering purchase of Pan American common stock should evaluate these bonds as an alternative to the common. Purchase of the bonds on margin may also be considered by the conservative investor if the common stock is selling well above the $8.75 area.

Note that, unlike the G. C. Computer bonds, it is not practical to hedge any of these three convertibles prior to the dates that the conversion terms are to be established. Since the convertibles price actions, up until these dates, will be essentially independent of their common stocks, a "hedge" position could result in losses as the shorted common stock rises in price. An exception would be Pan American if the common stock were to be trading at the $16.875 area. At that point, the Pan American bonds would advance along with any further price increase by the common. Even in this case, however, the short side of the position will have to be fully margined up until 90 days from the January 16, 1975 conversion date. The additional funds required to establish the hedge in Pan American would minimize the anticipated return on investment.

REAL ESTATE INVESTMENT TRUSTS—
DELAYED "WARRANTS"

Real Estate Investment Trusts have historically raised capital, at low-interest rates, by issuing convertible bonds or warrants. In recent times, the investment community has questioned the wisdom of holding convertible bonds yielding less than their related common stocks or holding REIT warrants which provide no yield at all. This has resulted in premature conversion of these securities, into their common stocks, to the dismay of the trust managements. It has also limited their ability to raise additional capital via the convertible bond or warrant routes.

To overcome this obstacle, an imaginative and new investment package was devised by Citizens and Southern Realty Investors in October 1972 and it has since been employed by other trusts. This package involved $100 units consisting of a straight 6¾ percent bond maturing in October 1978 plus a delayed "warrant." The "warrant" becomes exercisable into $125 worth of common stock on October 15, 1977, upon payment of $100 cash or surrender of the bonds at par value. If, at that time, the common stock is selling below $41.25, the "warrants" will not be exercisable but rather they will be redeemed by the trust at $25. If the common is trading above $50, the "warrants" will have a higher conversion value than $25—the purchase price per share will be equal to the lower price of $40 or 80 percent of the average stock price for the 10 trading days prior to October 15, 1977. In essence, the package offered investors a 6¾ percent current yield plus 25 percent (or more) capital appreciation over a five-year period—or about 10.6 percent yield to the "warrants" exercise date for a high quality short-term bond.

The package was similar to the Continental Investment delayed convertible bonds but offered greater flexibility since the straight bonds and "warrants" could be traded separately after the offering. Like Continental Investment, it also protected the company against near-term dilution of its common stock as the "warrants" are not exercisable until 1977.

Conservative investors seeking current yield plus modest long-term capital appreciation may find this type unit to be an attractive investment vehicle. Those investors, not desiring current income, would consider selling the bonds in the after market and holding (or adding to) the "warrants." Care should be exercised in placing orders to assure an acceptable yield to maturity. Also, if either or both parts of the package—bonds or "warrants"—are listed on an exchange, leverage may be employed to amplify the return on investment.

Note that, in all examples, the conversion terms will be based on the average price for the common stocks for a specified period of time prior to the conversion dates. The indicated conversion values will therefore be influenced by the trading pattern of the common stocks during this time period. If the common stock trends upward, the conversion value will increase while if the common stock declines in price the conversion value will be less.

Another element of risk for this type convertible is the possibility that the issuing company may go into bankruptcy prior to the effective conversion date. If this were to happen, the convertible's value would be subject to numerous and unpredictable factors.

FABRICATED CONVERTIBLES

As presented in Chapter 10, every convertible bond may be regarded as consisting of two separate components—a straight bond plus latent warrants to purchase common stock. To exercise the latent warrant, the investor surrenders the straight bond portion of his holding in lieu of cash. Keeping this analogy in mind, we can "fabricate" positions equivalent to convertible bonds by purchasing a combination of regular warrants along with straight bonds that may be used at par value in lieu of the cash exercise price.

A fabricated convertible has certain advantages over a conventional convertible bond. These include:

1. Greater flexibility since each of the two portions, warrants and straight bonds, may be purchased or sold separately.

136 *Dow Jones–Irwin Guide to Convertible Securities*

2. Greater leverage, based on current margin regulations, as the straight bond may be margined with as little as 30 percent compared to 50 percent for regular convertible bonds. This advantage will be of major importance when one is considering a safe hedge position.

To determine the number of warrants to be purchased along with each straight bond, simply divide the par value of the bond by the warrant's total exercise price. For example, consider a fabricated Daylin convertible bond consisting of the 5's–89 usable straight bond plus warrants to purchase one share of common stock for $22.50. Dividing the bond's $1,000 par value by the warrant's exercise price of $22.50 we get 44.44 ($1,000 ÷ $22.50 = 44.44), the number of warrants which, when added to the straight bond, forms the fabricated convertible.

The investment value of a fabricated convertible bond, assuming an efficient market, will normally be not too far below the market price of the straight bond. The conversion value of the Daylin fabricated convertible is 44.44 (number of warrants) times the market price of the Daylin common stock—the conversion of the fabricated convertible bond would result in receipt of 44.44 shares of common stock.

In May 1972, the three Daylin securities were trading at the following prices:

$$\text{Common stock} = \$22.00$$
$$\text{Warrant} = \$\ 7.00$$
$$5\text{'s--}89 \text{ bond} = 70\ (\$700)$$

The market price of the fabricated convertible was:

$$\$700 + (44.44 \times \$7.00) = \$1,010$$

The fabricated convertible's conversion value was:

$$44.44 \times \$22.00 = \$980$$

The Daylin fabricated convertible bond was selling at only a 3 percent premium over its conversion value and was an excellent candidate for either straight purchase or for hedging. Exhibit 13–2 illustrates a "bullish" hedge position. Note that the straight bonds were margined at 30 percent and the warrants at 55 percent,

EXHIBIT 13–2

WORK SHEET

WARRANT/USABLE BOND HEDGE EVALUATION

COMPANY _Daylin_   DATE _May 1972_

A. DESCRIPTION OF SECURITIES

Security	Description	Traded	Price	Yield %
Common stock		ASE	22	1.1
Warrant		ASE	7	
Usable bond	5's-89	ASE	70	7.1

Warrant exercise terms: _1.0_ shares for $ _22.50_ to _____

B. POSSIBLE HEDGE POSITION: Bullish _✓_, Neutral _____, or Bearish _____

Bonds purchased: _10_ M at $ _700_ each = $ _7,000_
Warrants purchased: _444_ shs. at $ _7.00_ each = $ _3,110_
Stock sold short: _222_ shs. at $ _22.00_ each = $ _4,880_

Investment: Bonds ($ _7,000_ + $ _50_ comm.) × _30_ % margin = $ _2,115_
           Warrants ($ _3,110_ + $ _80_ comm.) × _55_ % margin = $ _1,755_
           Total investment = $ _3,870_
Initial debit balance = $ _10,240_ − $ _3,870_ = $ _6,370_

C. PROFIT AND LOSS ESTIMATES—ASSUMING A 12-MONTH POSITION

Assumed stock price change	−50%	+50%	+100%	Other
Stock price	11	33	44	
Estimated warrant price	4	15	21½	
Estimated bond price	60	80	100	
Profit or (loss) − bonds	(1,000)	1,000	3,000	
− warrants	(1,330)	3,550	6,440	
− stock	2,440	(2,440)	(4,880)	
Commissions	(360)	(310) **	(320) **	( )
Estimated capital gain or (loss)	(250)	1,800	4,240	
Estimated return on investment	−6.5%	+46.5%	+110 %	%

D. ESTIMATED ANNUAL CASH FLOW

Bond interest received   = $ _500_
Less dividends paid on stock sold short   = (_55_)
Less estimated margin interest* = $ _6,370_ × _6.0_ % = (_380_)
Estimated cash flow   = $ _65_ = _1.7_ %

*Based on the initial debit balance, however, this will fluctuate as the short account is marked to the market. The indicated interest rate is also subject to change.

E. OTHER FACTORS _** It is assumed that warrants and bonds would be converted for closing out the position._

the rates prevailing at the time. The hedge position offered greater upside potential than purchase of the common stock at significantly less downside risk. There was also a small advantage in the cash flow from the hedge position which was greater than the common stock's yield.

BUYING CALL OPTIONS

What does the convertible conscious investor do when he "falls in love" with a stock which does not have an undervalued convertible or warrant? The obvious answer is to purchase the stock and hope that his expectations materialize. However, it is the author's opinion that a much better approach is the purchase of a call option for a fraction of the stock's price and the investment of the balance in safe hedging situations offering 15–20 percent annualized capital appreciation. In other words, the expert in convertibles should seldom or *never* buy a share of common stock!

For illustration purposes, suppose that one desires to buy 100 shares of stock currently selling at $50 which he believes will appreciate in value by 50 percent during the next 12 months. Should he buy the stock or a one-year call option for $750. If he choses the call, it will be assumed that the $4,250 balance will be invested in hedging or special situations providing a 20 percent return, or a net profit of $850 during the 12-month period (.20 × $4,250 = $850).

Upside Potential. If the common stock advances 50 percent as anticipated, the buyer of the stock would have received a profit of $2,500, less commissions. In comparison, the purchaser of the call would have obtained a net profit of $1,750 on the call ($2,500 − $750 = $1,750) plus the $850 profit on the $4,250 balance invested in hedges. The total gross profit for the proposed alternative would have been $2,600, or *more* than if one had simply purchased the common stock as was originally intended.

Downside Risk. If the common stock declined by 50 percent, instead of rising as hoped, the stock buyer would have lost half of his investment. How would the proposed alternative of a call option plus the balance invested in hedge positions have faired? The entire premium of $750 paid for the call would have, of course, been lost. However, the $850 earned on the funds invested in hedge positions would have resulted in a net *profit* of $100.

The convertible hedger clearly has far superior alternatives to buying common stocks.

BUYING CALL OPTIONS ON UNDERVALUED WARRANTS

The most dynamic call option that one can purchase is a call on a warrant, especially if the warrant is undervalued. One would normally expect that the percent premium paid for a call on a highly leveraged warrant would be at least twice that for a call on its common stock. However, this is not always the case. Apparently, call writers become overly impressed with high percentage premiums and frequently "jump" at offers exceeding 15 percent for a 6-month call or 20 percent for a one-year call, regardless of the inherent leverage of the security.

Call options on warrants plus cash may be a very viable alternative to the warrant plus cash approach. Or call options on warrants may be considered for part of a warrant hedge position. But, remember, always buy a sufficient number of warrants to permit short selling of the common stock at no margin on the short side as stock may not be sold short against a call option without depositing full margin against the short sale. In any case, be sure to work out the arithmetic before any investment decision is made.

WRITING CALL OPTIONS

Since a call option is identical to a short-term warrant, the writing (or sale) of a call against common stock held long in one's portfolio is similar to reverse warrant hedging and profit and loss calculations may be made accordingly. Major differences are the following:

1. The striking price of a call is reduced by any dividends paid on the common stock whereas a warrant is not so affected.
2. Since the striking price of a call option is usually set at the current market price of the stock, it will not be possible to establish the optimum situation where the stock is selling well below the striking price (the warrant's exercise price).
3. The premium received for writing the call option will probably not be as generous as the excessive prices paid by the investment public for short-term warrants.
4. Whereas warrants may be sold short having a life to expiration of up to three years or more, call options are usually written for only 12 months or less.

Although the above factors would tend to favor reverse warrant hedging over a call option writing program, hedging is much more limited from a selection standpoint—options may be written on a wide variety of common stocks. Another advantage to the call option writing program is that no margin is required for writing the call as it is for selling short a warrant. In fact, the premium received may be used to make additional investments.

A significant risk/reward improvement may be attained by writing call options (on common stocks) against undervalued convertible bonds or preferreds—in fact, this is the only area where the author would consider an option writing program to be comparable to the superior risk/reward opportunities available in convertible or warrant hedging. Writing options on common stocks against undervalued warrants may also be considered, but experience indicates that the market is much more limited as the call buyer is normally astute enough to purchase the favorably leveraged warrant instead of a call. Also, most brokerage firms impose higher margin requirements when calls are written against warrants as opposed to convertibles.

The holder of a substantial portfolio of convertibles should continuously offer call options on their related common stocks. If a bid is received, be sure to evaluate the risk/reward characteristics of the convertible/call position before acceptance. From a practical standpoint, one should determine in advance the amount he would like to receive for writing the call and at what price. This will permit a prompt decision when interest is expressed by a potential buyer. Remember, there is absolutely no reason to write a call option unless it improves the risk/reward aspects of your portfolio. Also, be sure that you are working with a brokerage firm that has an active option department and that the certificates, against which the options are written, are kept in your brokerage account.

If one is active in hedging convertibles he may also wish to offer call options against the convertibles. The initial hedge ratios will be established independently of potential calls. If a satisfactory bid is received, a portion of the common stock sold short may be closed out to accommodate the call options. A convertible hedge portfolio with some options written can be designed to make money in any type of market—bull, bear, or sideways.

Consider, for example, writing call options on Gulf Resources & Chemical common stock as part of the convertible bond hedge position presented in Exhibit 11–4 of Chapter 11. The straight hedge position would have involved the short sale of 900 shares of stock against 20 bonds. As illustrated by Exhibit 13–3, if two six-month call options were written for a premium of $150 each, the number of shares of stock sold short would be reduced to 800 to retain the neutral characteristic of the hedge. The potential upside and downside gains would be reduced somewhat by the

EXHIBIT 13–3

WORK SHEET

CONVERTIBLE BOND HEDGE WITH CALL OPTIONS SOLD

COMPANY __Gulf Resources + Chemical__   DATE __March 1973__

A. DESCRIPTION OF SECURITIES

Security	Description	Traded	Price	Yield %
Common stock		NYS	9½	0
Convertible bond	6¼–91	NYS	80	7.8

Bond's conversion value = __71.43__ shares x $ __9.50__ = $ __678__
Conversion premium   = $ __18__ %
Estimated investment value   = $ __60__

B. POSSIBLE HEDGE POSITION: Bullish_____, Neutral __✓__, or Bearish_____

Options sold: __200__ shs. at $ __150__ per 100 shs. for __6__ months = $ __300__
Bonds purchased: __20__ M at $ __800__ each   = $ __16,000__
Stock sold short: __800__ shs. at $ __9.50__ each   = $ __7,600__
Investment = ($ __16,000__ + __100__ comm.) x __50__ % margin   = $ __8,050__
Initial debit balance = $ __16,100__ − ($ __8,050__ + $ __300__)   = $ __7,750__

C. PROFIT AND LOSS ESTIMATES

Assumed stock price change	−50%	+50%	+100%	Other
Stock price	4¾		19	
Estimated bond price	65		140	
Profit or (loss) – bonds	(3,000)		12,000	
– stock	3,800	( )	(7,600)	
– options		( )	(1,900)	
Commissions	(455)	( )	675	( )
Estimated capital gain or (loss)	345		1,825	
Estimated return on investment	+4.3 %	%	+22.7 %	%

D. ESTIMATED CASH FLOW FOR LIFE OF OPTION

Premium received for call options   = $ __300__
Bond interest received = $ __1,250__ x __6__ /12   =   __625__
Less dividends paid on stock sold short   = (__0__)
Less estimated margin interest* = $ __7,750__ x __7.0__ % x __6__ /12 = (__270__)
Estimated net cash flow for __6__ months   = $ __655__ = __16.3__% (annualized)

*Based on the initial debit balance, however, this will fluctuate as the short account is marked to the market. The indicated interest rate is also subject to change.

E. OTHER FACTORS _____

inclusion of the call options but the annualized cash flow would be increased from 8.5 percent up to a very generous 16.3 percent.

GENERAL GUIDES FOR THE USE OF CALL OPTIONS IN A CONVERTIBLE HEDGING PROGRAM

1. *Buy* call options on undervalued warrants.
    - *a)* The call options will normally supplement a warrant hedge position as opposed to straight purchase for speculation.
    - *b)* The option length should be 6 months and 10 days or *more.*
    - *c)* Do not pay more than 20 percent for six-month calls or 30 percent for one-year calls—you will frequently be able to obtain even lower premiums.
    - *d)* Stagger your option purchases to smooth out the affect of market cycles.
    - *e)* Do not be too quick to take profits—remember that half of your options will probably be worthless on expiration. When options are purchased as part of a warrant hedge position they should normally be held until the day they expire.
2. *Buy* call options on common stock.
    - *a)* When a reverse warrant hedge has only one year remaining to expiration, consider buying call options on the common stock in lieu of holding the common. The funds released will probably provide greater profit potential in other situations.
    - *b)* When you "fall in love" with a stock that does not have an undervalued warrant or convertible, buy a long-term call option and invest the funds saved in high profit hedging situations.

3. *Sell* (write) call options on common stock against undervalued convertibles.
   a) The option length should be 6 months and 10 days or less.
   b) The convertible should be trading close to its conversion value.
   c) Expect to receive premiums ranging from 10 to 20 percent for a six-month call depending on the volatility of the common stock.
   d) Determine in advance the premium which you must receive to write the call—this will obviate the need for a hurried decision.
   e) Do not write call options on warrants.
   f) With few exceptions, do not write puts or straddle options and never write strips, straps, or spreads.
   g) Give your broker a written list of the stocks on which you will write call options. The list should be updated at least every three months.

DUAL-PURPOSE FUNDS

At recent price levels, the capital shares of the seven dual-purpose funds are some of the more interesting investment situations presently available. These funds are closed-end investment companies with portfolios consisting primarily of common stocks. The fund's ownership is divided equally into two classes of shares. The income shares receive all of the fund's dividends while the capital shares get all the capital gains.

Each fund has a specified terminal date at which time there will be a final accounting to both the income and capital shareholders. The income shares will be redeemed by the fund's sponsors on that date at a fixed redemption price plus dividend arrearages, if any. The remaining assets will go to the capital shareholders. Before the terminal date, neither class of shares can be redeemed;

however, all are traded in the marketplace. Like other closed-end funds, the market price of the capital shares may reflect either a discount or a premium in relation to net assets, and most have sold at discounts since their inception in 1967. But, unlike other closed-end funds, the terminal date provides a fixed point in time when they must sell at their net asset value.

The income shares may be evaluated on a yield-to-maturity basis as are bonds, recognizing that a serious stock market decline could reduce the fund's net assets to below the specified redemption price. The capital shares may be evaluated in a fashion similar to warrants and the previously discussed delayed convertibles since they will become "convertible" into cash at their net asset value on their terminal date. The net asset value, of course, will be directly related to the future market values of the securities held in the fund's portfolio and could even become nothing if the income shares consummed all of the fund's assets at that time. Exhibits 13–4 and 13–5 provide pertinent information on both types of securities.

EXHIBIT 13–4
The Income Shares

	Market Price 5/11/73	Minimum Annual Cumulative Dividend	Estimated Dividend 1973	Approx. Current Yield*	Redemption Price	Year	Approx. Yield to Maturity†
American DualVest	$13.00	$0.84	$0.87	6.7%	$15.00	1979	8.6%
Gemini Fund	14.00	0.56	1.19	8.5	11.00	1984	7.5
Hemisphere Fund	7.00	0.62	0.62	8.9	11.44	1985	10.9
Income and Capital Shares	10.38	0.50	0.90	8.7	10.00	1982	8.4
Leverage Fund of Boston	13.12	0.75	0.97	7.4	13.72	1982	7.8
Putnam Duofund	17.25	1.10‡	1.14	6.6	19.75	1983	7.6
Scudder Duo-Vest	8.50	0.64	0.64	7.5	9.15	1982	8.1

* Equals estimated dividend for 1973 divided by market price.
† Yield to maturity: based on estimated dividend for 1973 or minimum cumulative dividend (whichever is greater), market price, and redemption figures; no adjustments are made for possible dividend increases or decreases.
‡ Higher in future years.

EXHIBIT 13–5
The Capital Shares

	Symbol	Market Price 5/11/73	Net Asset Value*	Premium or Discount
American DualVest	ADV	$ 7.25	$ 9.01	−19.5%
Gemini Fund	GEM	12.38	16.67	−25.8
Hemisphere Fund	HEM	2.38	2.09	+13.6
Income and Capital Shares	ICS	7.88	11.33	−30.5
Leverage Fund of Boston	LFB	10.25	14.82	−30.8
Putnam Duofund	PUTNC	5.00	7.02	−28.8
Scudder Duo-Vest	SDV	7.25	10.23	−29.1

* After giving effect to arrearages, if any, of cumulative dividends and amortization of any difference between original paid-in capital and the redemption price of common shares.

At the present time, the capital shares offer attractive investment opportunities due to both their inherent leverage and their discounts below net asset values. Exhibit 13–6 illustrates the risk/reward characteristics for each of the funds based on possible changes in their total net asset values between now and their terminal dates. It should be noted that the lower priced shares provide the greatest upside appreciation potential but also have greater downside risk.

Does the purchase of these capital shares give the investor an advantage over the stock market as do the various convertible situations illustrated throughout this guide? This question may be answered by assuming that an investor splits his available

EXHIBIT 13–6

	Change in Value of Capital Shares at Terminal Date, Assuming Gain or Loss in the Portfolio of				
	−50%	−25%	0%	+50%	+100%
American DualVest	−100%	− 58%	+24%	+190%	+355%
Gemini Fund	− 77	− 21	+35	+146	+258
Hemisphere Fund	−100	−100	−12	+272	+556
Income and Capital Shares	− 92	− 24	+44	+179	+314
Leverage Fund of Boston	− 95	− 25	+45	+184	+323
Putnam Duofund	−100	− 93	+40	+308	+576
Scudder Duo-Vest	− 93	− 26	+41	+175	+308
Average	− 94%	− 50%	+31%	+208%	+384%

stock market funds between cash and equal investments in each of the seven dual-purpose funds. Assuming that the capital shares are held to their terminal dates and that the funds on average perform the same as the overall market, relative performance is estimated as follows:

	\multicolumn{5}{c}{Change in Value of Alternate Portfolios at Terminal Dates Assuming Gain or Loss in the Overall Stock Market of}			
	−50%	−25%	0%	+50%	+100%
Typical common stock portfolio.	−50%	−25%	0%	+ 50%	+100%
50% cash/50% dual-purpose funds.......................	−47	−25	+15	+104	+192

Since the interest earned on the cash retained should be about equal to dividends received from a typical stock portfolio, the dual-purpose funds offer a significant advantage to the long-term investor seeking professional money management. The obvious reasons for this characteristic are the current discounts below net asset value of the higher priced shares and the inherent leverage of the lower priced shares. If these factors did not exist, there would be no advantage.

One argument attempts to explain that discounts from net asset value are expected and reflect the higher downside risk that one assumes when he purchases dual-purpose fund stocks. The downside risk is certainly obvious, but, when one considers the greater upside potential, it compensates for the extra risk. Without exploring the arithmetic in detail, it is the author's conclusion that these securities should trade at net asset value, or slightly above, unless there are reasons to question the abilities of the fund's management. In fact, if the net asset value is only a small fraction of the total portfolio, the shares should trade at a premium (as were Hemisphere's) similar to long-term warrants. Exhibit 13–7 illustrates a suggested normal value curve. The recent market price relationships for the seven funds are also shown.

EXHIBIT 13-7

Normal Curve for Long-term Capital Shares of Dual-Purpose Funds

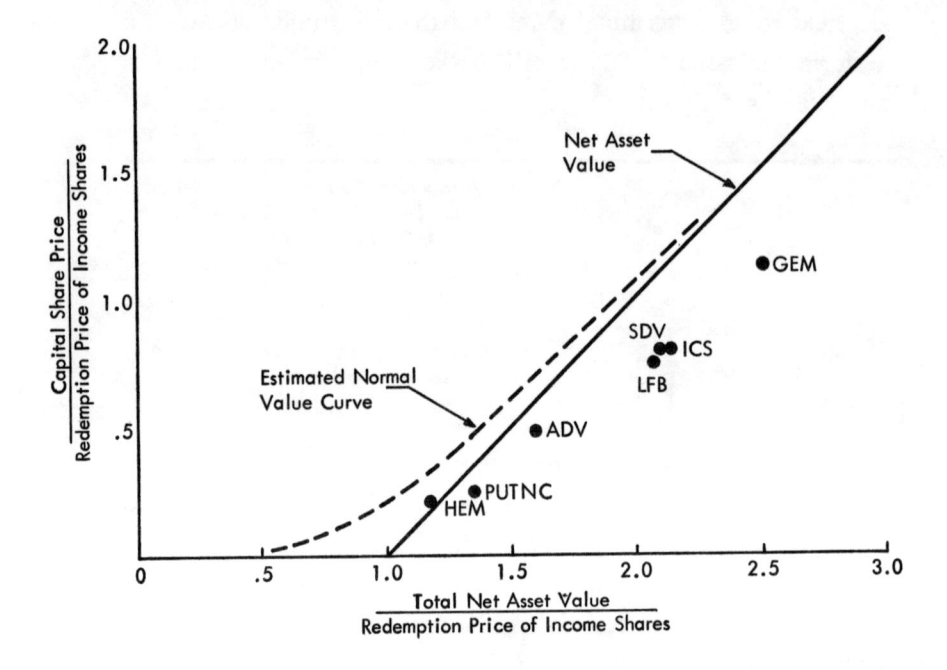

14

Margin Regulations

MARGIN is the amount of money that an investor deposits with his stockbroker if he desires to partially finance his investments. The balance is borrowed from the brokerage firm in compliance with rules established by the Federal Reserve Board under Regulation T (banks and other financial institutions are governed by the FRB's Regulation U). Under current regulations, for example, many common stocks may be purchased on as little as 65 percent margin, the remaining 35 percent being borrowed from the brokerage firm. Margin interest must be paid on the resulting debit balance but the loan need never be paid back until the account is closed.

In addition to Regulation T, which establishes initial margin requirements, the New York Stock Exchange has minimum requirements that must be maintained in the account. Most brokerage firms also have house maintenance requirements which are somewhat higher than the New York Stock Exchange's minimums.

If the equity in a margin account were to drop below the specified maintenance margin level, a margin call would be issued by the brokerage firm and requires that additional cash or marginable securities be deposited to bring the equity back up to the minimum level. The alternative is to liquidate a portion of the securities in the margin account.

Both the initial and maintenance margin requirements are subject to change without notice so one should stay in frequent contact with his broker to ascertain the current requirements. Different requirements may also be imposed from time to time on individual securities. Margin requirements prevailing at the present time are presented in Exhibits 14–1 and 14–2.

EXHIBIT 14–1
Initial Margin Requirements

Type of Security	Brokers (Regulation T)	Banks (Regulation U)
Common, Preferred and Warrants (Long or Short)		
Listed	65%	65%
OTC marginable*	65%	65%
OTC nonmarginable*	100%	Unregulated
Convertible Bonds (Long)		
Listed	50%	50%
OTC—convertible into listed or OTC marginable stock	100%	50%
OTC—convertible into OTC nonmarginable stock	100%	Unregulated
Straight Bonds (Long)		
Listed	Unregulated†	Unregulated
OTC	100%	Unregulated

* The Federal Reserve Board determines which OTC securities are marginable.

† The New York Stock Exchange requires 25 percent maintenance margin on listed straight bonds and most brokerage firms require 30 percent initial margin to provide a safety factor above the maintenance level.

APPLICATION OF MARGIN REGULATIONS IN A HEDGING PROGRAM

Although the use of margin is not normally recommended for the average investor, margin purchases and short sales (which

EXHIBIT 14–2

Typical Brokerage Firm Maintenance Requirements (listed and OTC marginable securities)

Long Side
  Common, preferred and warrants
    NYSE and ASE
      Securities selling at $3.00 and under................................... 100%
      From $3.125 to $10.00... 3 points
      From $10.125 and above... 30%
    Other exchanges and OTC marginable securities
      Securities selling at $4.00 and under................................... 100%
      From $4.125 to $10.00... 4 points
      From $10.125 and above... 40%
  Convertible bonds............................. 30% with minimum of 10 points
  Straight bonds................................ 25% with minimum of 10 points

Short Side (Common and Warrants)
  The greater of the above or the current NYSE minimum maintenance, to wit:
  NYSE and ASE
    Securities selling at $5.00 or less............... 2½ points or 100% whichever is greater
    Securities selling at $5.125 or above............ 5 points or 30% whichever is greater
  Other exchanges and OTC marginable securities
    Securities selling at $5.00 or less............... 2½ points or 100% whichever is greater
    Securities selling at $5.125 or above............ 5 points or 40% whichever is greater

    Note: Most brokerage firms also advise that their minimum requirements are intended for use only in diversified accounts, and in instances where the client's position in a given security is small. Where the account is not diversified, or where the customer's position is in blocks, or centered in a particular industry, or in volatile securities, proportionately higher requirements, dependent on the particular circumstances, may be charged.

must be executed in a margin account) are everyday tools of the convertible hedger. It is most important that he and his broker be knowledgeable of these requirements for effective planning, order executions, and management of the hedge portfolio. In addition to the basic requirements of Exhibits 14–1 and 14–2, the following points are also important.

1. The short sale of common stock against warrants, convertible bonds, or convertible preferred stock, held in the brokerage account, requires no margin on the short side. The warrants or convertibles may be margined according to the applicable rules of Exhibits 14–1 and 14–2.

2. Maintenance margin requirements of Exhibit 14–2 apply to one's total portfolio rather than to individual securities. For example, if the only security purchased was a $3 marginable warrant, the entire $3 would have to be deposited initially instead of the lower 65 percent as permitted by Regulation T. This is necessary to meet the maintenance margin requirement immediately after purchase. However, if the account also includes higher priced marginable securities, it might be possible to buy the additional $3 warrant at only 65 percent margin. To illustrate this phenomenon, consider the purchase of 200 shares each of both $3 and $15 securities, assuming that they are the only investments in the account.

Initial Margin
    200 × $15.00 × 65% = $1,950
    200 × $ 3.00 × 65% =   390
    Initial margin   = $2,340

Maintenance Margin
    200 × $15.00 × 30% = $ 900
    200 × $ 3.00 × 100% =   600
    Maintenance margin   = $1,500

Since the initial margin requirement of $2,340 exceeds the $1,500 maintenance requirement, both purchases may be made at 65 percent margin. Note that the New York Stock Exchange requires that the account have a minimum equity of $2,000 before any margin purchases may be made (some brokerage firms have higher minimums).

3. When warrants are sold short against common stock in a reverse hedge transaction, both sides of the position must be margined per the applicable initial margin requirements. Again, it may be possible to only deposit 65 percent for the short sale of a low-priced warrant and still meet the maintenance requirements depending on the other securities held in the portfolio.

15

Portfolio Management

YOU ARE the captain of your own investment destiny—your hedge portfolio of warrants, convertibles, options, and special situations. While managing this portfolio, you will be faced with numerous investment alternatives and important decisions. Your task may be simplified by the selection of only one approach to convertibles; i.e., the basic mechanical system for hedging undervalued warrants. Or it may be considerably more fun, and probably more rewarding, if you use your imagination and the many sophisticated investment tools at your disposal.

The following table summarizes the major techniques presented in this book and provides a quick determination of how the author believes they would normally be expected to perform in different type markets, bull, bear, or sideways. Comparisons are made on a 0 through 5 scale, with 5 denoting the highest and 0 the lowest degree of the characteristic.

YOUR BROKERAGE ACCOUNT

To execute short sales, a basic maneuver in a hedging program, all transactions must be made in a master margin account. This

	Bull Market	Sideways Market	Bear Market
Convertible bond portfolio	4	1	1
50 percent warrants/50 percent cash	5	1	0
Regular warrant hedges			
Bullish (the basic system)	5	0	3
Neutral	3	0	4
Bearish	0	0	5
Convertible bond hedges			
Bullish	3	2	2
Neutral	2	2	3
Bearish	1	2	4
Reverse warrant hedges	2	3	2
Call options written against convertible hedges	2	3	2

type account also permits one to leverage his investments, if desired, by borrowing money from the brokerage firm.

The master account will include several subaccounts. Five will most likely be employed by the convertible hedger. These are shown below, along with the initial margin requirements currently prevailing.

Cash account	—nonmarginable warrants and convertibles	—100%
Margin account	—warrants, common stocks, and preferred stocks	— 65%
	—options purchased	—100%
	—options written against convertibles	— 0%
Short account	—warrants sold short	— 65%
	—common stock sold short against warrants or convertibles	— 0%
Convertible bond account	—convertible bonds	— 50%
Straight bond account	—bonds usable at par value for exercising warrants	— 30%

Cash Account. In a convertible hedging program, the cash account will include warrants and convertibles which are traded over-the-counter and are nonmarginable (some OTC securities are marginable). The investor seeking maximum leverage, however, will generally avoid the over-the-counter market unless the security is presently marginable or is expected to be listed in the near future. An exception to this rule would be the purchase of a *highly leveraged* OTC warrant.

Margin Account. The margin account will usually include listed warrants and convertible preferred stocks. It will also contain nonmarginable warrants or convertibles if common stock is sold short against them. Their transfer from the cash account is required by Regulation T to permit short sales of common stock against them at no margin on the short side. If cash is required to collateralize the short sale of warrants, as in a reverse warrant hedge position, it will be deposited in the margin account as a credit entry, and will be offset against the debit balance for determining margin interest to be paid. Any options, purchased or written, will also be placed in the margin account. Call options bought must be paid for in cash as they have no collateral value. The premiums received for calls written will be credit entries in the margin account and will offset any debit balance or may be used for additional investments.

Bond Accounts. The convertible bond account will contain listed convertible bonds (and, depending on the brokerage firm, the short sales of common stock against the bonds might also be made in this account instead of the short account). The straight bond account will be employed when "fabricating" a convertible bond—the listed, usable bond will be purchased in this account.

Short Account. The short account will contain common stock sold short against warrants and convertibles, and warrants sold short in a reverse warrant hedge position. The short account will show a credit balance equal to the market value of the securities sold short. This account is normally adjusted weekly by your brokerage firm by a process called "marking to the market." If there was a decline in the total value of your short positions, the short account will be debited and the margin account credited with an equal amount. A rise in price will result in a credit to your short account and a corresponding debit entry in the margin account. Your brokerage loan, the debit balance in the margin account, will therefore fluctuate as the market value of your short positions change.

SELECTING A BROKERAGE FIRM

It is recommended that the manual, *The Better Idea, Total Investment Planning and Management System,* be consulted for in-depth guidelines for selecting a brokerage firm and a stockbroker. This manual emphasizes the need for obtaining the *right* brokerage firm for one's investment objectives and in selecting the *right* broker to provide the services you require and deserve. It includes detailed guidelines for aiding one in the evaluation and selection process.

From a convertible hedging standpoint, it has been the author's experience that many of the most reputable brokerage firms do not have comparable policies or capabilities in executing hedging transactions. These are some of the major factors to consider in determining which firm to do business with.

1. What is the minimum equity needed for opening a margin account? This may range from the New York Stock Exchange's minimum of $2,000 to considerably higher.
2. Will the firm permit you to sell short common stock, as specified by Regulation T, against margined warrants or convertibles without having to deposit additional funds against the short sale? Some do not; they probably don't understand the regulations. Look for another firm.
3. Will the brokerage firm execute and maintain short sales on securities that are difficult (but possible) to borrow? Some

firms will only permit you to sell short securities which are readily available from their clients' margin accounts. Find a firm that will make a reasonable effort to borrow the securities from other sources as required.
4. Be certain that the brokerage firm has an efficient back office and a margin department that is knowledgeable of Regulation T. Otherwise, you will be continuously annoyed by foul-ups. If this happens too often, find another firm.

SELECTING A BROKER

At this point, you should have your investment program firmly established and a sound basis for selecting a broker to work with. If you plan to make all of your own investment decisions, your selection problems will be nominal. Find a broker that provides good order executions, reporting, and the other services that you require.

If you need, or desire, a broker that has expertise in the complex world of convertibles, your problem will be most difficult as few brokers specialize in this area. It is recommended that you start your search by meeting with the manager of each firm under consideration and discuss with him your requirements and your profile of the ideal broker for you. After you have developed a list of broker candidates, then meet with each to determine if he (or she) is willing and able to provide the services you describe. If the broker you select does not live up to your expectations, find another one.

OPERATING AT MAXIMUM LEVERAGE

Since the safety of a carefully designed and diversified hedge portfolio is extremely high, most investors will employ maximum leverage permitted by current margin regulations. If you have not invested on margin in the past, and the thought disturbs you, do not disregard convertible hedging for that reason alone. Start with a nonleveraged portfolio—no debit balance on which you must pay margin interest. As you gain experience and confidence, and as your equity begins to build up, then gradually increase the amount of leveraged employed. It is recommended that any leveraged portfolio includes sufficient income-producing situations to avoid an equity decline in a sideways market from margin interest and dividends paid.

PORTFOLIO SELECTION AND DIVERSIFICATION

First, determine your investment objectives, income or long-term capital growth, or a combination of both. Then evaluate all situations which potentially meet these objectives. Depending on the amount you have available to invest, you may wish to select only a few of the best situations, or all of them that meet your minimum requirements—there won't be too many. If you plan to build up to a diversified portfolio of say 10 or more different positions, and this is certainly recommended by the author, do not invest in all of them at once. Select the few which look to be outstanding first. Then add new positions later—the marginal situations may become outstanding next week or next month—there is usually no great hurry. Or another brand new situation may become available.

Exhibit 15–1 provides a work sheet for planning your convertible hedge portfolio.

INVESTMENT SERVICES

An investment service which specializes in warrants and/or convertibles is an absolute necessity for the convertible hedger. It is recommended that trial subscriptions be taken from all of the

EXHIBIT 15-1

Position	Number Shares or Bonds	Purchases Price Each	Purchases Total Amount	Short Sales Price Each	Short Sales Total Amount	Margin Rate	Net Invest.	Annual Income Exp.
Bonds or preferreds	___	$___	$___			___%	$___	$___
Warrants	___	___	___					
Common stock	___			$___	$___			(___)
Bonds or preferreds	___	___	___					
Warrants	___	___	___					
Common stock	___			___	___			(___)
Bonds or preferreds	___	___	___					
Warrants	___	___	___					
Common stock	___			___	___			(___)
Bonds or preferreds	___	___	___					
Warrants	___	___	___					
Common stock	___			___	___			(___)
Bonds or preferreds	___	___	___					
Warrants	___	___	___					
Common stock	___			___	___			(___)
Bonds or preferreds	___	___	___					
Warrants	___	___	___					
Common stock	___			___	___			(___)
Bonds or preferreds	___	___	___					
Warrants	___	___	___					
Common stock	___			___	___			(___)
Bonds or preferreds	___	___	___					
Warrants	___	___	___					
Common stock	___			___	___			(___)
Bonds or preferreds	___	___	___					
Warrants	___	___	___					
Common stock	___			___	___			(___)
Bonds or preferreds	___	___	___					
Warrants	___	___	___					
Common stock	___			___	___			(___)
Totals			$___		$___		$___	$___

Estimated annual margin interest = $___ (debit balance) x ___% = (___)

Estimated annual net cash flow or (expense) = $___

few services available. Make sure that the one (or more) that you ultimately select provides exacting conversion terms and appropriate footnotes that explain the complex provisions inherent in some convertibles. Leverage projections should be soundly based and computerized to permit prompt and accurate adjustment for constantly changing price relationships. But, before you invest, be sure to make your own estimates and calculations of potential profit or loss—the work sheets illustrated in this guide are designed for quick and accurate computations.

	Frequency	Annual Cost	Areas Covered
The Value Line Convertible Survey 5 East 44th Street New York, New York 10017	Weekly	$192	Major warrants, convertible bonds and preferreds—emphasis on straight buys as opposed to hedging.
The R. H. M. Warrant & Stock Survey 220 Fifth Avenue New York, New York 10001	Weekly	$ 95	Most warrants plus selected low-priced stocks—reverse warrant hedges are sometimes recommended but not straight warrant hedges.
The R. H. M. Convertible Survey 220 Fifth Avenue New York, New York 10001	Weekly	$100	Most convertible bonds and preferreds—hedge positions are recommended.
C & P Warrant Analysis Box 123 Fort George Station New York, New York 10040	Bi-Weekly	$ 85	Most warrants—hedge and reverse warrant hedge situations are recommended.
FRA Warrant Service Box 13676 N. T. Station Denton, Texas 76203	Monthly	$ 76	Most warrants—hedge and reverse warrant hedge situations are recommended.

INCOME TAX CONSIDERATIONS

One's tax bracket, or the characteristic of the investment program, may play an important role in determining the best type of hedging program. An individual in a high tax bracket, for example, will probably lean toward long-term capital appreciation as opposed to a high cash flow. A pension fund, or other tax-sheltered plan, may wish to receive a high cash flow with only modest capital appreciation potential.

Once the type of hedging program is established, it is generally recommended that your investment decisions be made independently of possible tax consequences. But, keep in mind that a hedging program provides a great deal of flexibility toward achieving net long-term capital gains, even if an aggressive portfolio strategy is followed. For example, consider a warrant hedge position that has been held longer than six months and has achieved substantial paper profits from a bull market move. If it were closed out, the profits on the warrants would be long-term versus short-term losses on the common stock sold short (all short sales are short term regardless of the time held). These short-term losses could then be used to offset short-term profits from other trades made during the year.

PORTFOLIO TURNOVER STRATEGY

A continuous review of all positions taken and potential new situations will indicate opportunities for profits that will not be noticed by the investor who only evaluates his portfolio periodically. Experience indicates that optimum performance will be achieved by maintaining one's portfolio in the best situations available at the time. This will simply involve "leap frogging" from marginal positions held into new, mathematically superior, situations. The results of an aggressive posture will more than compensate for the additional brokerage commissions resulting from a high portfolio turnover strategy. Another approach is to trade the short side of a hedge position against the warrants or convertibles. Additional short sales are made as prices rise and a portion of the short position is covered during market declines. This technique will help improve performance during the dull sideways market at the expense of possibly lower profits if the initial position was held for a major price advance.

RECORD KEEPING

It is recommended that a log of all transactions be maintained on a continuous basis rather than waiting until income tax time. This will allow you to easily determine year-to-date performance

EXHIBIT 15–2

Security Transactions

No. of Shares or Bonds	Security	Purchase Data Date	Purchase Data Amount	Sale Data Date	Sale Data Amount	Capital Gain or (Loss) Short-Term	Capital Gain or (Loss) Long-Term

EXHIBIT 15–3

Investment Income

Date	Security	Dividends Received	Bond Interest Received	Accrued Bond Interest Paid	Net Bond Interest

EXHIBIT 15–4

Investment Expenses

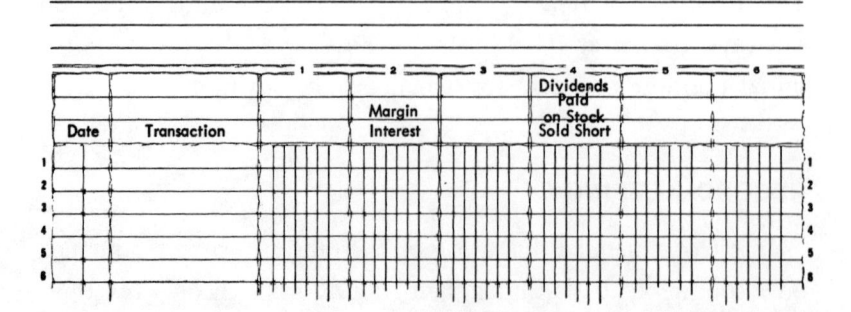

Date	Transaction	Margin Interest	Dividends Paid on Stock Sold Short	

and permit execution of orders throughout the year for optimum after-tax profit. All securities sold short may be kept in a separate log from securities purchased—since short sales are short term for tax purposes, regardless of the time period held, a separate log may simplify your tax bookkeeping. Exhibits 15-2 to 15-4 illustrate typical records maintained on standard accounting paper.

ACTION

If, upon completion of this guide, the reader desires to begin a convertible hedge program, Exhibits 15-5 and 15-6 provide general guidelines for planning, establishing, and managing the portfolio. They will also be of value to stockbrokers who specialize in the convertible securities field. Note, from Exhibit 15-6, that a broker who is skilled in convertibles, can be of valuable assistance to his clients, particularly in the areas of research and order execution.

The alternate approach, of course, is to retain the services of a professional money manager who specializes in this field. In view of the complexity and extraordinary effort involved in managing an intricate system such as this, professional management, by the few specalists trained to do so, is highly recommended. Their fee reflects the high level of expertise required, but is normally paid solely out of the expected high profits.

EXHIBIT 15–5

General Guides for Establishing a Convertible Hedge Program

1. Determine your investment objective:
   _____aggressive capital appreciation
   _____long-term capital appreciation at modest risk
   _____income plus modest long-term capital appreciation
2. How much capital is available for investment in the hedge program?
   Cash = $_____
   Securities to be sold = _____
   Loan value of securities to be held = _____
   Total capital for investment = $_____
3. Select investment areas of interest:
   _____warrant hedging
   _____convertible bond or preferred stock hedging
   _____reverse warrant hedging
   _____special situations
   _____options
4. Subscribe to one or more investment services specializing in convertibles.
5. Are you bullish or bearish on the stock market over the next year?
   _____bullish
   _____bearish
   _____no strong conviction
6. Evaluate available hedging situations and prepare profit and loss estimates for each based on possible price movements to the upside and downside (refer to work sheets in this book illustrating the various types of hedge positions).
7. How much leverage will be employed?
   _____no leverage
   _____no leverage initially but will employ leverage as profits build up.
   _____the maximum leverage, as permitted by Regulation T, will be employed immediately.
8. Determine the amount of portfolio diversification and cash flow desired. Prepare a portfolio plan based on the positions available which presently, or potentially, meet your objectives (Exhibit 15–1).
9. How closely will you watch your hedge portfolio?
   _____daily
   _____weekly
   _____monthly
10. Will you trade the short side of your hedge position against the warrants or convertibles or do you plan to hold the hedge positions for a major move?
    _____plan to trade
    _____plan to hold for a major price move.
11. Select a broker and open a margin account.
12. Prepare log sheets for recording all security transactions, investment income and expenses (Exhibits 15–2 to 15–4).

EXHIBIT 15–6

General Guides for Managing a Convertible Hedge Portfolio

	Investor or Money Manager	Stockbroker Skilled in Convertibles	Normal Stock Broker
Research			
Evaluate all convertibles on a continuous basis	X	X	
Prepare profit and loss estimates for best situations	X	X	
Evaluate and select positions to be taken	X		
Order Execution			
Determine strategy for taking or closing out a position	X	X	
Execute orders		X	X
Follow Positions			
Watch price action on a continuous basis	X	X	X
Determine when a position should be adjusted or closed out	X	X	
Make the decision to adjust or close out the position	X		
Administration			
Check order confirmations and monthly statements for correctness	X	X	X
Maintain ledgers for all transactions, income and expense items	X		
Compute equity periodically	X		
Determine strategy near the end of the year for tax purposes	X		
Prepare year end reports for tax purposes	X		

Warrants Which Are Possible Candidates for Hedging—January 1973

	Prices Common	Prices Warrant	Warrant Leverage Projections −50%	Warrant Leverage Projections +50%	Stock Yield %	Normal Value Band	Actual Value Band
Braniff Airways...............	15.62	16.62	−60	+ 95	nil	5	4
Carrier......................	28.38	8.25	−75	+110	1.5	5	2*
Daylin......................	16.25	4.75	−70	+110	1.5	5	4
General Host.................	13.62	1.88	−70	+115	nil	5	4
Goodrich, B. F...............	28.25	8.38	−65	+105	3.5	4	1*
Gould......................	32.38	8.38	−70	+115	2.9	4	2
LCA........................	38.00	11.50	−65	+ 95	nil	5	4
Leasco—1978................	19.12	5.00	−50	+110	2.1	4	5
Loews......................	46.75	18.12	−60	+115	2.5	4	2
Louisiana Land & Exploration..	43.25	12.00	−70	+125	2.3	4	2*
National General—New.......	32.75	6.50	−50	+165	1.5	5	1
NVF Co.....................	19.38	11.00	−65	+110	nil	5	1
United National..............	5.62	.88	−60	+130	nil	5	4
Warner Communications.......	36.88	12.38	−60	+100	0.7	5	3
Zayre......................	27.00	4.75	−65	+140	nil	5	1

Notes:
1. Refer to Appendix G for warrant terms and where securities are traded.
2. Leverage projections are the estimated percent that the warrant price would change if the price of the common stock declined 50 percent or advanced 50 percent during the next six months—courtesy of The Value Line Convertible Survey.
3. All warrants have a life to expiration of greater than three years.
4. All warrants are protected against dilution from stock splits or dividends.
5. As indicated by an asterisk (*), the normal value band should be reduced one level, below that based on the common stock's yield, since the historical price volatility has been below average. Volatility ratings were obtained from The Value Line Convertible Survey.

RECOMMENDED READINGS FOR INVESTORS INTERESTED IN WARRANTS, CONVERTIBLES, AND OPTIONS

Alverson, Lyle T. *How to Write Puts and Calls.* New York: Exposition Press, 1968.

"The Better Idea, Total Investment Planning and Management System," S. P. A. Industries, Inc., Glenview, Ill. 60025, 1972.

Evans, Morgan D., Jr. *Arbitrage in Domestic Securities in the United States.* West Nyack, N.Y.: Parker Publishing Co., Inc., 1965.

Filer, Herbert. *Understanding Put and Call Options.* New York: Crown Publishers, Inc., 1959.

Fried, Sidney. "The Speculative Merits of Common Stock Warrants," R. H. M. Associates, 220 Fifth Avenue, New York, N.Y. 10011, 1961.

Fried, Sidney. *Investing and Speculating with Convertibles.* New York: Crown Publishers, Inc., 1969.

Jenkins, David. *The Power of Leverage.* Larchmont, N.Y.: Investors Intelligence, Inc., 1966.

Kassouf, S. T. "Evaluation of Convertible Securities," Analytical Publishers Co., P.O. Box 361, New York, N.Y. 10011, 1966.

Schneider, Herman M. and Wintrub, Warren G. *Investor's Tax Savings Guide.* Princeton, N.J.: Dow Jones Books, 1967.

Schwartz, William and Spellman, Julius. "Guide to Convertible Securities," Convertible Securities Press, P.O. Box H, Lenox Hill Station, New York, N.Y. 10021, 1968.

Thorp, E. O. and Kassouf, S. T. *Beat the Market: A Scientific Stock Market System.* New York: Random House, Inc., 1967.

16

Can Anything Go Wrong?

THE NORMAL and expected risks associated with the purchase or hedging of convertible securities were illustrated throughout this handbook. Most of these risks can be reduced to nominal proportions by careful selection of one's positions, by portfolio diversification, including different types of situations, and by continuous portfolio management.

However, a major uncertainty in the area of convertibles at the present time—one that is not subject to the precise application of the mathematical techniques presented in this handbook—is the possibility that the common stock may be the target of a tender offer or a merger proposal by another company. In such an event, what are the options available to the holders of convertibles and what are the problems confronting them in comparison to owners of the common stock?

The common stockholder's situation is much simpler than that facing those owning convertibles. He simply evaluates the package offered to him as compared to his current holding. If it is concluded that the offer is advantageous, he then accepts the tender offer or votes in favor of the merger as the case may be. To assure a favorable response, the acquiring company must normally price its offer significantly above the stock's current market price. Thus, the majority of the stockholders will generally react positively by tendering their shares or by voting in favor of the proposed merger.

The owner of convertible securities generally faces a more complex set of circumstances. Since, in most cases, the convertible does not give its owner the right to vote on the affairs of the company, the tender offer will normally be made to the common stockholders and not to the convertible holders. In the event of a merger proposal, the convertible holder will be bound by the eventual decision, as determined by the stockholders, but cannot participate in the decision-making process. As a result, a convertible's normal market value, in relation to its common stock, could be seriously downgraded. It is, therefore, most important that holders of convertible securities understand how their investments might be affected by a tender offer or a merger proposal and what courses of action might be open, if any. This is of major importance to those holding hedge positions of long convertibles versus short common stock.

TENDER OFFERS

A tender offer made to common stockholders will generally cause a rapid advance by the common to the vicinity of the value of cash and/or securities being offered—a small discount below the offer is normal and reflects the time involved and the possibility that the offer may be withdrawn. Also, if the tender offer is made for just a portion of the outstanding common stock, a greater discount would be expected since all shares submitted might not be accepted.

Convertible bonds, preferred stocks or warrants, which are trading at their conversion values prior to the tender offer, must also advance along with the common stock since they could be converted to take advantage of the favorable offer. On the other hand, if they were trading at a premium over their conversion value, as would normally be the case, they would be expected to lag behind the common in anticipation of a pullback by the common upon expiration of the offer.

Anyone holding an outright long position in the convertible will most likely benefit from the tender although the price advance might not be as great as would be expected for the given stock advance. Those holding hedge positions, however, are likely to be disappointed as they might even experience a loss in their position as the shorted common advances a greater amount than the lagging convertible. If the short side of the position can be held throughout the tender period, the prices will probably readjust on the expected stock pull back and no harm would be done. However, if most stockholders tender their shares, it may not be possible to hold the short position as the stock lenders request the return of their certificates. This could cause a forced buy in of the short sales at what will probably be an unfavorable price for the hedge position.

Another complicating factor is whether there will be an active market for the common stock upon completion of the tender offer. A situation could develop where there is a large quantity of convertibles outstanding on a thinly traded stock. In this event, the convertible would probably not be viewed with favor by the investment community and might therefore trade at an abnormally low premium over its conversion value. It would, of course, be difficult, if not actually impossible, to hedge the undervalued convertible, as the common stock might not be available for short selling.

MERGER PROPOSALS

The rights of a convertible security are generally stated in the warrant agreement, the bond indenture, or the articles of incorporation for a preferred stock. These legal contracts normally protect the convertible, in the event of a merger, to the extent that it will become convertible into the same package that the common stockholders receive. In other words, if a convertible bond or preferred is convertible into two shares of common, and the common stockholders are offered two shares of the acquiring company for each share held of the target company, the bond or preferred will become convertible into four shares of the stock of the acquiring company. In the case of a warrant, the total exercise price would remain the same but twice as many shares would be received if the warrants were exercised.

In the typical merger, involving an exchange of common stock as illustrated above, the normal market values for the convertibles will probably not be significantly affected. The primary factors will be the volatility and yield of the new stock as compared to the old. For example, if Company A, whose common pays no dividend and has had historically high price volatility, is merged into Company B, whose common is relatively stable and pays a generous dividend, a Company A convertible would be expected to command a lower premium over its conversion value after the merger. A convertible's investment value may also change appreciably depending on the financial condition of the acquiring company as compared to the company being acquired.

Of much greater danger is the possibility that the merger package might contain nonequity securities; i.e., cash, straight bonds, or notes. If it is not protected against an exchange involving nonequity securities, the convertible would have even less reason to command a premium over its conversion value, since the volatility of the package might be abnormally low. An extreme example, and one that might be tested in the courts by a class action lawsuit, was the effect on Far West Financial warrants as a result of a proposed merger with Leasco Corp. in December 1972.

FAR WEST FINANCIAL WARRANTS—WHAT WENT WRONG?

On December 18, 1972, Far West Financial common stock closed at 12¾ on the New York Stock Exchange and their warrants at 2¾ bid in the over-the-counter market. At these prices, the warrants, which were exercisable at $24 until November 1974 and then $26.50 until their November 1979 expiration date, were considered to be reasonably priced. The following day, Leasco Corp. announced an agreement to acquire Far West Financial common stock for $18 cash via the merger route. The result of this announcement was a quick 15 percent advance by Far West Financial's common stock but a devastating decline by the warrants to below $1 bid. What went wrong? Why should the announcement of a favorable merger agreement have such a negative impact on a long-term option to purchase Far West Financial common? The apparent answer was in the complex, and little understood, legal instrument called the warrant agreement. This agreement stipulated in essence, as do virtually all warrant agreements, that in the event of a merger, the warrant's exercise price and expiration date would remain the same and that the warrant holder would be entitled to receive whatever package is given to the common shareholders in the merger. Since the "package" proposed to the stockholders was $18 cash, the Far West Financial warrant would supposedly become the right to purchase $18 cash for $24 cash—in other words, by a simple agreement between the managements of the two companies, the warrants would apparently become worthless, to the obvious benefit of the stockholders of both companies.

In addition, there was a reported further complication because the announced merger would have technically entailed the liquidation of Far West Financial. The warrants would, therefore, have expired after the exchange although this made little difference since they would become worthless anyway under the proposed merger terms agreed to between the management of the two companies.

As mentioned previously, a class action lawsuit has been filed on behalf of the warrant holders of Far West Financial. It therefore remains to be seen whether convertibles are not, in fact, protected against a "washout" of their premiums over conversion values by the common stockholders. For example, did the prospectus, under which these warrants were originally issued and sold to the public, clearly indicate this as a possible risk? Were the warrant purchasers given a copy of the warrant agreement, which included these apparent risks, along with the prospectus at the time they bought the warrants? Who was to blame—the underwriter, the company, or the Securities and Exchange Commission? There are many questions that remain to be answered.

NATIONAL GENERAL WARRANTS—WHAT WENT WRONG

As was illustrated by Exhibit 7-2 of Chapter 7, the National General new warrant was the most undervalued, listed warrant at the end of 1972—it closed the year at $6.50 while its common stock was at $32.75 (at a price of $32.75 for the common, the normal value for this long-term warrant was approximately $11).

Was the abnormally low warrant price discounting a potential disaster similar to the Far West Financial warrant? The warrant holders did not have long to wait for the answer. In early January, American Financial and National General announced that they had agreed to a "consolidation" and that National General stockholders would be offered a package consisting of about half equity in American Financial and the remaining half comprising a combination of cash and notes. What impact did this announcement have on the National General warrants? Following is an excerpt from an article in the March 19, 1973 issue of *Barron's*.[1]

Merger or Tender Offer?

The deal was not a bad one for NGC stockholders, since the package has an estimated value of about $41; however, it created countless headaches for the warrant-holders. For one thing, American Financial had not made up its mind whether the acquisition was to be made by formal merger or via tender offer. If by a merger, the NGC warrants would become a call on this heavily non-equity package at $40 until 1978. If there were to be a tender offer for NGC common, the warrants could continue to call NGC stock at $40 until expiration.

The warrant-holders' problem in evaluating the offer was that they had no way of knowing how successful a tender for the common would be. If, for extreme example, all or nearly all of NGC common were tendered, the warrants would become a call on a stock with limited or no marketability. Furthermore, at that point, American Financial could vote its NGC shares for a formal merger and squeeze out the warrant-holders with no compensation at all, a la Leasco-Far West. Not surprisingly, the warrants plummeted 30% in value to 4¾ in less than an hour's trading, at which point trading was halted.

Subsequently, American Financial announced that the consolidation would be made via tender; then, because of a combination of adverse publicity

---

[1] Daniel Turov, "Trampled Rights—Warrant Holders Have Become an Oppressed Minority," *Barron's* March 19, 1973.

and a warrant-holders' class action suit, it announced a separate tender for all the NGC warrants at $6.75, the closing price at the time the consolidation intent was announced. While this may assuage some warrant-holders, it remains grossly inadequate.

. . .

Safety Valve

An investor who purchases a call on equity should be safeguarded in the case of merger or acquisition from having that call on equity become either a call on non-equity or a call on nothing. Security regulations should stipulate that in the event of consolidation, a warrant-holder must be guaranteed that his warrants become a call on the equivalent amount of equity in the acquiring or merged company.

The mathematics of implementing such a rule are really quite simple. For example, at the time Leasco announced its proposed $18 offer for Far West, Leasco itself was trading near 18. What could be simpler than for the Far West warrant to become a warrant to buy one share of Leasco at the same $24/$26.50 exercise price until 1979?

National General warrants, at the time the offer was announced, had an intrinsic negative value of $7 ($40-$33), and American Financial was trading at 19½. What could be simpler and more equitable than having each NGC warrant become a warrant to purchase two shares of American Financial at $23 until 1978? The warrant would still have an intrinsic negative value of $7 ($23-19.50 x 2).

The publicity surrounding these transactions, coming as it were back-to-back, has cast a pall over all warrants. Investors have reacted by dumping them en masse. In the first two months of 1973, only five of the American Stock Exchange's 79 warrants have advanced, four are unchanged, and an incredible 70 have declined.

Those investors, who had purchased Far West Financial or National General warrants prior to these announcements, either lost a great deal of money, or made less profit than was commensurate with the risks they had assumed, depending on their specific purchase costs. Those who had established "conservative" hedge positions of long warrants versus short common stock literally took a *financial bath*. How can the securities industry permit companies to raise funds by the sale of warrants, or other convertible securities, at normal and expected premiums over conversion values, then employ the proceeds in the operation of their businesses to the obvious benefit of the common stockholders, and later "wash out" these securities by such a simple act as a merger announcement? Note that the latent warrant portion of a convertible bond or preferred stock would be affected in the same manner as a regular warrant, thus the entire convertible area would be subject to the same abuse.

It is believed by the author that positive steps *must* be taken *immediately* by the securities industry to protect the rights of those investors who purchase warrants and other convertibles—*creditability must be restored!* An initial step was suggested in the April 2, 1973 issue of *The Value Line Convertible Survey*. Their entire editorial is worth repeating.

A Proposed Bill of Rights for Warrant Holders

The purchaser of a warrant willingly assumes an above-average degree of risk in hopes of high capital gains. One of these risks should not, however, be the danger of being quickly wiped out in a merger. Regulations should be established immediately to protect the warrant holder from such a disaster. In our view, such regulations should be instituted by the New York and American Stock Exchanges to protect not only warrant holders but also corporations who may wish to issue warrants in the future.

Like the weather, everyone is talking about it, but nobody seems to be doing anything about it!

The rights of warrant holders are in serious jeopardy and, unless regulations are enacted to protect this vulnerable class of investors, we will witness a further retreat to the sidelines by investors who feel that they are not being treated fairly. By now just about everybody has heard the story, but it bears repeating once more for the record.

THE GOOD OLD DAYS

There was a time, not too long ago, when the warrant holder could count on a fair shake when his company was being acquired. The typical warrant agreement stipulates that in a merger, the warrant becomes an option to purchase whatever package is offered in exchange for the underlying common stock, with the total exercise price and expiration date remaining unchanged.

This was fine for the great bulk of cases, but it created a potential inequity for warrants selling at a premium, especially when the underlying common stock was selling below the per-share exercise price of the warrant. In the latter case, a warrant could be rendered worthless by an exchange of cash, debt, or other consideration with negligible volatility. Warrant holders never needed to be concerned about this, however, because it was standard operating procedure for the acquiring company to correct the inequity by offering a separate deal for the warrants.

When LTV acquired Wilson & Co., it offered $12.50 cash for each outstanding Wilson & Co. share. The Wilson & Co. warrant, which had been an option to purchase one share of common at $16.63, would then become an option to buy $12.50 cash for $16.63. To correct this absurd situation, LTV offered to exchange one of its $40 warrants for each Wilson & Co. warrant. Another recent example was PepsiCo's acquisition of Wilson Sporting Goods for cash. Again, the Wilson Sporting Goods warrants would have become worthless if not for PepsiCo's offer of $3.50 cash for each warrant, approximating the fair value of the warrant based upon the offer for the common.

UNFORTUNATE PRECEDENTS

Under the announced merger proposal under which Leasco will pay $18 cash for all shares of Far West Financial, each Far West warrant will become worthless. Each Far West warrant is currently an option to buy one share of Far West Common for $24. Based on the $18 offer for the common, a fair offer for the warrants would be about $5. But Leasco has so far refused to make such an offer. To our knowledge this is the first instance of grossly inequitable treatment of a warrant. For further details of this sordid example, see Page 381 of the January 1st issue.

Right on the heels of this first precedent, American Financial announced its intention to gain control of National General via a tender offer initially valued at about $40 for each National General share. Following a class action suit and a great deal of adverse publicity, American Financial finally offered $6.75 cash for each National General new warrant. We recommended acceptance of the offer as the best available alternative. But the offer could hardly be called equitable: based on a $40 offer for the common, a fair offer for the National General new warrants would have been about $15, more than double the paltry offer that materialized.

WHO GETS HURT?

The way we see it, the present situation is disadvantageous to nearly everybody. The hazards to the warrant holder are obvious. He stands the risk of seeing the entire value of his holdings wiped out in a flash. Furthermore, other investors, aware of this possibility, will be very hesitant to buy warrants—especially those without tangible value. The result of this must be a deterioration in the overall level of warrant premiums (a phenomenon that appears to have already begun). And no matter how cheap a warrant without tangible value may be, there is still the risk of a 100% loss due to a merger. Effectively, therefore, the price of a warrant can't realistically discount this kind of disaster.

Corporations will feel the effects of lower premiums when they issue warrants. They will find they have to accept much lower prices than in the past, thereby increasing the cost of raising capital. Moreover, warrants will become unacceptable as part of a merger proposal once investors realize that devious managements can subsequently wipe out the value of the warrants by clever manipulation.

The major stock exchanges should be concerned because the sudden 'wipe-out' of a warrant certainly goes contrary to the principles of an orderly market. Only three years ago warrants achieved an aura of "respectability" when the New York Stock Exchange rescinded its ban on listing warrants. This new status is now being eroded rapidly as warrant holders realize that they are not being treated equitably.

A MODEST PROPOSAL

Convinced that it is in everyone's interest to solve the problem as soon as possible, we suggest that the New York Stock Exchange and American Stock Exchange take the initiative and build into their listing requirements certain provisions which will protect the rights of the warrant holder.

It should be required that whenever a company is acquired in an exchange of its common for cash, straight debt or other nonvolatile securities, then there must be a separate exchange for the warrants. The exact makeup of the package offered for the warrant can be left up to the acquiring company. The only restriction would be that the market value of the package be worth at least as much as the fair market value of the warrants sans the merger based upon a common stock price equal to the value of the package given to the common shareholders.

As an example, in the American Financial—National General offer, the package (of equity, notes, and cash) to be exchanged for each share of National General common was worth about $40.50 at the time of the announcement. American Financial should have been required to estimate (with the help of an investment banker) what the normal value of the National General new warrant would be with the common at 40½; the resulting value of each warrant would be about $15. The warrant holders would then be offered a package worth at least that amount, with the contents of the package left to the discretion of American Financial.

We further suggest that the exchanges require that all listed companies abide by this rule in any acquisitions they may make. In addition to mergers, we urge that these regulations also cover any tender offer in which the acquiring company stands the chance of gaining at least 50% control of the outstanding common stock of the target company. And these regulations should cover convertible bonds and convertible preferreds as well as warrants.

A FINAL WORD

We believe that the individual investor's confidence in the stock market has been badly shaken by his experiences over the past few years. We also firmly believe that a restoration of this lost confidence is essential to a healthy, sustained bull market.

We therefore urge the New York and American Stock Exchange to quickly enact the proposals that we have suggested here before investors take another "bath." Our suggestions provide corporations with enough freedom of choice so as not to inhibit them from making acquisitions while protecting the rights of the warrant holders and convertible holders.

Appendix A

Straight Bonds Usable at Par Value in Exercising Warrants

Warrant	Bond Coupon and Maturity	Traded	Bond Price	Warrant Exercise Price	Effective Exercise Price	Available*	Fn.
Allegheny Airlines—1987	5.5 –87	ASE	62	18.00	11.16	+ 35	
Avco	7.5 –93	NYS	84	56.00	47.04	− 45	
Braniff Airways	5.75 –86	NYS	70	73.00	51.10	− 5	
Brown	9.0 –90	PAC	83	16.50	13.70	− 96	1
Chris Craft Industries	10.0 –85	PAC	93	25.00	23.25	− 40	
Daylin	5.0 –89	ASE	70	22.50	15.75	− 90	
Frontier Airlines	5.5 –87	ASE	60	12.06	7.24	+ 48	
Fuqua Industries—1973	7.0 –88	NYS	84	43.50	36.54	− 54	
General Host	7.0 –94	PAC	70	40.00	28.00	− 30	
Guardian Mortgage Invest	6.75 –86	ASE	91	37.00	33.67	− 86	
ITEL—1979	6.75 –89	OTC	59	29.12	17.18	+ 58	2
LTV (JLI)	6.75 –94	ASE	64	37.50	24.00	+ 43	3
Leasco—1987	5.75 –87	ASE	72	16.50	11.88	+100	
Loews	6.875–93	NYS	85	37.50	31.87	+ 60	
NVF	5.0 –94	PAC	54	22.05	11.91	+ 29	
Northwest Industries	7.5 –94	NYS	91	25.00	22.75	− 89	
PSA	6.0 –87	NYS	76	23.40	17.78	+ 40	
Rapid American	7.5 –85	NYS	82	35.00	28.70	− 59	
Security Mortgage Invest	6.0 –82	OTC	77	16.00	12.32	− 40	4
Tenneco—1979	6.0 –79	NYS	92	32.17	29.60	+ 86	
Trans World Airlines	6.50 –78	NYS	90	22.00	19.80	+ 48	
United Brands—1978	6.75 –88	NYS	77	69.00	53.13	+ 69	
United National	7.5 –88	ASE	70	10.00	7.00	− 55	

* Is the usable bond issue large enough for exercise of the entire warrant issue? + means yes, − means no. The number following + gives the percentage of the bond issue required for full exercise of the warrant issue. The number following − gives the percentage of the warrant issue that can be exercised by using the full bond issue.

Footnotes:
1. Bonds are traded flat since interest may be paid in common stock in lieu of cash.
2. Bonds are identified as SSI Computer.
3. Jones & Laughlin Industries bonds—usable at par through 4/1/74 only.
4. Their 7.25's–82 bonds are alternately usable at par value.

Appendix B

Calculations for Plotting the Normal Value Curve for Long-Term Warrants (common stocks have high price volatility and pay no dividends)

$W = \sqrt{E^2 + S^2} - E$ Where: W = adjusted warrant price
S = stock price
E = adjusted exercise price

S/E	W/E	S/E	W/E
0.1	0.005	2.1	1.326
0.2	0.020	2.2	1.417
0.3	0.044	2.3	1.508
0.4	0.077	2.4	1.600
0.5	0.118	2.5	1.693
0.6	0.166	2.6	1.786
0.7	0.221	2.7	1.879
0.8	0.281	2.8	1.973
0.9	0.345	2.9	2.068
1.0	0.414	3.0	2.162
1.1	0.487	3.1	2.258
1.2	0.562	3.2	2.354
1.3	0.640	3.3	2.448
1.4	0.720	3.4	2.544
1.5	0.803	3.5	2.641
1.6	0.887	3.6	2.736
1.7	0.972	3.7	2.832
1.8	1.059	3.8	2.930
1.9	1.147	3.9	3.026
2.0	1.236	4.0	3.123

Appendix C

Stock Volatility Calculations

$$V = \frac{H - L}{\frac{1}{2}(H + L)}$$

Where: V = Volatility
H = Stock's high for the year
L = Stock's low for the year

Common Stock	1970 Low–High	V	1971 Low–High	V	1972 Low–High	V	3-Year Average V
American Tel. & Tel.	40.38–53.88	.29	40.75–53.88	.28	41.12–53.50	.26	.28
Braniff Airways	6.25–11.50	.59	8.12–17.00	.71	13.25–20.25	.42	.57
Carrier	17.62–26.50	.40	21.38–32.38	.41	22.12–31.00	.33	.38
Commonwealth Edison	28.12–40.50	.36	34.50–43.88	.24	32.00–40.12	.23	.28
Daylin	9.88–23.50	.82	16.50–27.88	.51	14.25–25.12	.55	.63
General Development	14.50–32.35	.76	23.75–33.75	.35	12.25–35.38	.97	.69
General Host	6.62–14.75	.76	9.50–23.25	.84	12.62–21.88	.54	.71
Goodrich, B. F.	19.75–34.00	.53	25.62–35.00	.31	23.62–32.25	.31	.38
Gould	12.25–25.62	.71	20.50–30.62	.43	29.88–40.75	.31	.48
Leasco	7.00–30.50	1.25	15.50–26.75	.53	17.00–24.50	.36	.71
Loews	16.25–40.50	.85	34.00–57.50	.51	43.00–60.50	.34	.57
Louisiana Land & Exploration	35.00–66.50	.62	40.50–52.00	.25	38.50–55.50	.36	.41
McCrory	13.75–26.75	.62	18.00–31.62	.55	21.00–32.12	.42	.53
NVF Co.	8.25–18.62	.77	8.62–20.25	.80	15.25–21.88	.36	.64
National General	9.00–20.25	.74	15.75–29.50	.61	21.50–34.75	.47	.61
Tenneco	17.50–24.88	.35	21.62–29.62	.31	23.00–29.62	.25	.30
United National	3.62–8.00	.75	4.00–7.00	.55	4.62–6.88	.39	.56
Warner Communications	20.88–36.00	.53	25.88–39.38	.41	31.25–50.25	.47	.47
Zayre	20.00–42.50	.72	30.00–47.25	.45	23.62–39.75	.51	.56

Appendix D

Selling Securities Short

To SELL short is to sell securities that one does not own. The securities are borrowed for you by your broker from another customer who holds them in a margin account, or from another brokerage firm. The funds received from the sale are held by the brokerage firm lending the securities as collateral against the borrowed securities. At some future time, the investor must cover his short sale by buying the same amount of securities he originally sold short for return to the lender.

THE UP-TICK RULE

With but a few technical exceptions, securities may be sold short only on an "up-tick" or a "zero-plus tick"—the last change in the securities price must have been an increase. This regulation was designed to prevent speculators from driving down the price of a security by uncontrolled short selling.

SHORT-EXEMPT SALES

The up-tick rule does not apply when securities are sold on a short-exempt basis. To qualify as exempt, the seller must give his broker irrevocable instructions to convert bonds, preferreds or warrants and to deliver the stock received upon the conversion to cover the short sale.

MARGIN RULES

Short sales may be made only in a margin account. Cash or marginable collateral must be deposited against the short sale in accordance with applicable margin regulations. No additional collateral is required if the short sale is made against convertibles or warrants providing that they are convertible within 90 days. This exception recognizes the safety of a short sale made against a convertible security.

MARKING TO THE MARKET

Once a short sale is made and the price of the security changes, the brokerage firm will adjust the balance in the short account to reflect current prices. This process is called "marking to the market" and simply involves debit and credit entries between the short account and the regular margin account. If the securities sold short decline in price, the short account is debited and an offsetting credit entry is made in the margin account. If the securities rise in price, the margin account is debited and the short account credited. The credit balance in the short account will then equal the current market value of the securities sold short.

DIVIDENDS

Since a short sale creates excess stock held long by other investors, the short seller must pay any dividends that are paid by the company. For this reason securities which do not pay dividends are generally more suitable for selling short to avoid the cost of making up the dividends.

SHORT SQUEEZE

When excessive short selling takes place in a particular security and it becomes difficult or impossible to borrow the security, a temporary squeeze may take place. The rush to cover by the "squeezed" short sellers may force prices up sharply. A squeeze may also develop if a tender offer is made for the common stock or warrant.

Appendix E

Optimum Short to Long Ratio for Hedge Positions in Undervalued Warrants

THE BASIC system, as presented in Chapter 6, was based on a short to long ratio of 1.3—that is, common stock equaling 130 percent of the market value of warrants purchased was sold short. This ratio offered an approximate break-even position in a declining market and it was believed that this would produce optimum long-term performance results.

To verify this conclusion, consider alternate hedge positions in the previously discussed undervalued warrant having these characteristics.

Upside leverage	= 2.6
Downside leverage	= 0.65
Mathematical advantage	= $\frac{2.6}{1.0} \times \frac{0.50}{0.65}$ = 2.0

We will assume that the market undergoes a major cycle wherein common stocks decline 50 percent and then advance 100 percent, or vice versa. In either event, a portfolio of representative stocks would be exactly even upon completion of the cycle. Three alternate hedge positions will be evaluated.

Bullish hedge—1.30 short to long ratio
Neutral hedge—1.95 short to long ratio
Bearish hedge—2.60 short to long ratio

Assuming that $1,000 worth of warrants are purchased at 70 percent margin (investment = $700), anticipated performance results are computed as follows for both downside and upside phases of the market cycle.

	Stock Price Move	
	−50%	+100%
Bullish Hedge		
Downside		
Profit on stock sold short = $1,300 × 50%...	$ 650	
Loss on warrants purchased = $1,000 × 65%...	(650)	
Upside		
Profit on warrants purchased = $1,000 × 260%..		$2,600)
Loss on stock sold short = $1,300 × 100%..		(1,300)
Net profit or (loss).............................	$ 0	$1,300
Return on investment..........................	0%	+186%
Neutral Hedge		
Downside		
Profit on stock sold short = $1,950 × 50%...	$ 975	
Loss on warrants purchased = $1,000 × 65%...	(650)	
Upside		
Profit on warrants purchased = $1,000 × 260%..		$2,600
Loss on stock sold short = $1,950 × 100%..		(1,950)
Net profit or (loss).............................	$ 325	$ 650
Return on investment..........................	+46%	+93%
Bearish Hedge		
Downside		
Profit on stock sold short = $2,600 × 50%...	$1,300	
Loss on warrants purchased = $1,000 × 65%...	(650)	
Upside		
Profit on warrants purchased = $1,000 × 260%..		$2,600
Loss on stock sold short = $2,600 × 100%..		(2,600)
Net profit or (loss).............................	$ 650	$ 0
Return on investment..........................	+93%	0%

Note that commissions, margin interest and dividends paid on stock sold short (if any) were excluded to simplify the calculations.

Appendix E 189

The return on investment estimates for the alternate hedge positions are summarized in the following table. Common stock and warrants purchased on a cash basis are also shown for comparison purposes along with a 50 percent warrants/50 percent cash position. The indicated overall gain is based on compounding the results achieved for each of the two phases of the market cycle.

	Stock Price Move		
Alternate Investments	−50%	+100%	Overall Gain
Straight Purchases			
Common stock	−50%	+100%	0%
Warrants	−65%	+260%	+ 26%
50% warrants/50% cash	−32%	+130%	+ 55%
Warrant Hedge Positions			
Bullish	0%	+186%	+186%
Neutral	+46%	+ 93%	+182%
Bearish	+93%	0%	+ 93%

All of the warrant hedge positions would have outperformed any of the straight purchases. It is noted that the bullish hedge achieved optimum performance even without a long-term upward bias to the market. Also, the lower commissions and stock dividends paid (if any) would increase the actual net difference for the bullish hedge over the neutral hedge.

Appendix F

Warrants Evaluated during the Six-Year Study—1967 through 1972

Security	Stock Price	Warrant Price	S/E	W/E	Normal Value Band	Actual Value Band	Action	Fn.
January 1967								
Atlas..................	2.62	1.50	0.42	0.24	5	6		
First National Realty....	0.75	0.38	0.13	0.06	5	6		
Hilton Hotels...........	32.00	6.75	0.64	0.14	4	3	Buy	
Indian Head............	19.62	8.50	0.98	0.42	4	6		
National General........	11.75	4.25	0.78	0.28	5	6		
Realty Equities.........	7.38	3.50	0.93	0.35	5	5		
Uris Buildings..........	16.25	6.12	1.38	0.49	5	2	Buy	
July 1967								
Atlas..................	3.88	2.25	0.62	0.36	5	6		
First National Realty....	1.62	0.44	0.28	0.06	5	6		
Hilton Hotels...........	59.12	19.75	1.18	0.39	5	3	Buy	
Indian Head............	28.25	13.25	1.13	0.53	4	6		
National General........	17.00	7.00	1.13	0.47	5	5		
Realty Equities.........	12.38	6.25	1.55	0.62	5	1	Buy	
Uris Buildings..........	21.25	11.88	1.80	0.95	5	3	Hold	(b)
January 1968								
Allegheny Airlines......	15.88	10.00	1.74	1.10	5	6		
Atlas..................	6.25	3.75	1.00	0.60	5	6		
Braniff Airways.........	47.62	20.88	0.82	0.36	5	6		
First National Realty....	1.75	0.88	0.30	0.13	5	6		
Frontier Airlines........	20.00	10.12	1.67	0.84	5	3		(b)
Hilton Hotels...........	82.50	32.12	1.65	0.64	5	1	Buy	

Appendix F 191

Security	Stock Price	Warrant Price	S/E	W/E	Normal Value Band	Actual Value Band	Action	Fn.
Indian Head	41.88	25.25	1.68	1.01	5	6		
Lerner Stores	17.50	8.12	1.17	0.54	4	5		
National General	24.75	13.75	1.65	0.92	5	5		
Realty Equities	10.00	6.12	1.26	0.61	5	5	Hold	
Uris Buildings	33.25	22.75	2.82	1.82	5	NR	Sell	(f)
July 1968								
Atlas	6.62	3.50	1.06	0.56	5	6		
Braniff Airways	22.88	28.50	1.18	0.49	5	4	Buy	
First National Realty	3.50	1.62	0.60	0.24	5	6		
Frontier Airlines	15.75	10.62	1.31	0.89	5	6		
Gulf & Western	48.38	18.38	0.88	0.33	5	5		
Hilton Hotels	104.62	58.88	2.09	1.18	5	2	Hold	(b)
Indian Head	36.00	19.88	1.44	0.80	5	6		
Lerner Stores	22.88	12.50	1.52	0.83	5	6		
Ling-Temco-Vought	106.25	61.75	1.32	0.77	5	6		
Realty Equities	25.25	20.50	3.17	2.05	5	NR	Sell	(f)
Trans World Airlines	37.25	24.88	1.88	1.26	4	6		
January 1969								
Atlas	7.62	4.50	1.22	0.72	5	6		
Braniff Airways	21.88	28.50	1.20	0.52	5	5	Hold	
Frontier Airlines	11.38	7.75	1.35	0.92	5	6		
Gulf & Western	51.25	18.12	0.93	0.33	5	4	Buy	
Hilton Hotels	134.00	82.00	2.68	1.64	5	NR	Sell	(f)
Indian Head	42.00	26.00	1.68	1.04	5	6		
Leasco Data Processing	122.00	66.50	1.40	0.76	5	6		
Lerner Stores	28.25	17.50	1.88	1.17	5	6		
Ling-Temco-Vought	98.00	41.25	1.58	0.60	5	1	Buy	
LTV Aerospace	42.12	26.50	1.97	1.24	5	6		
LTV Ling Altec	13.25	6.75	1.04	0.53	5	6		
Loew's Theatres	50.00	33.88	1.68	1.14	5	6		
McCrory	36.00	16.25	1.80	0.81	4	1	Buy	
National General—New	47.12	20.50	1.18	0.51	5	5		
National Industries	23.75	14.88	1.11	0.70	5	6		
Okonite	28.00	13.50	1.33	0.64	4	5		
Pacific Southwest Airlines	26.62	16.00	1.52	0.91	4	6		
TST Industries	8.00	5.25	0.92	0.60	5	6		
Wilson & Co	37.12	13.75	1.49	0.55	4	1	Buy	
Wilson Sporting Goods	20.88	11.38	1.37	0.75	4	6		
July 1969								
AMK	25.88	8.00	0.56	0.17	4	6		
Allegheny Airlines	15.62	11.50	1.45	1.06	5	6		
Atlas	6.00	3.88	0.96	0.62	5	6		
Braniff Airways	14.50	16.50	0.85	0.32	4	6	Sell	
Budget Industries	16.25	6.88	1.16	0.49	4	5		
Commonwealth United	10.62	5.38	0.62	0.31	5	6		

192   Dow Jones–Irwin Guide to Convertible Securities

Security	Stock Price	Warrant Price	S/E	W/E	Normal Value Band	Actual Value Band	Action	Fn.
Daylin	32.50	11.75	0.72	0.26	5	6		(g)
Elgin National Industries	12.25	3.88	0.56	0.44	5	6		
Frontier Airlines	9.88	6.00	1.36	0.83	5	6		
General Host	24.00	5.62	0.60	0.14	5	4	Buy	(g)
Gulf & Western	26.25	8.25	0.48	0.15	5	6	Sell	
Indian Head	28.25	14.00	1.13	0.56	4	6		
Kaufman & Broad	37.75	18.62	1.16	0.57	5	6		
Leasco Data Processing	32.50	14.50	0.93	0.42	5	6		
Lerner Stores	24.50	14.50	1.63	0.97	4	6		
Ling-Temco-Vought	40.00	13.12	0.78	0.23	4	4	Hold	
LTV Aerospace	24.00	11.38	1.20	0.57	4	6		
LTV Ling Altec	7.25	4.00	0.66	0.36	4	6		
Loew's Theatres	32.00	13.88	1.14	0.49	5	5		
McCrory	24.25	8.88	1.21	0.44	3	3	Hold	(a)
National General	29.62	16.38	1.98	1.09	5	3		(b)
National General—New	29.62	8.62	0.74	0.22	5	4	Buy	
National Industries	11.50	5.62	0.54	0.26	5	6		
Pacific Southwest Airlines	16.62	9.25	1.01	0.56	4	6		
Rapid American	23.88	8.88	0.68	0.25	4	6		
Ward Foods	27.62	7.38	0.46	0.12	4	6		
Whittaker	21.88	7.50	0.44	0.15	5	6		
Wilson & Co	24.25	6.88	1.12	0.32	3	2	Hold	(a)
January 1970								
AMK	30.38	8.75	0.66	0.19	5	5		
Allegheny Airlines	12.12	8.50	1.35	0.94	5	6		
Atlas	4.12	2.75	0.77	0.51	5	6		
Bangor Punta	18.62	4.38	0.34	0.08	4	6		
Bluebird	7.00	3.50	0.65	0.33	5	6		
Budget Industries	17.75	7.88	1.27	0.56	4	4		
Chris-Craft Industries	10.75	3.38	0.45	0.13	5	6		
Daylin	35.88	13.25	0.80	0.30	5	6		(g)
Elgin National Industries	8.38	2.75	0.38	0.31	5	6		
Fibreboard	24.38	11.25	1.08	0.50	4	6		
Frontier Airlines	7.88	4.25	1.31	0.70	5	6		
General Host	14.50	3.50	0.36	0.09	5	6	Sell	(g)
Gould	36.75	8.50	0.67	0.15	4	3	Buy	
Gulf & Western	20.38	6.38	0.38	0.12	4	6		
Indian Head	24.12	10.88	0.96	0.44	4	6		
International Controls	13.88	6.00	0.66	0.29	5	6		
Kaufman & Broad	49.00	22.25	1.51	0.68	5	3	Buy	
Kinney National Services	30.25	8.75	0.82	0.24	5	4	Buy	
Leasco Data Processing	29.12	14.12	0.84	0.41	5	6		

Appendix F   193

Security	Stock Price	Warrant Price	S/E	W/E	Normal Value Band	Actual Value Band	Action	Fn.
Ling-Temco-Vought	27.00	7.62	0.66	0.17	3	4	Sell	
LTV Ling Altec	4.50	2.62	0.48	0.28	4	6		
Loew's Theatres	37.38	16.00	1.42	0.61	5	3	Buy	
McCrory	23.75	7.62	1.19	0.38	3	2	Hold	(a)
National General	19.38	12.12	1.29	0.81	5	5		
National General—New	19.38	6.38	0.48	0.16	5	6	Sell	
National Industries	9.12	3.50	0.43	0.16	5	6		
Okonite	9.88	4.00	0.64	0.26	5	6		
Pacific Southwest Airlines	26.25	14.75	1.60	0.90	5	6		
Rapid-American	18.75	6.75	0.54	0.19	4	6		
Trans World Airlines	25.75	13.75	1.56	0.83	5	5		
United National	7.62	3.50	0.64	0.29	5	6		
Ward Foods	27.62	8.25	0.46	0.14	4	6		
Whittaker	17.62	7.12	0.35	0.14	5	6		
Wilson & Co	19.75	5.25	0.91	0.24	2	2	Hold	(a)

July 1970

Security	Stock Price	Warrant Price	S/E	W/E	Normal Value Band	Actual Value Band	Action	Fn.
AMK	14.50	3.62	0.32	0.08	4	6		
A-T-O	6.88	2.38	0.23	0.08	5	6		
Alleghany	6.38	4.88	1.70	1.30	4	6		
Allegheny Airlines	13.62	8.88	1.51	0.99	5	6		
Atlas	2.62	1.50	0.62	0.36	5	6		
Avco	12.62	2.75	0.23	0.05	5	6		(g)
Bangor Punta	7.00	1.88	0.13	0.03	5	6		
Bluebird	3.88	1.62	0.36	0.15	5	6		
Budget Industries	7.62	2.12	0.54	0.15	5	6		
Chris-Craft Industries	6.00	1.25	0.25	0.05	5	6		
Daylin	12.38	4.25	0.55	0.19	5	6		(g)
Elgin National Industries	5.25	1.75	0.24	0.20	5	6		
Fibreboard	17.50	5.75	0.78	0.26	4	5		
Frontier Airlines	4.12	2.62	0.86	0.54	5	6		
General Host	8.00	1.25	0.20	0.03	5	6		(g)
Gould	23.50	4.75	0.43	0.09	3	5	Sell	
Gulf & Western	12.75	3.50	0.24	0.06	4	6		
International Controls	6.25	2.12	0.25	0.08	5	6		
Kane-Miller	9.00	4.00	0.41	0.18	5	6		
Kaufman & Broad	32.12	13.88	1.48	0.64	5	3	Buy	
Kinney National Services	21.38	5.50	0.58	0.15	5	5	Hold	
Leasco Data Processing—1987	8.50	4.50	1.03	0.55	5	6		
Leasco Data Processing—1978	8.50	3.50	0.24	0.10	5	6		
Lerner Stores	20.25	10.50	1.35	0.70	4	6		
Ling-Temco-Vought	13.12	3.75	0.13	0.03	5	6		

Security	Stock Price	Warrant Price	S/E	W/E	Normal Value Band	Actual Value Band	Action	Fn.
L-T-V (Okonite)	13.12	1.88	0.38	0.13	5	6		
LTV Ling Altec	2.62	1.38	0.39	0.20	5	6		
Loew's Theatres	20.00	8.00	0.76	0.30	5	6	Sell	
McCrory	15.38	3.50	0.77	0.18	2	2	Hold	(a)
NVF Co	9.62	4.25	1.46	0.64	5	3		(c)
National General	10.00	5.00	0.67	0.33	5	6		
National General—New	10.00	2.75	0.25	0.07	5	6		
National Industries	4.50	1.88	0.21	0.09	5	6		
Northwest Industries	10.00	3.88	0.57	0.22	5	6		
Pacific Southwest Airlines	16.75	8.38	1.19	0.60	5	6		
Trans World Airlines	11.12	5.88	0.84	0.44	5	6		
United National	4.50	1.75	0.38	0.15	5	6		
Uris Buildings	10.12	12.25	1.91	1.09	4	4		
Ward Foods	9.50	2.62	0.16	0.04	4	6		
Whittaker	6.00	2.75	0.12	0.06	5	6		
Wilson & Co	8.88	3.25	0.44	0.16	1	6	Sell	
January 1971								
A-T-O	8.38	2.88	0.24	0.08	5	6		
Allegheny Airlines	10.25	6.62	1.10	0.68	5	6		
Atlas	2.38	1.25	0.56	0.30	5	6		
Avco	12.50	3.38	0.22	0.06	5	6		(g)
Bangor Punta	8.00	2.50	0.15	0.05	5	6		
Bluebird	5.00	2.00	0.47	0.19	5	6		
Budget Industries	8.25	2.75	0.59	0.20	5	6		
Chris-Craft Industries	8.25	1.88	0.35	0.07	5	6		
Continental Telephone	25.25	7.75	1.13	0.35	4	2	Buy	(d)
Daylin	19.00	7.62	0.84	0.34	5	6		(g)
Fibreboard	26.62	10.12	1.18	0.45	4	4		
Frontier Airlines	5.00	2.25	0.88	0.40	5	6		
General Host	9.88	1.75	0.25	0.04	5	6		(g)
Gulf & Western	19.38	4.75	0.36	0.09	4	6		
Indian Head	26.00	10.00	1.04	0.40	4	4		
International Controls	12.00	3.62	0.47	0.14	5	6		
Kane-Miller	18.38	7.12	0.84	0.32	5	6		
Kaufman & Broad	44.75	23.75	2.06	1.10	5	1	Hold	(b)
Kinney National Services	29.00	7.25	0.78	0.20	5	3	Buy	
Leasco Data Processing—1987	16.00	10.50	1.70	1.12	5	6		
Leasco Data Processing—1978	16.00	6.75	0.46	0.19	5	6		
Ling-Temco-Vought	10.38	2.62	0.10	0.02	5	6		
LTV (Okonite)	10.38	1.25	0.32	0.10	5	6		
LTV Ling Altec	1.75	.88	0.31	.16	5	6		
Loews	34.88	14.00	1.22	0.49	5	4	Buy	

Appendix F

Security	Stock Price	Warrant Price	S/E	W/E	Normal Value Band	Actual Value Band	Action	Fn.
McCrory.............	17.75	5.12	0.89	0.26	2	3	Sell	
NVF Co...........	8.75	4.88	1.21	0.67	5	6		
National General.......	16.12	7.12	1.08	0.48	5	6		
National General—New.	16.12	3.12	0.40	0.08	5	6		
National Industries......	6.00	2.12	0.28	0.10	5	6		
Northwest Industries....	17.50	8.00	0.95	0.43	5	6		
Pacific Southwest Airlines.............	20.38	9.75	1.32	0.63	5	5		
Rapid-American........	10.62	3.50	0.30	0.10	5	6		
United Brands........	16.50	4.25	0.36	0.09	4	6		
United National........	4.62	2.00	0.39	0.17	5	6		
Ward Foods...........	10.75	2.62	0.18	0.04	4	6		
Whittaker.............	7.50	3.00	0.15	0.06	5	6		
July 1971								
Affiliated Capital.......	11.75	7.75	1.23	0.78	5	6		
A-T-O................	10.88	3.75	0.31	0.11	5	6		
Allegheny Airlines......	13.88	8.25	1.38	.79	5	6		
Atlas.................	3.00	1.88	0.59	0.37	5	6		
Avco.................	13.50	4.50	0.24	0.08	5	6		(g)
Bangor Punta..........	11.38	4.62	0.21	0.09	5	6		
Braniff Airways........	9.75	14.00	0.69	0.33	5	6		
Brown................	8.62	3.75	0.52	0.23	5	6		(g)
Budget Industries.......	7.12	3.00	0.51	0.21	5	6		
Chris-Craft Industries....	7.25	2.38	0.31	0.09	5	6		
Chrysler..............	27.50	13.50	0.81	0.40	4	6		
Continental Telephone...	23.25	7.38	1.04	0.33	4	3	Hold	(d)
Daylin................	21.25	7.38	0.94	0.33	5	4	Buy	(g)
Equity Funding.........	40.25	26.62	1.59	1.05	5	6		
Fibreboard............	25.38	11.75	1.13	0.52	4	6		
Flying Tiger............	39.88	24.88	1.35	0.80	5	6		
Frontier Airlines........	6.00	4.25	0.94	0.67	5	6		
General Host..........	16.62	4.12	0.42	0.10	5	6		(g)
Gould................	36.25	8.62	0.66	0.16	4	3	Buy	
Gulf & Western........	28.88	9.75	0.54	0.18	4	6		
Indian Head...........	32.00	15.25	1.28	0.61	4	5		
International Controls...	10.12	3.25	0.40	0.13	5	6		
Kane-Miller...........	16.38	7.25	0.74	0.33	5	6		
Kaufman & Broad......	63.00	41.00	2.91	1.89	5	NR	Sell	(f)
Kinney Services........	34.25	12.25	0.92	0.33	5	5	Hold	
Ling-Temco-Vought.....	14.38	8.25	0.15	0.07	5	6		
LTV (Okonite).........	14.38	4.88	0.45	0.38	5	6		
LTV Ling Altec........	2.88	2.75	0.35	0.34	5	6		
Leasco—1987..........	18.00	10.50	1.76	1.03	5	5		
Leasco—1978..........	18.00	7.62	0.52	0.22	5	6.		
Loews................	54.25	27.88	1.85	0.95	5	2	Hold	(b)
Louisiana Land & Exploration..........	44.25	16.50	1.09	0.41	4	4		

Security	Stock Price	Warrant Price	S/E	W/E	Normal Value Band	Actual Value Band	Action	Fn.
NVF Co.	12.88	6.75	1.63	0.85	5	4		(c)
National General—New.	24.38	7.50	0.61	0.19	5	6		
National Industries	7.25	3.50	0.34	0.16	5	6		
Northwest Industries	27.50	18.25	1.37	0.91	5	6		
Pacific Southwest Airlines	29.00	18.00	1.82	1.13	5	6		
Rapid-American	14.38	5.38	0.41	0.15	5	6		
United Brands	14.75	4.75	0.32	0.10	4	6		
United National	4.62	1.75	0.31	0.12	5	6		
U.S. Smelting	25.62	6.50	0.39	0.10	4	6		
Wards Foods	11.62	4.00	0.19	0.07	5	6		
Whittaker	11.25	4.75	0.22	0.10	5	6		
January 1972								
A-T-O	9.88	2.75	0.28	0.08	5	6		
Affiliated Capital	10.00	5.75	1.05	0.58	5	6		
Allegheny Airlines	13.88	8.38	1.40	0.81	5	6		
Atlas	2.25	1.12	0.45	0.22	5	6		
Avco	16.00	4.62	0.29	0.08	5	6		(g)
Bangor Punta	9.75	3.12	0.18	0.06	5	6		
Braniff Airways	15.88	19.12	1.01	0.39	5	5		
Brown	8.00	2.62	0.48	0.16	5	6		(g)
Budget Industries	7.62	2.88	0.54	0.21	5	6		
Carrier	47.25	17.25	1.15	0.42	5	4		(d)
Chris-Craft Industries	5.50	1.38	0.23	0.06	5	6		
Chrysler	28.62	13.75	0.84	0.40	4	6		
CMI Investment	48.88	23.88	1.54	0.75	5	4		(b)
Continental Telephone	22.38	6.38	1.00	0.28	4	2	Hold	(e)
Daylin	23.75	8.25	1.06	0.37	5	4	Buy	(g)
Equity Funding	35.25	23.62	1.40	0.94	5	6		
Fibreboard	24.00	10.50	1.07	0.47	4	6		
Flying Tiger	38.88	25.38	1.32	0.82	5	6		
Frontier Airlines	5.50	3.25	0.86	0.51	5	6		
General Development	25.88	9.00	0.92	0.32	5	4	Buy	
General Host	17.50	4.00	0.44	0.10	5	6		(g)
Gould	44.25	11.25	0.80	0.20	4	3	Buy	
Gulf & Western	28.38	8.62	0.53	0.16	4	6		
Indian Head	28.25	12.12	1.13	0.48	4	5		
International Controls	6.75	1.75	0.27	0.07	5	6		
Kane-Miller	15.25	6.25	0.69	0.28	5	6		
Kinney Services	31.25	9.75	0.84	0.26	5	4	Buy	
Ling-Temco-Vought	10.75	5.00	0.14	0.04	5	6		
LTV (O-A)	10.75	3.25	0.15	0.12	5	6		
LTV Ling Altec	2.25	1.50	0.13	0.09	5	6		
Leasco—1987	21.00	12.00	1.82	1.04	5	5		
Leasco—1978	21.00	7.75	0.60	0.22	5	6		
Loews	46.38	22.00	1.44	0.68	4	4	Hold	

Appendix F   197

Security	Stock Price	Warrant Price	S/E	W/E	Normal Value Band	Actual Value Band	Action	Fn.
Louisiana Land & Exploration	51.12	18.50	1.26	0.46	5	3	Buy	(d)
NVF Co.	15.38	6.88	1.56	0.70	5	3		(c)
National General—New	25.00	6.38	0.62	0.16	5	4	Buy	
National Industries	7.12	3.00	0.33	0.14	5	6		
Northwest Industries	33.75	22.25	1.35	0.89	5	6		(g)
Pacific Southwest Airlines	25.00	15.62	1.41	0.88	5	6		
Rapid-American	16.75	5.38	0.48	0.15	5	6		
Tesoro Petroleum	38.50	26.25	1.39	0.95	5	6		
United Brands	10.75	3.38	0.23	0.07	4	6		
United National	5.50	1.25	0.37	0.08	5	6		
Ward Foods	12.25	3.75	0.20	0.06	5	6		
Whittaker	10.38	4.38	0.21	0.09	5	6		
July 1972								
A-T-O	12.12	4.88	0.35	0.14	5	6		
Allegheny Airlines—1987	19.50	13.75	1.85	1.25	5	6		
Allegheny Airlines—1979	19.50	10.75	1.08	0.60	5	6		
Altec	1.75	1.00	0.10	0.06	5	6		
Atlas	2.25	1.12	0.45	0.22	5	6		
Avco	14.62	4.12	0.26	0.07	5	6		(g)
Bangor Punta	16.12	3.88	0.30	0.07	5	6		
Braniff Airways	15.75	21.62	0.97	0.43	5	6		
Brown	11.00	3.62	0.67	0.22	5	6		(g)
Budget Industries	8.50	2.88	0.61	0.20	5	6		
Carrier	44.25	14.75	1.08	0.36	5	3	Buy	(d)
Chris-Craft Industries	7.00	1.62	0.30	0.06	5	6		
Chrysler	30.88	15.12	0.91	0.44	4	6		
Continental Telephone	21.00	4.88	0.94	0.22	3	1	Hold	(e)
Cott	6.88	2.38	0.46	0.16	5	6		
Daylin	17.75	6.00	0.79	0.27	5	5	Hold	(g)
Diversified Industries	3.62	1.50	0.39	0.16	5	6		
Equity Funding	36.25	21.50	1.44	0.85	5	6		
Fibreboard	22.38	10.50	1.02	0.47	4	6		
Frontier Airlines	10.38	7.12	1.43	0.98	5	6		
General Development	33.25	11.88	1.20	0.42	5	3	Buy	
General Host	17.00	3.25	0.42	0.08	5	5		(g)
Gould	32.75	10.75	0.89	0.29	4	4	Hold	
Gulf & Western	38.00	12.62	0.71	0.23	5	6		
Indian Head	26.62	12.88	0.89	0.43	4	6		
Kane-Miller	9.75	3.88	0.40	0.16	5	6		
LCA	38.62	13.12	0.83	0.28	5	5		
LTV	12.62	5.88	0.17	0.05	5	6		
LTV (O-A)	12.62	3.00	0.18	0.11	5	6		

Security	Stock Price	Warrant Price	S/E	W/E	Normal Value Band	Actual Value Band	Action	Fn.
Leasco—1987	18.62	9.62	1.59	0.82	5	5		
Leasco—1978	18.62	5.75	0.54	0.16	5	6		
Loews	53.50	23.62	1.66	0.73	5	2	Buy	
Louisiana Land & Exploration	44.75	14.50	1.10	0.36	4	3	Hold	(d)
NVF Co	17.38	9.50	1.76	0.86	5	2		(c)
National General—New	23.75	5.88	0.59	0.15	5	5	Hold	
National Industries	6.62	2.50	0.31	0.12	5	6		
Northwest Industries	32.00	18.62	1.28	0.75	5	6		(g)
Pacific Southwest Airlines	26.00	15.62	1.46	0.88	5	6		
Rapid-American	16.12	5.00	0.46	0.14	5	6		
Rossmoor	11.00	4.88	0.88	0.39	5	6		
Telex	9.00	5.00	0.82	0.45	5	6		
Tesoro Petroleum	44.25	26.88	1.60	0.97	5	6		
United Brands	14.00	3.25	0.30	0.07	5	6		
United National	5.88	1.25	0.39	0.08	5	6		
UV Industries	26.75	6.75	0.40	0.10	4	6		
Ward Foods	11.00	3.00	0.18	0.05	5	6		
Warner Communications	48.38	19.12	1.31	0.52	5	3	Buy	
Western Pacific	16.38	6.75	0.80	0.33	5	6		
Whittaker	8.75	3.12	0.18	0.06	5	6		
January 1973								
A-T-O	9.50	2.62	0.27	0.08	5	6		
Allegheny Airlines— 1987	16.25	9.75	1.49	0.86	5	6		
Allegheny Airlines— 1979	16.25	8.38	0.90	0.47	5	6		
Altec	1.38	.75	0.08	0.04	5	6		
Atlas	2.75	1.50	0.44	0.24	5	6		
Avco	15.50	3.62	0.28	0.06	5	6		(g)
Bangor Punta	17.75	3.88	0.33	0.07	5	6		
Braniff Airways	15.62	16.62	0.92	0.31	5	4	Buy	
Brown	11.62	4.12	0.70	0.25	5	6		(g)
Budget Industries	11.75	4.12	0.84	0.29	5	5		
Carrier	28.38	8.25	1.04	0.30	5	2	Buy	(d)
Chris-Craft Industries	6.25	1.25	0.27	0.05	5	6		
Chrysler	40.88	17.00	1.20	0.50	4	4		
Continental Telephone	25.75	5.50	1.15	0.25	4	1	Sell	(b)
Cott	4.38	1.25	0.29	0.08	5	6		
Daylin	16.25	4.75	0.72	0.21	5	4	Buy	(g)
Diversified Industries	2.75	1.25	0.30	0.14	5	6		
Frontier Airlines	7.62	4.62	1.09	0.66	5	6		
General Development	13.75	4.00	0.50	0.14	5	6	Sell	
General Host	13.62	1.88	0.34	0.05	5	4	Buy	(g)
Gould	32.38	8.38	0.88	0.23	4	2	Buy	

Security	Stock Price	Warrant Price	S/E	W/E	Normal Value Band	Actual Value Band	Action	Fn.
Gulf & Western	34.50	10.75	0.64	0.20	5	6		
Indian Head	25.75	8.88	0.86	0.30	4	5		
Kane-Miller	14.38	6.12	0.59	0.25	5	6		
LCA	38.00	11.50	0.81	0.25	5	4	Buy	
LTV	9.50	3.50	0.13	0.03	5	6		
LTV (O-A)	9.50	1.50	0.14	0.05	5	6		
Leasco—1987	19.12	9.38	1.66	0.81	4	3		(b)
Leasco—1978	19.12	5.00	0.55	0.14	4	5		
Loews	46.75	18.12	1.45	0.56	4	2	Buy	
Louisiana Land & Exploration	43.25	12.00	1.07	0.30	4	2	Buy	(d)
Molybdenum	15.88	7.38	1.06	0.49	5	6		
NVF Co	19.38	11.00	1.90	0.89	5	1	Buy	
National General	32.75	6.50	0.82	0.16	5	1	Buy	
National Industries	4.38	1.50	0.20	0.07	5	6		
Northwest Industries	30.75	15.62	1.23	0.62	4	6		(g)
Pacific Southwest Airlines	20.75	11.62	1.17	0.65	5	6		
Rapid-American	20.00	5.25	0.57	0.15	4	5		
Rossmoor	10.00	3.12	0.80	0.31	5	6		
Telex	5.62	2.75	0.51	0.25	5	6		
Tesoro Petroleum	38.88	22.00	1.41	0.80	5	6		
United Brands	11.62	2.38	0.25	0.05	5	6		
United National	5.62	0.88	0.38	0.05	5	4	Buy	
UV Industries	26.75	6.38	0.41	0.10	4	6		
Ward Foods	8.75	1.62	0.15	0.03	5	6		
Warner Communications	36.88	12.38	1.00	0.33	5	3	Buy	
Western Pacific	13.50	4.88	0.66	0.24	5	6		
Whittaker	7.38	2.75	0.15	0.06	5	6		

Footnotes:
   a) Normal rating band was below band 4 (stock yield greater than 4 percent). Warrants were therefore rated "hold" if previously purchased but could not be considered as a current "buy," even if they were undervalued.
   b) Warrants were selling above the 2.0 leverage line but below 1.67. They were therefore rated "hold" if previously purchased but could not be considered as a current "buy."
   c) Warrants would have been a "buy" except that their usable bonds were selling at an excessive discount. Alternate S/E and W/E calculations were made based on a higher bond price.
   d) A value rating of two levels below normal would have been required for a "buy" rating to compensate for the low-price volatility of the common stock. Hold and sell decisions would also have been adjusted by an additional band level accordingly.
   e) Warrant was rated "hold," if previously purchased, as its life to expiration was less than three years but greater than two.
   f) Where an "NR" (not rated) is shown for the "actual value band," the warrant was above the 1.67 leverage line (a "sell" action) and was shown in the tables only when a previous "buy" action was indicated.
   g) The usable bond was not considered in computing S/E and W/E factors since there were an insufficient number available for exercise of the complete warrant issue.
   h) The warrant was rated a "sell" as its life to expiration was less than two years.

Appendix G

Exercise Terms for Warrants Having Common Stocks Listed on The New York or American Stock Exchanges

Warrant	Traded Common-Warrant	No. Shs.	Total $	Eff. to	Expiration Date	Usable Senior Security	Fn.
APL....................	NYS-OTC	1.000	28.00	12-31-88	12-31-88		
A-T-O...................	NYS-MID	1.000	30.00	10-15-73	10-15-78		
			35.00	10-15-78			
Affiliated Capital...........	ASE-ASE	1.153	10.00	3-26-75	3-26-75		
Alison Mortgage Investors....	ASE-OTC	1.000	19.00	12-15-75	12-15-75		
Alison Mortgage Investors....	ASE-OTC	1.000	27.50	12-15-76	12-15-76		
Alleghany.................	NYS-ASE	1.000	3.75	perp.	none		
Allegheny Airlines..........	ASE-ASE	1.040	18.00	4- 1-87	4- 1-87	5.5 -87	
Allegheny Airlines..........	ASE-ASE	1.000	18.00	4-12-77	4-12-79		1
			25.00	4-12-79			
Allied Artists Pictures.......	ASE-PAC	1.000	4.50	5-15-75	5-15-75		
Allied Products.............	NYS-OTC	1.000	58.00	7- 1-83	7- 1-83	7.0 -84	
Altec.....................	ASE-ASE	1.000	17.00	5- 1-78	5- 1-78		
Altec "Aug."..............	ASE-OTC	1.000	5.91	8-15-78	8-15-78		
American Century Mortgage...	NYS-ASE	1.000	23.00	6-30-75	6-30-75		
American Fletcher Mortgage...	ASE-ASE	1.000	25.00	1-31-75	1-31-75		
American Medicorp..........	NYS-OTC	1.000	35.00	12-31-74	12-31-74		
American Metal Climax......	NYS-OTC	1.000	47.50	10- 1-77	10- 1-77	8.0 -86	2
American Motors............	NYS-OTC	1.050	12.00	10- 1-76	10- 1-76		
American Realty Trust.......	ASE-ASE	1.000	9.62	9-30-76	9-30-76		
American Ship Building......	NYS-OTC	1.050	30.00	8- 1-76	8- 1-76		
American Tel. & Tel.........	NYS-NYS	1.000	52.00	5-15-75	5-15-75		
Associated Mortgage Inv......	ASE-OTC	1.000	28.25	12-14-73	12-14-73	10.0 -73	
Atico Mortgage Investors.....	NYS-ASE	1.000	15.00	12-31-79	12-31-79		3

Appendix G 201

Warrant	Traded Common-Warrant	No. Shs.	Total $	Eff. to	Expiration Date	Usable Senior Security	Fn.
Atico Mortgage Investors.....	NYS-OTC	1.000	21.00	4–30–81	4–30–81		
Atico Mortgage Investors.....	NYS-OTC	1.000	23.00	10–31–82	10–31–82	6.75 –82	
Atlas.........................	NYS-ASE	1.000	6.25	perp.	none	$1.00 Pfd.	4
Avco..........................	NYS-NYS	1.000	56.00	11–30–78	11–30–78	7.5 –93	
AVEMCO.......................	ASE-OTC	1.000	8.25	9– 9–74	9– 9–74		
BT Mortgage Investors.......	ASE-OTC	1.000	24.00	1–31–77	1–31–77		
Bangor Punta.................	NYS-ASE	1.038	55.00	3–31–81	3–31–81		5
Barnett Mortgage Trust.......	NYS-OTC	1.000	28.50	9– 1–76	9– 1–76	6.75 –91	
Barnett Mortgage Trust.......	NYS-OTC	1.000	20.00	4– 1–80	4– 1–80		
Beneficial Std. Mtg...........	ASE-ASE	1.000	20.00	7–14–75	7–14–75		
Beneficial Std. Mtg...........	ASE-OTC	1.000	27.75	3– 1–77	3– 1–77		
Bluebird.....................	ASE-ASE	1.000	10.75	4– 9–74	4– 9–74		
Braniff Airways..............	NYS-ASE	3.183	73.00	12– 1–86	12– 1–86	5.75 –86	
Brown........................	NYS-ASE	1.000	16.50	5–15–80	5–15–80	9.0 –95	
Budget Industries............	NYS-PAC	1.000	14.00	10–31–79	11– 1–83	6.0 –88	6
			17.00	10–31–81			
			20.00	11– 1–83			
Builders Invest. Group........	NYS-OTC	1.000	25.00	12– 7–76	12– 7–76		
C. I. Mortgage Group........	NYS-ASE	1.000	20.00	12– 1–80	12–1–80		
CMI Investment..............	ASE-ASE	1.000	31.75	8–26–76	8–26–76		
Cameron-Brown Invest........	NYS-OTC	1.000	25.00	11–15–76	11–15–76		
Carrier.......................	NYS-ASE	1.000	27.33	7–15–76	7–15–76		
Chris-Craft Industries.........	NYS-PAC	1.053	25.00	6– 1–79	6– 1–79		7
Chrysler.....................	NYS-NYS	1.000	34.00	5–15–76	5–15–76		8
Citizens & Sthn. Realty.......	NYS-OTC	0.500	10.00	10– 1–75	10– 1–75		
Citizens Mortgage Inv.........	ASE-ASE	1.000	15.00	12–10–74	12–10–74		
Colwell Mortgage Trust.......	ASE-ASE	1.000	20.00	12–15–74	12–15–74		
Colwell Mortgage Trust.......	ASE-OTC	1.000	29.37	9–30–73	9–30–76		
			31.37	9–30–76			
Commonwealth Edison A.....	NYS-NYS	1.000	30.00	4–30–81	4–30–81		9
Commonwealth Edison B.....	NYS-NYS	1.000	30.00	4–30–81	4–30–81		9
Continental Illinois Realty....	NYS-OTC	1.000	20.00	4– 2–74	4– 2–74		
Continental Telephone........	NYS-ASE	1.000	22.38	11– 5–74	11– 5–74		
Cott..........................	ASE-ASE	1.000	15.00	1–31–77	1–31–82		
			20.00	1–31–82			
Cousins Mortgage & Equity...	NYS-ASE	1.000	24.62	2–28–77	2–28–77		
Daylin.......................	NYS-ASE	1.000	22.50	3–21–89	3–21–89	5.0 –89	10
Diversified Industries.........	NYS-ASE	1.000	9.25	7–15–76	7–15–76		
Dreyfus......................	NYS-OTC	1.000	45.00	8–25–79	8–25–79		11
Duro-Test....................	ASE-OTC	1.033	10.58	9–30–77	9–30–77		
E-Systems....................	ASE-OTC	0.520	21.30	8–15–78	8–15–78		
Elgin National Industries.....	NYS-ASE	0.400	8.24	11–15–73	11–15–73		
Equity Funding..............	NYS-ASE	1.000	25.25	12– 1–75	12– 1–75		
Far West Financial...........	NYS-OTC	1.000	24.00	11– 1–74	11– 1–79		
			26.50	11– 1–79			
Federated Development.......	NYS-OTC	1.000	16.00	12–31–75	12–31–75		
Fibreboard...................	NYS-ASE	1.000	22.50	12– 1–78	12– 1–78		
Fidelco Growth Investors.....	ASE-ASE	1.000	25.00	9– 1–75	9– 1–75		
Fidelity Mortgage Inv.........	NYS-OTC	1.000	22.25	3–15–79	3–15–79		
Financial Gen'l Bnkshs........	ASE-OTC	1.600	10.64	6–15–78	6–15–78		
First of Denver Mortgage.....	ASE-ASE	1.000	20.00	10– 6–75	10– 6–75		
First Mortgage Investors......	NYS-OTC	1.000	11.25	12–15–77	12–15–77		
First Mortgage Investors......	NYS-OTC	1.000	23.00	6–30–75	6–30–79		
			25.00	6–30–79			

	Traded Common-	Exercise Terms			Expiration Date	Usable Senior Security	Fn.
Warrant	Warrant	No. Shs.	Total $	Eff. to			
First Penn Mortgage Trust....	NYS-OTC	0.500	10.00	7–23–74	7–23–74		
First Penn Mortgage Trust....	NYS-OTC	0.500	14.12	9– 1–75	9– 1–75		
First Union R. E. Equity......	NYS-OTC	1.000	12.75	12– 1–76	12– 1–76		
Flying Tiger..................	NYS-ASE	1.000	17.85	12–31–75	12–31–75		
Frontier Airlines.............	ASE-ASE	1.000	12.06	3– 1–87	3– 1–87	5.5 –87	
Fuqua Industries.............	NYS-OTC	1.140	43.50	12–31–73	12–31–73	7.0 –88	
Fuqua Industries.............	NYS-OTC	1.000	50.00	12–31–77	12–31–80		
			55.00	12–31–80			
General Development.........	NYS-NYS	1.020	28.25	7–15–78	7–15–78		13
General Host.................	NYS-PAC	1.000	40.00	1–31–79	1–31–79	7.0 –94	
Goodrich, B. F..............	NYS-ASE	1.000	30.00	8–15–79	8–15–79		
Gould.......................	NYS-ASE	1.000	36.37	6–29–76	6–29–76		14
Granite Mgmt. Services.......	ASE-OTC	1.207	45.00	11–16–73	11–16–73		
Great American Mtge.........	NYS-OTC	2.000	40.00	11– 1–75	11– 1–75		
Great Basins Petroleum.......	ASE-PAC	1.000	2.75	8–27–76	8–27–76		
Greyhound..................	NYS-NYS	1.000	23.50	5–14–80	5–14–80		
Guardian Mortgage Inv.......	NYS-ASE	1.000	37.00	7–15–76	7–15–76	6.75 –86	
Gulf & Western Industries.....	NYS-NYS	1.027	55.00	1–31–78	1–31–78		3
Gulf Mortgage & Realty......	ASE-ASE	1.000	20.00	3–31–76	3–31–76		
Gulf South Mortgage Inv......	ASE-ASE	1.000	20.00	2–20–77	2–20–77		
Hoerner Waldorf.............	NYS-OTC	1.000	30.00	10–31–73	10–31–73		
Holiday Inns.................	NYS-OTC	1.000	24.75	6–18–75	6–18–75		
Hospital Mortgage Group.....	ASE-ASE	1.000	25.00	2–16–77	2–16–77		
Indian Head.................	NYS-ASE	1.000	25.00	5–15–75	5–15–90		
			30.00	5–15–80			
			35.00	5–15–85			
			40.00	5–15–90			
Inexco Oil Co. B.............	ASE-OTC	1.000	20.00	7– 1–74	7– 1–74		
Instrument Systems...........	ASE-OTC	1.000	40.00	5–28–81	5–28–81		15
International Tel & Tel.......	NYS-OTC	see Fn	50.00	11– 1–76	11– 1–76		16
Intersystems.................	ASE-OTC	2.000	20.00	4– 1–76	4– 1–76		
Iowa Beef Processors..........	NYS-OTC	1.050	25.00	9–15–75	9–15–75		
ITEL........................	ASE-OTC	1.000	6.25	5– 1–78	5– 1–78		
ITEL........................	ASE-OTC	1.120	29.12	1–15–79	1–15–79	6.75 –89	17
Kane-Miller.................	NYS-ASE	1.000	22.00	1–15–75	1–15–80		
			24.25	1–15–80			
Kaufman & Broad............	NYS-ASE	1.000	10.84	3– 1–74	3– 1–74		
Kidde, Walter & Co...........	NYS-OTC	1.077	48.50	6–15–77	6–15–77		
LCA........................	ASE-ASE	1.000	46.75	5–29–77	5–29–77		
LTV........................	NYS-ASE	1.970	115.00	1–15–78	1–15–78		
LTV........................	NYS-OTC	1.109	40.00	1–15–78	1–15–78		
LTV (JLI)....................	NYS-OTC	0.647	37.50	4– 1–79	4– 1–79	6.75 –94	18
LTV (O-A)..................	NYS-ASE	0.400	28.00	7–15–78	7–15–78		
Larwin Mortgage Inv.........	NYS-OTC	1.000	32.00	4–15–77	4–15–77		
Larwin Realty & Mortgage....	ASE-ASE	1.000	20.00	12–27–76	12–27–76		
Leasco......................	NYS-PBW	1.000	16.50	7– 1–87	7– 1–87	5.75 –87	
Leasco......................	NYS-ASE	1.000	34.80	6– 4–78	6– 4–78		
Lerner Stores.................	ASE-ASE	1.000	15.00	8–31–82	8–31–82		3
Liberty Loan.................	NYS-ASE	1.000	19.50	11– 1–74	11– 1–79		
			22.00	11– 1–79			

Appendix G 203

Warrant	Traded Common-Warrant	No. Shs.	Total $	Eff. to	Expiration Date	Usable Senior Security	Fn.
Lincoln American	ASE-OTC	1.000	15.12	8–14–74	8–14–79		
			17.12	8–14–79			
Loews	NYS-ASE	1.000	37.50	11–29–76	11–29–80	6.875–93	
			40.00	11–29–80			
Louisiana Land & Exploration	NYS-ASE	1.000	40.50	6–15–76	6–15–76		19
MDS-Atron	NYS-OTC	0.250	17.00	1–31–75	1–31–75		20
McCrory Corp.	NYS-ASE	1.000	20.00	3–15–76	3–15–76		
McCrory Corp.	NYS-ASE	1.000	20.00	3–15–76	3–15–81		
			22.50	3–15–81			
McDonough	ASE-OTC	1.000	18.00	5– 1–80	5– 1–80		
Midland Mortgage Inv.	ASE-OTC	1.000	12.50	9–30–74	9–30–74		
Mobile Oil	NYS-ASE	1.000	47.50	8– 1–75	8– 1–75		21
Molybdenum	NYS-ASE	1.000	15.00	4– 7–77	4– 7–77		
Mortgage Trust of Amer.	NYS-OTC	1.000	19.00	11– 6–74	11– 6–74		
NVF Co.	NYS-PAC	1.450	22.01	1–31–79	1–31–79	5.0 –94	
National General	NYS-OTC	0.285	4.97	2–28–74	2–28–74		
National General	NYS-ASE	1.000	15.00	5–15–74	5–15–74		22
National General	NYS-ASE	1.000	40.00	9–30–78	9–30–78		
National Industries	NYS-ASE	1.000	21.40	10–31–78	10–31–78		
Nortek	ASE-OTC	1.000	34.00	5– 1–74	4–30–79		
			38.00	4–30–79			
North Amer. Mtge. Inv.	NYS-OTC	1.000	24.00	12– 2–74	12– 2–74		
North Amer. Mtge. Inv.	NYS-ASE	1.000	31.12	3–31–79	3–31–79		
Northwest Industries	NYS-NYS	1.000	25.00	3–31–79	3–31–79	7.5 –94	
Old Town	ASE-OTC	1.000	17.64	6– 6–74	6– 6–79		
			22.54	6– 6–79			
Ozark Airlines	ASE-OTC	1.000	8.00	12–31–78	12–31–78		
PNB Mtge & Realty Inv.	ASE-ASE	1.000	20.00	12–31–74	12–31–74		
PSA	NYS-ASE	1.000	23.40	10– 1–77	10– 1–77	6.0 –87	
Palomar Mortgage Inv.	ASE-ASE	1.000	16.50	3–21–77	3–21–77		
Permaneer	ASE-OTC	1.000	17.00	10– 4–74	10– 4–74		
Phoenix Steel	ASE-OTC	1.013	7.69	12–31–79	12–31–79		
Pneumo Dynamics	ASE-OTC	1.000	14.00	6–30–75	6–30–75		
Presidential Realty	ASE-OTC	1.000	14.00	3–31–75	3–31–75		
Puritan Fashions	ASE-OTC	1.000	6.18	8– 1–81	8– 1–81		
Rapid American	NYS-ASE	1.000	35.00	5–15–94	5–15–94		23
Realty ReFund Trust	ASE-OTC	1.000	20.00	6–14–74	6–14–74		
Republic Mortgage Inv.	NYS-ASE	1.000	20.00	6–30–74	6–30–74		
Rockwood Computer	ASE-OTC	1.277	50.00	1–15–79	1–15–79	8.5 –79	
Rollins International	ASE-OTC	1.000	15.50	9–30–76	9–30–76		
Rossmoor	ASE-ASE	1.000	12.50	7–15–76	7–15–76		
Ryder System	NYS-ASE	1.000	12.50	8– 5–75	8– 5–75		
Security Mortgage Inv.	ASE-ASE	1.000	16.00	5– 1–79	5– 1–79	6.0 –82	24
Standard Prudential	NYS-OTC	1.000	15.00	12–31–83	12–31–83		23
Sutro Mortgage Inv.	NYS-PAC	1.000	20.00	4–15–74	4–15–76		
			22.00	4–15–76			
Sutro Mortgage Inv.	NYS-ASE	1.000	20.00	6– 1–77	6– 1–77		
TFI Companies	ASE-OTC	1.000	8.00	9–27–75	9–27–75		
Tampa Electric	NYS-OTC	1.000	23.00	12–31–76	12–31–76		
Telex	NYS-ASE	1.000	11.00	11– 1–76	11– 1–76		

204 Dow Jones–Irwin Guide to Convertible Securities

Warrant	Traded Common-Warrant	No. Shs.	Total $	Eff. to	Expiration Date	Usable Senior Security	Fn.
Tenneco	NYS-ASE	1.070	32.17	4- 1-79	4- 1-79	6.0 -79	
Tenneco	NYS-NYS	1.000	24.25	11- 1-75	11- 1-75		
Tesoro Petroleum	NYS-ASE	1.000	27.62	8-24-76	8-24-76		
Texas Industries	NYS-OTC	1.000	32.75	1-16-78	1-16-78		
Texas International	ASE-PAC	1.000	9.00	5-31-75	5-31-74		
Textron	NYS-ASE	1.000	8.75	5- 1-74	5- 1-74		25
			10.00	5- 1-79			
			11.25	5- 1-84			
Trans World Airlines	NYS-ASE	1.000	22.00	12- 1-73	12- 1-73	6.5 -78	
Tri-Continental	NYS-OTC	3.130	22.50	prep.	none		
Tri-South Mortgage Inv.	NYS-OTC	0.500	10.00	12- 2-74	12- 2-74		
Triangle Pacific Forest	NYS-OTC	1.040	24.00	11-15-73	11-15-73		
USM	NYS-OTC	1.073	39.00	7-24-82	7-24-82		26
U V Industries	NYS-ASE	1.000	66.00	1-15-79	1-15-79		27
Unionamerica Mortgage	ASE-ASE	1.000	20.00	12-31-74	12-31-74		
United Brands	NYS-OTC	2.000	69.00	3- 1-78	3- 1-78	6.75 -88	
United Brands	NYS-ASE	1.000	46.00	2- 1-79	2- 1-79		
United Foods	ASE-OTC	1.000	3.50	4-15-79	4-15-79		
United National	ASE-ASE	1.000	12.00	12-31-73	12-31-76		
			15.00	12-31-76			
United National	ASE-ASE	1.000	10.00	5-28-78	5-28-78	7.5 -88	
United Telecommunications	NYS-NYS	1.000	17.50	10-14-75	10-14-75		
U.S. Leasing Real Estate	ASE-ASE	1.000	25.00	12-31-80	12-31-80		28
Uris Buildings	NYS-ASE	2.122	12.50	5- 1-75	5- 1-75		
Ward Foods	NYS-ASE	1.000	60.00	1- 2-79	1- 2-79		3
Warner Communications	NYS-ASE	1.000	37.00	1- 8-80	1- 8-80		29
Webb (Del E.)	ASE-OTC	1.000	6.25	12- 1-75	12- 1-75		
Wells Fargo Mortgage Inv.	NYS-OTC	0.500	10.00	7- 1-74	7- 1-74		
Western Pacific Industries	NYS-ASE	1.000	20.50	1-10-77	1-10-77		
Whittaker	NYS-ASE	1.000	50.00	5- 5-79	5- 5-79		
Williams Companies	NYS-NYS	1.000	20.00	1- 1-76	1- 1-76		
Wolverine Industries	ASE-OTC	1.000	10.50	6- 1-73	6- 1-78		
			12.25	6- 1-75			
			14.00	6- 1-78			
Work Wear	ASE-OTC	1.000	17.75	10- 1-77	10- 1-77		
Zapata	NYS-OTC	1.000	15.00	2-28-77	2-28-77	6.5 -77	
Zayre	NYS-OTC	1.000	40.00	8-31-76	8-31-76		

Footnotes:
1. Not protected for dilution up to 8 percent.
2. Bonds are usable at 92.6 percent of par.
3. Not protected for dilution up to 5 percent.
4. $1.00 preferred usable at $20 par value. Warrants are not protected for stock dividends.
5. Callable at $55, company may permit the use of certain debt securities at market in lieu of cash.
6. Bonds are usable only after 11/1/78.
7. Not protected for stock dividends up to $0.50 in value per year.
8. Issued by Chrysler Financial.
9. Warrant is alternately convertible into .333 shares of common stock at any time without payment.
10. Callable at $5.35 when common has traded above $28 for 30 continuous days.
11. Callable at $25.
12. Callable at $50.

13. Warrants were issued by City Investing and are identified as City Investing.
14. Maximum dilution from stock dividends is 10 percent over life of warrant.
15. Company may reduce exercise price and/or increase the number of shares issuable upon exercise and/or permit the use of debt securities in lieu of cash.
16. Exercise terms are .5212 shares of common plus .05 shares of "K" preferred.
17. Bonds are SSI Computer.
18. Bonds are usable through 4/1/74 only.
19. Issued by Amerada Hess.
20. Converts into Mohawk Data Science common stock.
21. Issued by Northern Natural Gas.
22. 5.0–84 usable at par if warrants have not been detached.
23. Callable at $20. Not protected for dilution up to 5 percent.
24. 7.25–82 alternately usable at par.
25. Not protected for dilution up to 2 percent.
26. 9 percent guaranteed loan stock 1982 usable at par. Company may reduce exercise price up to 25 percent or increase usability of loan stock to a maximum of 133 percent of par.
27. Not protected for dilution up to 3 percent. Maximum dilution from stock dividends on common is 15 percent over life of warrant.
28. Callable at $5 after 12/31/74.
29. The "warrant" is actually the "C" preferred paying $0.05 annual dividend.

Appendix H

Terms Applying to Convertibles, Warrants, and Hedging

Accrued Interest. Interest earned on a bond since its last interest payment date. The buyer of the bond pays the market price plus accrued interest to the seller and is entitled to the next interest payment in full. Exceptions include bonds in default and income bonds, which are traded flat (without accrued interest).

Adjusted Exercise Price. The warrant's exercise price divided by the number of shares receivable upon exercise. Where senior securities are usable at par in lieu of cash, the exercise price is first reduced by their discount below par to determine the effective exercise price. The effective exercise price is then divided by the number of shares to arrive at the adjusted exercise price.

Adjusted Warrant Price. The market price of the warrant divided by the number of shares receivable upon exercise.

Adjustment of Conversion Terms. Changes in conversion terms which may be provided for under the terms of the conversion privilege or by virtue of the implementation of an antidilution clause.

Antidilution Clause. Provisions contained in most convertibles and warrants which call for the adjustment of the conversion or exercise terms in the event of stock splits, stock dividends, or the sale of new stock at a price below the conversion price of existing warrants or convertibles. In some cases, no adjustment is made for stock dividends under 2 percent to 5 percent in any single year.

Arbitrage. A simultaneous purchase and sale of identical or similar securities for an immediate profit upon conversion. This technique generally involves the purchase of a convertible bond or preferred that is trading at a price below its conversion value and the sale of its common stock.

Attached. Warrants are frequently attached to other securities, usually bonds. The security specifies the time and terms under which the warrants may be detached. The bonds and warrants may also trade individually or as units.

Bearer Bond. A bond whose principal and interest are payable to its holder without specifying any name—the opposite of a registered bond.

Bond. A certificate of debt issued by a government, municipality, or corporation to the bondholder, where by the issuer promises to pay interest on a regular basis and to repay the face amount of the bond on a specified date.

Bond Indenture. The contract under which bonds are issued. It describes such terms of the agreement as interest rate, interest payment dates, date of maturity, redemption terms, conversion privileges, and the security for the loan.

Bond Price Quotation. Bonds are quoted as a percentage of par. Thus, 90 means 90 percent of a $1,000 bond, or $900. 110 means 110 percent of par or $1,100.

Break-even Time. The time period in which a convertible bond or preferred will recapture the premium paid over conversion value through extra income when bond interest or preferred dividends exceed the common stock's dividend.

Callable. Term applying to securities which contain a provision giving the issuer the right to retire the issue prior to its maturity date.

Call Option. An option to buy stock under specified terms which include the price, the time period, and the number of shares.

Call Price. The amount of money a corporation is obliged to pay if it chooses to redeem its senior securities. In the case of bonds, the call price is usually expressed as a percentage of par. In the case of preferred stock, the call is the price per share. The call price normally starts somewhat above par and is reduced periodically.

Capital Gain or Loss. A profit or loss from the sale of securities. A capital gain or loss may be either short term (six months or less) or long term (more than six months).

Change in Terms. See "Adjustment of Conversion Terms."

Closed-end Fund. An investment company having a fixed number of common shares outstanding and not having the obligation to redeem the shares at net asset value, as compared with a mutual fund. The market price of closed-end fund shares will fluctuate based on supply demand conditions in the marketplace.

Common Stock. Securities which represent an ownership interest in the corporation, also called "capital stock." Common stockholders assume greater risk than do preferred stockholders or bondholders, but generally exercise greater control and may gain the greater reward in the form of dividends and capital appreciation if the business is successful.

Conversion Parity. Either the price at which common stock must sell for the market price of the convertible to equal its conversion value, or the price at which the convertible must sell for it to equal the current market value of the common shares to be received upon conversion. If the convertible is trading at a premium above conversion parity, it is generally better to sell the convertible and buy the stock rather than to convert.

Conversion Ratio. The number of shares of common stock for which a convertible bond or preferred stock is exchangeable. For bonds, the ratio is normally expressed as the number of shares per $1,000 bond. For preferreds, the ratio is expressed as the number of shares per share of preferred stock.

Conversion Value. The worth of a convertible bond or preferred if it were converted into common stock. It equals the number of shares to be received upon conversion times the current market price of the common. For a warrant, it equals the number of common stock shares per warrant times the current market price of the common, less the exercise price.

Convertible Bond. A bond which may be exchanged, at the option of the holder, into common stock or other security in accordance with the terms of the bond indenture.

Convertible Hedge. A market operation in which the investor buys or holds a convertible bond or preferred and sells the common stock short against it. The amount of common sold short may vary up to the number of shares to be received upon conversion.

> ***Half Hedge.*** Half the number of shares to be received upon conversion are sold short. The investor is seeking profits on the upside at reduced downside risk.
>
> ***Full Hedge.*** The full number of shares of common are sold short. The investor is seeking profits in a declining market as the bond price levels out near its investment value while the common stock continues to fall.

Convertible Preferred Stock. An equity security, senior to the common stock, which may be exchanged, at the option of the holder, into common stock or other security in accordance with the terms of the conversion privilege.

Coupon Bond. Bonds with coupons attached.

Coupons. Certificates attached to a bond which represent the right to periodic interest payments. The coupons are clipped as they become due and are deposited in a bank for payment.

Cum Dividend. With the dividend.

Cumulative Preferred. A preferred stock which provides for omitted dividends (arrearages) to be paid before dividends may be paid on the company's common stock.

Current Yield. The yield on a bond figured by simply dividing the annual amount of interest by the current market price of the bond.

Debenture. A bond—an unsecured long-term certificate of debt issued by a corporation.

Debenture with Warrants. A bond issue which has a specified number of warrants attached to each bond. Provisions are usually made for the detachment of the warrants after a specified date. See "Attached."

Debt Security. A bond or note.

Default. Failure of the bond issuer to meet a contract obligation, such as payment of interest, maintenance of working capital requirements, or payment of principal via a sinking fund or at maturity.

Delayed Convertibility. A convertible bond, preferred, or warrant which does not become convertible until some future date.

Dilution. The increase in the amount of common stock issued by a corporation due to conversion of warrants and convertibles. Dilution also refers to the issuing of additional common stock.

Discount. The amount by which a bond may be selling below its par value.

Effective Exercise Price. Where senior securities are usable at par in lieu of cash, the warrant's exercise price is reduced by the discount below par to determine the effective exercise price.

Equity. In a margin account, equity represents the difference between the market value of securities held in the account and the amount owed on them.

Ex-dividend. A stock trading without its current dividend. The seller of the stock on the ex-dividend date will receive the dividend.

Exercise. Surrendering a warrant with the exercise price in exchange for the common stock. When a warrant is about to expire, or when terms are about to change, exercise may be mandatory. See "Forced Conversion."

Expiration Date. The date on which a conversion privilege ends. If the option or warrant has value, it must be exercised on or before the expiration date or it will become worthless.

Ex-warrants. Bonds trading without warrants attached.

Fabricated Convertible. The combination of warrants plus bonds which are usable for exercise purposes at par value in lieu of cash is called a fabricated convertible and is equivalent to a regular convertible bond.

Flat. Bonds trading without accrued interest.

Forced Conversion. When convertibles are called for redemption, or there is an adverse change in their conversion terms, or an upcoming expiration date, the holders of convertible securities may be forced to convert or to sell them to someone else who will convert. This is necessary to avoid a loss of value.

Guaranteed Bond. A bond which includes a provision that the interest and principal will be paid by a company other than the debtor company in case of default.

Hedge. A position which includes securities which have been both purchased and sold short to take advantage of the price disparity between the related securities. See "Convertible Hedge," "Reverse Warrant Hedge," and "Warrant Hedge."

Hypothecate. To pledge securities as collateral for a loan while still retaining ownership of the securities.

Income Bond. A bond on which interest payments are contingent upon earnings.

Income Preferred. A preferred stock on which dividend payments are contingent upon earnings.

Indenture. A contract or written agreement between a corporation and the holders of its securities, such as a bond indenture. See "Bond Indenture."

Interest Rate. The cost of borrowing money determined by supply and demand and the nature of the loan.

Investment Floor. The price at which a convertible bond or convertible preferred stock would not be expected to sell below upon a decline by the related common stock. See "Investment Value."

Investment Value. The estimated value of a convertible bond or preferred stock without giving any consideration to its conversion privilege. Also known as the investment floor.

Latent Warrants. The difference between the market value of a convertible bond or preferred stock and its investment value represents the premium that investors are willing to pay for the conversion privilege. This premium over investment value represents the market value for the convertible's latent warrants.

Leverage. Leverage is obtained by the use of borrowed money to finance a portion of one's investments or by the purchase of securities which contain inherent leverage such as warrants or call options. The use of leverage will normally amplify both potential profits and losses.

Life to Expiration. The time remaining before a warrant or call option expires or before a conversion privilege expires.

Long. This represents ownership of securities.

Maintenance Margin. Minimum equity requirements that must be maintained in a margin account as established by the New York Stock Exchange or the brokerage firm.

Margin. The amount of money and/or securities deposited with the brokerage firm to finance part of the cost of purchasing securities. The Federal Reserve Board establishes the minimum requirements through its Regulation T.

Margin Account. An account with your brokerage firm in which securities are purchased on margin or in which securities are sold short.

Margin Interest. The interest paid to the brokerage firm on the debit balance in the margin account.

Marking to the Market. An adjustment to the credit balance in an account having securities sold short to reflect current market prices.

Mathematical Advantage. The advantage offered by an undervalued convertible or warrant over purchase of its common stock. See "Risk/Reward Ratio."

Maturity Date. A fixed date when the company must redeem a bond by paying the full face value to the bondholder.

Negative Leverage. Leverage which exerts downward price pressure such as a convertible or warrant which is overpriced.

Normal Value. A mathematically determined value for a convertible or warrant in relationship to the current market value of the related common stock.

Normal Value Curve. A graphical representation of a convertible's or warrant's normal value at any price level for the related common stock.

OTC. Over-the-counter, unlisted securities.

Option. A contractual privilege representing the right to buy or sell securities at a given price within a specified period of time.

Overpriced Convertible. A convertible or warrant which is currently trading above its normal value.

Par. The face value of a bond or preferred stock.

Parity. See "Conversion Parity."

Perpetual Warrant. A warrant which has no expiration date.

Plus Cash. A convertible bond or convertible preferred stock that requires an additional cash payment upon conversion.

Positive Leverage. Leverage which exerts upward price pressure such as a convertible or warrant which is undervalued.

Puts and Calls. Options which provide the right to sell or buy a fixed amount of common stock at a given price within a fixed period of time. A put gives the holder the right to sell (or "put") the stock and a call the right to buy the stock.

Redemption. The act of retiring part or all of a bond issue prior to its maturity date. When a convertible bond issue is called by the issuing company and the bond is selling above the redemption price, it is equivalent to a forced conversion of the issue.

Registered Bond. A bond which is issued in the name of the holder as opposed to a bearer bond. If the bond is fully registered, or registered as to both principal and interest, interest is paid by check to the holder. Most recent issues of convertible bonds are fully registered.

Regulation T. A Federal Reserve Board regulation which establishes the maximum amount of credit that brokers may extend to their customers for the purpose of buying securities on margin.

Regulation U. A Federal Reserve Board regulation which establishes the maximum amount of credit that banks may advance to their customers for the purchase of securities.

Reverse Warrant Hedge. The short sale of a warrant against the purchase of the related common stock or securities which are convertible into the common.

Right. Usually refers to a short-term option to subscribe to a new issue of securities and is given by the company to existing stockholders.

Risk/Reward Ratio. A simple formula for determining whether a convertible or a warrant offers a mathematical advantage over its common stock. Assuming that the common will either double in price or drop in half (other price movements may also be used) the risk/reward ratio for the convertible may be computed as follows:

$$\text{Risk/Reward ratio} = \frac{\text{Upside leverage}}{1.00} \times \frac{.50}{\text{Downside leverage}}$$

A ratio in excess of 1.0 would indicate a positive advantage.

Securities. Includes bonds, preferred stocks, common stocks, and warrants.

Senior Securties. Bonds or preferred stocks which have a prior claim over the common stock in the distribution of interest or dividends, or to assets in case of liquidation.

Senior Securities Usable at Par Value in Lieu of Cash. Securities usable at par value in lieu of cash when exercising a warrant. If the usable senior securities are selling below par, the warrant's exercise price is reduced by the percentage discount to determine the effective exercise price.

Short Covering. The purchase of a security to return it to the lender to close out a prior short sale.

Short Interest. The total amount of securities sold short in the market. A report is issued each month covering all issues on the New York and American Stock Exchanges in which there was a significant short position.

Short Position. Securities sold short and not covered as of a particular date.

Short Sale. The sale of a security which one does not own with the hope of buying it back at a lower price at some future time for a profit.

Short Squeeze. A sharp increase in the price of a security as a result of panic short covering or difficulty in borrowing the security to maintain the short position (as in a tender offer).

Stock Dividend. The issuance of small amounts of stock (usually 5 percent or less) in lieu of a cash dividend. This technique is normally employed by companies which desire to conserve cash for expansion purposes and so forth.

Subordinated. Subject to the prior claim of other senior securities and usually not secured by any specific property. Most convertible bonds are subordinate to regular bonds issued by the company.

Sweetener. Market slang for a warrant issued with other securities to enhance the marketability of the package.

Tangible Value. See "Conversion Value."

Undervalued Convertibles. A convertible or warrant which is currently trading below its normal value.

Unit. A package of securities issued and traded in units such as bonds and warrants.

Up-tick. A term used to designate a transaction made at a price higher than the preceding transaction. Short sales may only be executed on an up-tick.

Warrant. A negotiable security issued by a company which represents a long-term option to purchase common stock from the company on specified terms.

Warrant Agreement. A contract from the company or written agreement between a corporation and the holders of its warrants.

Warrant Hedge. A market operation in which the investor buys or holds a warrant and sells the common stock short against it. The amount of common sold short may vary up to the number of shares to be received upon exercise of the warrants but the actual amount is determined in advance to accomplish one of the following objectives.

> *Bullish Hedge.* A sufficient amount of common is sold short to simply limit downside risk while seeking profits upon an upside move.
>
> *Neutral Hedge.* Extra common is sold short to seek profits in either a rising or declining market.
>
> *Bearish Hedge.* This hedge is designed for profits on the downside while limiting risk if prices were to advance.

When Detached. A form of "when issued" transaction when securities are issued as a package and are not separable for a period of time.

When Issued. This term indicates a conditional transaction in a security which has been authorized for issuance but not as yet actually issued.

With Warrants. Bonds quoted "ww" means that warrants are still attached and the price of the package includes both the bond and warrants.

Writing Options. The sale of a call option against stock or convertibles held in one's portfolio.

Yield. The dividends or interest paid annually by a company on a security, expressed as a percentage of the current market price of the security.

Yield to Maturity. The effective yield of a bond, taking into account its premium or discount from par, if one were to hold it to maturity when it is expected to be redeemed by the company at par value.

Index

A

Accounts; *see* Brokerage account
Accrued interest, 162, 206
Adjusted exercise price, 3, 19–20, 41, 43–44, 206
Adjusted warrant price, 19–20, 41, 43–44, 206
Alternatives to the basic system, 86–92
    continuous review of all opportunities, 86–88
    fine tuning the hedge portfolio, 88–90
    over-the-counter warrants, 88
    predicting major market swings, 90–92
    trading against a warrant hedge position, 90
Amerada Hess warrant; *see* Louisiana Land & Exploration warrant
American DualVest, 145–48
American Financial Corp., 173–80
American General Convertible Securities, 102
American Stock Exchange, 2, 54, 128, 177, 179–80
American Telephone & Telegraph, 127, 183
    reverse warrant hedge, 118–25
    warrant, 1–2, 24
Antidulition clause, 4, 206
Application of margin regulations in a hedging program, 150–52
Arbitrage, 12, 129, 207

B

Back office, 157
Bancroft Convertible Fund, 102
Bankruptcy, 114, 118
Barron's, 174
Basic system, 35–36, 53–85
    anticipated performance, 57–59
    evaluating, establishing and maintaining positions, 54–56, 60–61
    performance results, 70–85
    six-year study, 61–68, 190–99
Bear markets, 57–58, 63, 65, 70–74, 80, 82, 90–91, 97
Beat the Market, 115, 167
Better Idea, Total Investment Planning and Management System, 156, 166

217

Books on warrants, convertibles and
    options, 166–67
Braniff Airways, 183
    5.75's–bond, 19–20, 181
    warrant, 4, 19–20, 62–63, 65–67,
        71, 166
Brokerage account, 153–56
    cash account, 154–55
    convertible bond account, 155
    margin account, 155
    short account, 155–56
    straight bond account, 155
Brokerage firm; see Selecting a brokerage firm
Budget Industries 6's–88 bond, 7
Bull markets, 58–59, 62, 65, 70–74,
    82, 90–91
Buy-in, 114, 170
Buying on margin, 37, 48, 77–80,
    83–85, 99, 103, 130–31, see
    also Hedging on margin
Buying power, 57–58

C

C & P Warrant Analysis, 160
Calculations for plotting the normal
    value curve for long-term warrants, 182
Call provisions, 100, 103, 114
Call options, 117–18, 126, 138–44,
    155, 207
Callable warrants, 7–10
Carrier Corp., 183
    warrant, 24, 64–67, 72, 166
Cash account; see Brokerage account
Cash flow, 105–6, 109, 113, 115,
    122–23
Certificates kept in brokerage account, 37, 103–4, 113
Chase Convertible Fund, 102
Check lists; see Worksheets
C. I. Convertible Fund, 102
Citizens and Southern Realty Investors delayed warrant, 134–35
City Investing warrant; see General
    Development warrant
Closed-end funds, 102, 208
Closing out a convertible bond hedge
    on the upside, 109, 114

Commonwealth Edison, 183
    warrant, 24
Continental Investment Corp. 9's–90
    convertible bond, 129–31, 134
Continental Telephone warrant, 63–
    64, 66, 72
Conversion value, 208
    convertibles, 93–95, 103, 105
    warrants, 11–13
Convertible bonds and preferred
    stocks, 93–104, 117, 125–26
    bonds versus preferreds, 98–100
    conversion value, 94–95
    convertible funds, 101–2
    convertibles versus warrants/cash,
        100–01
    general guides, 103–4
    investment value, 93–94
    latent warrants, 95–96
    opportunities in undervalued convertibles, 96–97
Convertible bonds versus convertible
    preferred stocks, 98–100
    brokerage commissions, 99
    call provisions, 100
    continuity of payments, 98–99
    interest and dividend payments, 98
    margin buying, 99
    maturity, 98
    safety, 98
    tax consequences, 99–100
Convertible funds, 101–2
Convertibles versus warrants/cash,
    100–01
Converting warrants and convertibles,
    12, 109, 114
Covering warrants sold short before
    expiration, 117, 122

D

Daylin, Inc., 183
    fabricated convertible bond, 136–
        38
    5's–88 bond, 8–9, 181
    warrant, 8–9, 64–67, 72, 166
Debit balance, 111, 117, 121
Delayed convertibles, 128–33
Delayed warrants, 133–35

Index 219

Diversification, 51–52, 84, 113, 115–16, 158–59
Dividends, 98–99, 162
Dividends paid on stock sold short, 50, 52, 84, 113, 185
Dual-purpose funds, 144–48

E

Effective exercise price, 5–6, 19–20, 41, 43–44
Exercise price, 3, 95
Exercise terms, 3–7
Exercise terms for warrants having common stocks listed on The New York or American Stock Exchanges, 200–05
Exercise value; *see* Conversion value
Extention of warrant life, 116, 118

F

Fabricated convertibles, 135–38, 155, 211
　advantages over conventional convertible bonds, 135–36
　hedging, 137–38
Far West Financial warrant, 172–80
Federal Reserve Board; *see* Regulations T and U
Financial Analysts Journal, 69
Fine tuning a hedge portfolio, 88–90, 109
FRA Warrant Service, 160

G

G. C. Computer convertible bond, 128–29
Gemini Fund, 145–48
General Development, 183
　warrant, 64, 66, 72
General guides for:
　buying convertibles, 103–4
　buying warrants, 36–37
　establishing a convertible hedge program, 164
　hedging convertibles, 113–14
　hedging warrants, 50–51
　managing a convertible hedge portfolio, 165
　reverse warrant hedging, 115–18

General guides for—*Cont.*
　use of call options in a convertible hedge program, 143–44
General Host, 183
　7's–94 bond, 7, 181
　warrant, 7, 63, 65–68, 71, 166
Goodrich, B. F., 183
　warrant, 24, 166
Gould, Inc., 183
　warrant, 63–67, 71–72, 166
Gulf Resources & Chemical convertible bond hedge, 110–13, 141–43
Gulf & Western Industries warrant, 63, 66, 71

H

Harbor Fund, 102
Hedging convertibles, 105–14, 209
　actual hedge position in Gulf Resources & Chemical, 110–13
　bearish hedges, 106–9
　bullish hedges, 106–8
　closing out a bond hedge on the upside, 109
　general guides, 113–14
　hedging XYZ Company bonds, 105–9
　neutral hedges, 106–13
　possible risks, 114
Hedging on margin, 157–58
　convertibles, 107–14
　warrants, 47–52, 57–59, 83–84, 92
Hedging warrants, 38–52
　bearish hedges, 44–47, 52, 187–89, 215
　bullish hedges, 44–47, 52, 55, 187–89, 215
　general guides, 50–51
　hedging with borrowed funds, 47–49
　neutral hedges, 44–47, 52, 55, 187–89, 215
　performance results from the basic system, 80–85
　possible risks, 52
　recent candidates, 166

Hemisphere Fund, 145–48
Hilton Hotels warrant, 62–63, 66, 71

I

Income and Capital Shares, 145–48
Initial margin requirements, 149–52
Interest
  bond, 98–99, 162
  margin, 52, 98, 162
Intrinsic value; see Conversion value
Investment services, 158–60
Investment value, 93–94, 97, 100–101, 103, 105–6, 211

K–L

Kaufman & Broad warrant, 63–64, 66, 71–72
Keyes Fibre warrant, 8
Kinney National Services warrant, 63–66, 71–72, 87, see also Warner Communications warrant
Latent warrants, 93, 95–96, 100, 135, 211
LCA Corp. warrant, 65, 67, 166
"Leap frogging," 161
Leasco Corp., 172–80, 183
  warrant, 166
Leverage
  margin buying, 47, 52, 157–58, 211
  warrant leverage, 24–26, 28, 30–31, 36, 44, 55–57, 66, 73
Leverage Fund of Boston, 145–48
Ling-Temco-Vought; see LTV Corp.
Listed warrants, 2, 60
Loews Corp., 183
  6.875's–93 bond, 5–6, 181
  warrant, 3, 5–6, 63–66, 71–72, 166
Loew's Theatres; see Loews Corp.
Louisiana Land & Exploration, 183
  warrant, 24, 64–67, 72, 166
LTV Corp., 177
  5's–88 bond, 6, 40–49
  warrant, 6, 40–49, 53, 63, 66, 71
  warrant hedge, 40–49

M

McCrory Corp., 183
  warrant, 63, 66, 71–72
Maintenance margin requirements, 80, 149–52, 212
Margin account; see Brokerage account
Margin buying; see Buying on margin and Hedging on margin
Margin interest, 52, 84, 162
Margin rules and regulations, 117, 139, 149–52, 185
Marking to the market, 155–56, 185
Mathematical advantage, 212
  convertibles, 103, 106, 111, 113
  warrants, 31, 33, 36, 44, 50, 73, 103
Maximum warrant price, 15
Mechanical system; see Basic system
Merger proposals, 51–52, 168–69, 171–72, see also Tender offers
Minimum value; see Conversion value
Money managers skilled in convertible hedging, 163
Mutual funds, 102

N

National General, 96–97, 173–80, 183
  4's–90 convertible bond, 94–97
  new warrant, 63–67, 71–72, 87, 166, 173–80
  old warrant, 18, 20
Neutral market; see Sideways market
New York Stock Exchange, 2, 40, 54, 80, 88, 118, 130, 149, 152, 156, 177, 179–80
Normal value curves for warrants, 17–29
  basic formula, 18, 182
  standard curves, 28–29
NVF Company, 183
  5's–94 bond, 181
  warrant, 65, 67, 166

O

Opportunities in undervalued convertibles, 96–97

Index 221

Optimum short to long ratio for hedge positions in undervalued warrants, 55–56, 66, 187–89
Over-the-counter securities
 common stocks, 54
 convertibles, 154–55
 warrants, 2, 54–55, 60, 88, 154–55

P

Pacific Petroleums reverse warrant hedge, 126
Pacific Southwest Airlines
 6's–87 bond, 19–20, 181
 warrant, 19–20
Pan American World Airways 7.5's–98 convertible bond, 131–33
PepsiCo, 177
Portfolio management, 153–67
 brokerage account, 153–56
 investment services, 158–60
 operating at maximum leverage, 157–58
 portfolio selection and diversification, 158–59
 portfolio turnover strategy, 161
 record keeping, 161–63
 selecting a broker, 157
 selecting a brokerage firm, 156–57
 tax considerations, 160–61
Portfolio turnover strategy, 161
Premium over conversion value, 13, 95, 100
Premium over investment value, 94, 101
Proposed Bill of Rights for Warrant Holders, 176–80
PSA Inc., see Pacific Southwest Airlines
Putnam Duofund, 145–48

R

Real Estate Investment Trusts
 delayed warrants, 133–35
 warrants, 22, 55, 116
Realty Equities warrant, 62, 66, 71
Recommended readings, 166–67
Record keeping, 161–63

Regulation T, 48, 129, 149–50, 152, 155–57, 213
Regulation U, 149–50, 213
Reverse warrant hedging, 115–26, 140, 213
 A. T. & T. hedge, 118–25
 general guides, 115–18
R.H.M. Convertible Survey, 160
R.H.M. Warrant & Stock Survey, 160
Risk factors
 convertible hedging, 114, 168–80
 delayed convertibles, 135
 reverse warrant hedging, 116–18
 warrant hedging, 52, 168–80
Risk/reward ratio; see Mathematical advantage

S

Scudder Duo-Vest, 145–48
Securities and Exchange Commission, 173
Selecting a broker, 157
Selecting a brokerage firm, 156–57
Selling securities short; see Short selling
Short account; see Brokerage account
Short-exempt sales, 184–85
Short selling, 156–57, 184–86
 common stocks, 36, 39, 50, 52, 55–56, 113, 129, 155–56, 161, 163, 170
 warrants, 115–26, 155–56
Short squeeze, 170, 185–86
Sideways markets, 52, 59, 64–65, 70–74, 83–84, 90, 161
Source Capital, Inc., 102
Special situations, 127–38
Sperry Rand reverse warrant hedge, 125
Stockbrokers, 157, 163, 165
Straight bonds usable at par value; see Usable bonds

T

Tangible value; see Conversion value
Tax considerations, 12, 84, 99–100, 109, 160–61
Tender offers, 51–52, 168–70

Tenneco, Inc., 183
  warrant, 24, 87–90
Terms applying to convertibles, warrants and hedging, 206–16
Trading against a hedge position, 52, 59, 90, 161
Turnover strategy; *see* Portfolio turnover strategy
Turov, Daniel, 174

U

Undervalued warrants, 1–2, 30–37, 54–56, 68–69, 166
United National, 183
  7.5's–88 bond, 181
  convertible preferred, 131
  old warrant, 65, 67–68, 166
Universal American reverse warrant hedge, 125–26
Up-tick, 184, 215
Uris Buildings warrant, 62, 66, 71
Usable bonds, 5–7, 55, 87, 155, 181

V–W

Value Line
  convertible survey, 160, 176
  1,500 stock average, 70, 77–78, 82–83, 85
Volatility, 37, 47, 50, 52, 55, 61, 105, 116
  stock volatility calculations, 183
Wall Street Journal, 102
Warner Communications, 183
  warrant, 65–67, 72, 166, *see also* Kinney National Services warrant
Warrants, 1–37
  adjusted exercise price, 3, 19–20
  adjusted warrant price, 19–20
  alternative to common stock, 1, 31–36
  arbitrage, 12
  callable warrants, 7–9
  certificates, 37
  changes of exercise terms, 3
  check list for initial evaluation, 10
  conversion value, 11–13
  definition, 1

Warrants—*Cont.*
  effective exercise price, 5–6, 19–20
  exercise into common stock, 5, 12
  exercise price, 3
  exercise terms, 3
  expiration date, 4–5
  factors affecting normal value, 21–24
  general guides for buying warrants, 36–37
  leverage, 24–26, 28, 30–31, 36, 44, 52, 55–56
  long-term warrants, 4–5, 36, 50, 52
  mathematical advantage, 31, 33, 36, 44, 50
  maximum price, 15
  normal value bands, 22–23
  normal value curves, 17–29
  normally priced, 31–33
  origination, 2
  overpriced warrants, 30, 37, 51
  perpetual warrants, 4
  premium, 13
  protection against stock splits and stock dividends, 3–4
  reduction of exercise price, 9
  senior securities usable at par value, 5–7, 43, 55
  short-term, 4–5, 37, 52
  speculative value, 11–13
  undervalued warrants, 1–2, 30–37
  warrant/common stock price relationships, 11–16
  where traded, 2
Warrant/cash investment approach, 31–33, 35, 40, 76–78, 100–101
Warrants evaluated during the six-year study, 190–99
Wilson & Co. warrant, 63, 66, 71, 177
Wilson Sporting Goods warrant, 177
Worksheets
  for evaluating long-term warrants, 29
  for hedging convertible bonds, 112
  for hedging warrants, 49

Worksheets—*Cont.*
   for hedging warrants/usable bonds, 137
   for initial evaluation of a warrant, 10
   for planning a convertible hedge portfolio, 159
   for reverse warrant hedging, 119–21

Worksheets—*Cont.*
   for writing call options against a convertible bond hedge, 142

Y–Z

Yield advantage; *see* Cash flow
Zayre Corp., 183
   warrant, 166

This book has been set in 12 point Garamond #3, leaded 3 points, and 11 point Garamond #3, leaded 2 points. Chapter numbers are set in 24 point Helvetica Medium; chapter titles are set in 18 point Helvetica. The size of the type page is 25 by 43 picas.